George Melville Baker

The Drawing-Room Stage

"MY BROTHER'S KEEPER."

George Melville Baker

The Drawing-Room Stage

ISBN/EAN: 9783337340971

Printed in Europe, USA, Canada, Australia, Japan

Cover: Foto ©Thomas Meinert / pixelio.de

More available books at **www.hansebooks.com**

MY BROTHER'S KEEPER.

THE DRAWING-ROOM STAGE:

A SERIES OF ORIGINAL

DRAMAS, COMEDIES, FARCES,

AND

ENTERTAINMENTS FOR AMATEUR THEATRICALS AND SCHOOL EXHIBITIONS.

BY

GEORGE M. BAKER,

AUTHOR OF "AMATEUR DRAMAS," "THE SOCIAL STAGE," "THE MIMIC STAGE," "A BAKER'S DOZEN HUMOROUS DIALOGUES," ETC.

ILLUSTRATED.

BOSTON:
LEE AND SHEPARD, PUBLISHERS.
NEW YORK:
LEE, SHEPARD AND DILLINGHAM.
1873.

Entered, according to Act of Congress, in the year 1872,
BY GEORGE M. BAKER,
In the Office of the Librarian of Congress, at Washington.

Stereotyped at the Boston Stereotype Foundry,
19 Spring Lane.

PREFACE.

As "The Social Stage," "The Mimic Stage," and "Amateur Dramas" are still "live" books in the publishers' catalogue, and greedy amateurs are crying for "more," the author is confident that he will not wear his welcome out by the publication of "The Drawing-room Stage;" although, as it contains his fiftieth dramatic composition, the title of a "prolific writer," so often applied, for good or ill, to those who play frequent engagements upon the world's broad stage with pen and ink in "sock and buskin," may fairly be fastened upon him. This, certainly, is not always a meritorious distinction, and would be poor satisfaction to the author for his efforts, should not a few grains of truth and thought be found in his acres of caricature and burlesque. This volume, like its predecessors, is designed to present original and healthy entertainment for the home circle, the exhibition hall, and the school platform. The same plans which characterize the former volumes may be found here — the doing away with elaborate scenery and costumes, the absence of strained and unnatural "spouting," and, as far as possible in dealing with every-day characters, the omission of "slang." Were this latter excluded altogether, a *good* play might be written, but the best-natured audience would fail to find "characters," or to be amused, and the strongest railer against this "custom of American society" be the first to turn his back upon the tedious performance. For the many favorable notices by the press of his previous works, the author returns thanks; to his unfavorable critics, he can only say, that as dramatic composition with him is but a pastime, and not an occupation, perfection should not be expected.

CONTENTS.

		PAGE
MY BROTHER'S KEEPER.	*A Drama.*	7
THE REVOLT OF THE BEES.	*An Allegory.*	69
A TENDER ATTACHMENT.	*A Farce.*	85
AMONG THE BREAKERS.	*A Drama.*	107
GENTLEMEN OF THE JURY.	*A Farce.*	171
THE SEVEN AGES.	*A Tableau Entertainment.*	187
THE BOSTON DIP.	*A Comedietta.*	215
THE DUCHESS OF DUBLIN.	*A Farce.*	241

ALL the Plays in this **book are** furnished separately by the publishers. Price 15 cents **each.**

MY BROTHER'S KEEPER.

A DRAMA IN THREE ACTS.

CHARACTERS.

ABEL BENTON, Merchant.
MATTHEW ALLEN, ⎫
RICHARD CARNES, ⎬ his Clerks.
CHARLES BENTON, ⎭
JOB LAYTON (Scraps), a Rag-picker.
GRACE BENTON, Abel's daughter.
RACHEL ALLEN, Matthew's sister.
BETSEY BENTON, Abel's sister.

COSTUMES.

ABEL BENTON. Blue coat, white vest, white necktie, dark pants, gray wig, side whiskers.

MATTHEW ALLEN and RICHARD CARNES. Act 1 and 2, Business suits. Act 3, Evening dress.

JOB LAYTON. Act 1, Ragged coat fastened at the waist with a rope, rough iron-gray wig, rough beard, dark pants, large boots unblacked, dark necktie, old hat. Act 2, Black pants and coat, white vest, white necktie, hair and beard trimmed. The dress should be good but slouchy.

CHARLES BENTON. Act 1, Dark pants, white shirt, a large wet

handkerchief thrown loosely about his neck, boots in his hand, and coat over his arm, socks on his feet, hair dripping wet. Sprinkle the clothes with bits of isinglass for a general soused appearance; change to Base Ball suit, with the letter G on breast. Act 2, Business suit. Act 3, Neat evening dress.

GRACE BENTON. Act 1, Fashionable summer dress, with shawl and hat. Act 3, White evening dress, rich and tasty.

RACHEL ALLEN. Acts 1 and 2, Neat and pretty street dress. Act 3, White.

BETSEY BENTON. Act 1, Black silk dress, scant, old-fashioned shawl and hat, gray front of hair. Act 3, Black silk dress, white bertha, front, and cap.

ACT 1. SCENE. — ABEL BENTON'S *counting-room. Desk against wall,* R. *Desk against wall,* L. *Writing table,* C., *with drawer opening at back. Chairs before desks,* R. *and* L. *Chair* R. *of table. Lounge behind table,* C. *On desks inkstands, pens, paper, &c. The entrances are from* R. *and* L.: *that on the* R. *is from the warehouse and the street; that on the* L. *leads to* ABEL BENTON'S *private room.* RICHARD CARNES *discovered seated at desk,* L.

Richard. 56 — 65 — 72 — 81 — 90. Figures, figures, figures! I'm heartily tired of this drudgery, day after day, casting up columns that add no sum total to my earthly happiness. If one could be as lucky as our head centre, Abel Benton, patience would indeed be a virtue. But he's one in a thousand. First a rag-picker, a searcher in cast-out heaps of rubbish for scraps of paper, rags, old junk, anything that by accumulation could produce a few pennies with which to keep soul and body together; then, by the usual stages of honest industry, rising to the more honorable position of peddler, proprietor of a small junk shop, general speculator in paper stock, and now gathering rags from every quarter of the globe, supplying almost every paper-mill in the country; with an income sufficient to glut the appetite of the most luxurious, and a name A 1 on the street; while I, with a rich and stingy old father, am forced to drudge in the counting-room of this opulent rag-picker for a meagre salary, keep myself, and grow rich on expectation. O, it's a funny world — 7 — 16 — 21 — a remarkably facetious old globe — 32 — 37 — 41. Hallo; who's there?

Enter SCRAPS, R., *with a basket. In all his scenes his eyes are roving about the stage, and in this Act he picks up scraps of rags and paper, which should be left about for that purpose.*

Scraps. Eh, hey! (*Puts his hand to his left ear with this word, always.*) O, if you please, Mr. Carnes, here's my ticket from the warehouse; twenty-five cents — white, all white, four pounds and a quarter — just twenty-five cents. Hey, Mr. Carnes.

Rich. (*takes ticket, and gives* SCRAPS *scrip from desk*). Twenty-five cents; and is that the extent of your day's pickings, Scraps?

Scraps. Hey? Yes, that's all. Pickings is hard, Mr. Carnes.

Rich. O, you'll never amass a fortune at this rate. Look at the shining example of successful rag-picking at the head of our house, and stir your stumps a little more lively, Scraps.

Scraps. Hey? Stir my stumps? O, no, can't do it. I've got the gout with too high living. Ha, ha! high living! I think I'll retire, and live on my fortune; ha, ha! my fortune! That's good; that's exceedingly good.

Rich. You're an old sinner, Scraps. Now I've no doubt you have a snug sum stowed away in one of our banks.

Scraps. Hey?

Rich. You'll cut up rich one of these days. In which of our banks do you deposit?

Scraps. Cut up pranks, at my time of life — no, no.

Rich. (*rises, crosses, looks off*, R., *then comes down* R. *of* SCRAPS). Now, look here, Scraps; you're not so deaf as you appear. I happen to want a hundred dollars. Lend it to me. I'll pay you ten per cent.; the banks only give you six. Let me have a loan —

Scraps. Hey? Let you alone? I can't hear, you know. You're on the wrong side.

Rich. (*angrily crosses to* L., *pushing* SCRAPS *back as he passes*). Bah! you old fool! None so deaf as those who won't hear. (*Sits at desk.*)

Scraps (*pointing* L.). Is Mr. Benton in there, Mr. Carnes?

Rich. Yes, he's in there, and very busy settling his last year's business. Not to be disturbed.

Scraps. O, he's a rich un, he is, and once he was as mean and dirty a rag-picker as I am. We were chummies then, we were; ha, ha! not very chummy now — not very. He was a chap what saved his money; mine went as fast as it came. He took to books; I took to billiards. He loved study; I loved sport. And so the road in which we picked parted one day; he crawled up hill, and I down. Now he's a looking off over his vast possessions from the top of the hill, and I'm picking away in the mud, far, far below. Let this be a warning to you, Mr. Carnes.

Rich. Warning to me? What do you mean?

Scraps. O, you know what I mean. You're fond of billiards, and theatres, and — the tiger — you know you are; and I know it too, for I've watched you many a night. Now Abel Benton don't like this. Here are you and Mr. Matthew Allen, equally trusted. He delights in books, you in billiards; and depend upon it both of these, like everything else about here, will be weighed on Abel Benton's scales, and, when they do, billiards will kick the beam.

Rich. You miserable street grubber, do you dare to threaten me? Leave the room at once.

Scraps. Yes, billiards is mighty captivating.

Rich. (*seizing a ruler, and approaching* SCRAPS, *who backs to* R.). Clear out, you croaking vagrant.

Scraps. But it takes money, Mr. Carnes, it takes money.

Rich. Fool, take that! (*Raises the ruler. Enter quickly,* R., MATTHEW.)

Matthew (*steps between,* **and arrests** DICK'S *arm*). Easy, Dick, easy. Scraps' head is not thick, and the ruler is very thin. Don't spoil either.

Rich. Insolent old fool! Were I master here, he should never show his ugly face in this place. (*Goes to desk.* L.)

Mat. Then I'm very glad you're not, Dick. Scraps

is a very worthy old fellow. Since you and I have been clerks for Mr. Benton, daily, winter and summer, he has dropped in upon us, and I, for one, should miss him.

Scraps. Thank you, Mr. Allen.

Rich. O, you've found your ears, have you.

Scraps. I haven't but one, Mr. Carnes; the other's stopped, and I'm glad of it, for a poor old chap like me gets many a hard word flung at him, that can't touch the heart-strings when there's a closed door between. I'm much obliged to you, Mr. Allen. Mr. Carnes wanted to put me out, but, bless you, I don't mind it. I'm never put out, never; and mark me, *I* shan't be the one put out here — no, no. (*Exit*, R.)

Rich. The meddling old scamp!

Mat. Dick, you seem out of sorts to-day. What is the trouble between you and Scraps?

Rich. Nothing you can mend. Any news of the Elmyra?

Mat. She has just been telegraphed.

Rich. Any private signals?

Mat. Yes, English rags, full freight, consigned to Abel Benton.

Rich. Of course — low market, high prices, and just in the nick of time the Elmyra sails into Abel Benton's pocket with a cargo of five thousand dollars in gold. The old scrub!

Mat. And who is old scrub?

Rich. The governor, the head centre, Abel Benton, of course.

Mat. Gently, Dick, gently. He deserves more respect. He has been a kind master to you and me.

Rich. Well, he ought to have made money enough by this time to retire and give us a chance. Now, here's the case of the Elmyra. You foretold a short market; you proposed sending an agent across the water. Your advice was taken; it has proved a success: yours was the venture; to you should come the profits.

Mat. Dick, you are unreasonable. Listen: that ship sailing into port reminds me that seven years ago I stood on the deck of a vessel sailing into this same port. Coming to this country from old England, a lad of fourteen, leaving behind me the fresh-tufted grave of my mother, the only protector I had in the world, my only companion my sister, four years younger. Dick, you have father and mother, rich and powerful friends, everything about you comfortable and pleasant. You never knew what it is to cry with hunger, to shiver with cold, as I did in the old country; you never stood, as I stood then, on the deck of a vessel with not a cent in my pocket, knowing not what awaited me amid the domes and spires of the city we were nearing fast. If you had, Dick, if you had suffered all this, and then felt upon your shoulder the hand which fell upon mine as I leaped ashore, looked into the kindly face that I looked into, you would strain every faculty of your being to serve the interests of so kind a benefactor as Abel Benton.

Rich. Benefactor, indeed! I tell you, Matt, you think too little of yourself. Benton is shrewd. I've no doubt he read in your face, at first sight, the energy and spirit by which he has profited. You've given him hard work for every dollar expended.

Mat. Then, there's my sister. He has been like a

father to her. She is treated in his house as a daughter, every wish gratified, almost spoiled by his indulgence.

Rich. Well, he doesn't spoil us by indulgence. His old-fashioned notions put double work upon us. He won't have a safe, but requires one of us to sleep here every night. It's very lucky nothing has ever disappeared from the warehouse, for I believe he would discharge us on mere suspicion.

Mat. He's an odd man, Dick, and no one can tell to what his whims may lead; but with clear consciences, and determination to do our best, we need not fear his changing humors. (*Sits at desk,* R.)

Charley (*outside,* R.). Old rags! old rags! (*Enter,* R.) Here you are, now, a prime lot, a little damaged by salt water. Who bids? Going, going.

Mat. Why, Charley, where did you come from?

Chas. (*takes handkerchief off his neck, and wrings out the water*). The bottom of the sea. "The sea, the sea, the boundless sea." I'm a river god, a mermaid, — Charley Benton as a live mermaid; his first appearance on any stage.

Mat. Come, Charley, be sober.

Chas. Sober! Do you know where I've been? I've been in the depths of sobriety — at the bottom of the bay. I can lead you to the spot where the flounders are thickest, for I've floundered among them; where the smelts congregate, for I've smelt 'em; where the rock is in the cradle of the deep, for I went straight for it — red hot.

Rich. You've been overboard.

Chas. Considering my present humid appearance, that was not a very remarkable guess.

Mat. And you are wet through.

Chas. Thank you; that's a very dry remark. Any more interesting news?

Mat. If you don't change your clothes at once you'll be laid up for a month.

Chas. Thank you; any fool could tell me that; but don't trouble yourself; I've a dry suit in the loft.

Mat. But what sent you overboard?

Chas. My love of business. I was hurrying down the wharf to catch sight of the Elmyra, and — somebody's been shortening that wharf, for, before I knew it, I was in the briny, and bound for the bottom.

Rich. You lummux, walked overboard?

Chas. Exactly; clamoring for help, which did not arrive until I'd been down clamming at the bottom.

Mat. Well, run and change your clothes.

Chas. My base ball uniform is up stairs, and if I can keep out of the governor's way, I'm all right. Mum, boys, for he's down on the manly sport. He knows nothing of the glories of the base ball field, and if he finds me in that rig I shall catch it. (*Exit,* R.)

Rich. Clumsy chap. Served him right.

Mat. Hold on, Dick. There's the faintest shadow of a mystery here. Charley may have accidentally walked overboard, but he took precious good care to remove his boots first. Did you notice? They were as dry as mine. You'll find there is more in this than appears on the face of it.

Rich. Matt, you're always finding excuses for him.

Mat. Am I? Well, it's because he's a noble-hearted fellow. If he's not a driving business man, it's because he has a rich father, and does not feel the need of exertion. It's time Mr. Benton was informed of the arrival of the Elmyra. Where away to-night, Dick?

Rich. The usual round: a little billiards, a peep into the theatres, and a good time generally. Will you go with me?

Mat. No, I thank you, Dick. It's my night on guard here, and, besides, I don't fancy your sport. Ah, Dick, it's a pity you're so fond of it. If Mr. Benton should get an inkling of your predilections, 'twould go hard with you. Have a care, old boy, have a care. (*Exit*, L.)

Rich. (*at desk*, L.). Have a care, indeed! Preach away, parson. You fancy you are feathering your nest by the remarkably moral life you lead. Bah! With all my love for sport, I can hold my place in old Benton's warehouse. He trusts me as fully as he does you; confides to me as important business as he does to you. I have the advantage in being the oldest, and shrewdness enough to keep my pleasures from being noticed by the head centre. But I'd like to see you, Matt Allen, taken down a peg, and if ever I have the chance, you shall be brought to your level, depend upon it. (*Writes.*)

Enter SCRAPS, *cautiously*, R.

Scraps (*aside*). I've been hunting everywhere for Master Charley. O, he's a sly one. Hullo! there's Mr. Carnes again. Ho, ho! he'd break my head, would he? he'd turn me out, would he? We shall see. It's time Abel Benton knew the snake he is warming. O, I'll reward him for his kindness.

Enter CHARLEY, R., *in base ball dress. Snatches the basket from* SCRAPS, *and covers his head with it.*

Scraps. Help! murder! help! (*Extricating himself from basket.*) Hallo, Master Charley! Up to your old tricks, hey?

Chas. Tricks, indeed! I was only filling your basket with what it so much needs — old rags, old rags.

Scraps. Now — now — now — you're a funny dog, Master Charley. But, my eyes, how fine you're rigged! Going sojering, hey?

Chas. Sojering? No. This is the emblematic costume of the Gooseneck Base Ball Club. Ain't it gay, red hot.

Rich. Red hot! It will be well warmed if the governor catches you.

Chas. But I don't mean he shall. When he takes the field, "I'm out on the fly." Ah, Dick, you should join us. It's glorious sport.

Rich. Bah! it's so fatiguing and so dirty!

Chas. It may be for you, lily fingers. You'd rather spend your time in a smoky billiard room. But for me, give me the free air, the green field, strong, tough fellows striving for the mastery, every muscle alive with health, sharp eyes, eager hands, quick legs, the strike, the run, the catch. O, it's glorious! Hey, Scraps?

Scraps. O, yes. How much do you get for it?

Chas. O, pshaw, Scraps! don't be mercenary. Get fame, glory. (*Takes a small leather case from his pocket, and opens it.*) Look at that. That's what we get for it. There's a badge to be presented to Bob Dyke, our pitcher, this evening, as a slight token of the Goosenecks' appreciation of his valuable services. And I'm to make the presentation speech. Ain't it gay?

Scraps. Well, 'tis handsome. And you to make a speech? I declare, I should like to hear you make a speech.

Chas. Would you? Then you shall. You shall be the pitcher, not exactly the figure, but you'll do for a rehearsal now. You stand there. (*Places him in* C., *and goes down*, R.) Ahem! ahem! Renowned pitcher —

Scraps. Hey?

Chas. Now what's the matter with you?

Scraps. Why, you're on the wrong side.

Chas. (*crossing to* L.). All right. I forgot the impediment. Now then. Renowned — O, stand up; present a dignified aspect.

Scraps. Hey? Me present. I thought you was a going to do that.

Chas. O, you're a muff. Stand up; throw out your chest. There, that's better. Now. Renowned pitcher! champion of the ball field, model of muscular manliness — O, hold up your head, will you?

Scraps. How can I hear if I hold up my head?

Chas. Shut up! Paragon of perfect proportions, politest of peripatetic pitchers, how much we owe thee!

Scraps. Not a cent. Mr. Carnes settled —

Chas. Shut up! As we look back to the glorious victories achieved on Potter's field, we see thy noble form animated with a spirit bold and daring —

Scraps. Hey? Spirits? 'Pon my word I never drank a drop; and as for swearing —

Chas. Shut up! In the front of battle, winning renown for the Goosenecks. We would express our gratitude; and it devolves upon me, the humble instrument of our victorious nine, to present you this slight token of our appreciation of your valuable services. Take it, prize it for the giver's sake; take it, wear it over your noble heart. (*Enter,* L., MR. BENTON, *followed by* MATTHEW ALLEN.) Take it —

Mr. Benton (*takes badge*). Thank you, and once in my possession I shall preserve it; depend upon that, Charley Benton.

Chas. (*crosses to* R.). The governor. Foul ball.

Scraps. Is that all, Charley?

Mr. B. So, sir, in spite of my repeated warnings, I find you tricked out in a garb I have forbidden, making a fool of yourself when you should be attending to business. Shame, shame, Charles! I thought you were more of a man.

Chas. Yes, sir, it's a mistake; I — I — I know it's wrong, but I tumbled overboard a while ago, and as I was very dry — no, wet — I —

Mr. B. Tumbled overboard?

Chas. Yes, accidentally — not on purpose — walked overboard.

Scraps. Don't you believe it, Abel Benton; don't you believe it. It's a lie; a downright lie.

Chas. Scraps, I'll break your head.

Scraps. Hey? You're on the wrong side. O, I know him, Abel Benton, I know him, the smooth-tongued villain, and I'll expose his wickedness too.

Mr. B. Well, Job, what do you know?

Scraps. I know all about it. It's the common talk

on the wharf; and if I have but one ear; that's wide open.

Chas. Scraps, if you say another word —

Scraps. Hey? — O, you're on the wrong side. O, he's a deep one. An hour ago he was on the wharf — this scoundrel. Walking coolly down the wharf. Just before him was a little ragged, dirty girl —

Chas. Scraps, Scraps, your life's in danger.

Scraps. Hey? — You're on the wrong side. Creeping along, picking up chips, and this rogue, this scamp, close behind her. She reached the end of the wharf —

Chas. Scraps, another word, and I'll strike —

Scraps. Hey? — You're on the wrong side, I tell you. — Her foot slipped, and over she went; and this villain, this cold-blooded villain —

Mr. B. Looked coolly on.

Scraps. Cool, — his boots were off in a second, and over he went, seized the child, and held her head above water until they were both drawn out. Look at him! look at the calm, cool, calculating villain. O, he's a deep one.

Mr. B. Charles, is this true?

Chas. I'm sorry to say it is, sir.

Mr. B. Sorry! Charley, my boy, you're a noble — Hem! yes, sir, you have disobeyed my orders, and I shall see that you are punished. As for this trinket, I'll take care of it. (*Unlocks drawer in table,* C., *deposits the case, and then locks drawer.*) Here it is safe, but you see it no more. (*Exit,* L.)

Chas. Out on the badge. Scraps, I've a great mind to pommel you.

Mat. No you won't, Charley, for he's defended you. Give me your hand. You're an honor to the house.

Scraps. What did I tell you? Villany is always found out, always.

Chas. O, I'll be even with you, Scraps.

Scraps. Hey? — You're on the wrong side.

Chas. We've had quite enough of your interference; so go.

Scraps. Yes, I'll go down on the wharf, and hunt up more of your crimes. O, you're a sly one; deceive your father, hey! walk overboard, hey! Ha, ha! you'll catch it. Ha, ha! (*At door,* R.) I say, Charley, red hot, red hot! (*Exit,* R.)

Mat. Dick, here's Foley's invoice. You copy that, and I'll take Dixon's. They must both go by next mail. (*Sits at desk,* R.)

Rich. (*at desk,* L.). All right, Matt.

Chas. (*sits on table,* C.). "I saw it but a moment, but methinks I *don't* see it now." The renowned pitcher's badge has gone into the governor's drawer, and how the renowned pitcher is to get it, and how the subscriber is to present it to the renowned pitcher, are questions of vital importance, in fact, red hot. The governor won't give it up; but I must have it.

Rachel (*outside,* R.). Goodness gracious, I shall die, I know I shall.

Betsey (*outside,* R.). Do behave yourself, Rachel Allen. I declare, you mortify me to death.

Rachel. Can't go another step. (*Enters,* R., *with her arms full of bundles. She drops them in a heap on the floor,* R., *and falls on her knees.*) It's no use. It's that last camel hair shawl that broke this camel's back. Why, hallo, Charley!

Chas. And hallo, Shellie! what's the matter?

Enter AUNT BETSEY, R., *shaking her parasol at an imaginary foe outside.*

Betsey. Don't you look at me! Don't you dare to look at me! Mind your business, impudence.

Chas. What's the matter, Aunt Betsey?

Betsey. Do look at that impudent — Go away, I say. Don't stand gawking at me. S'pose he never saw a woman afore. Jest like 'em; they're all alike.

Chas. (*looking off*, R.). Why, he isn't looking at you, Aunt Betsey.

Betsey. I tell you he is. I know he is. You can't fool me.

Chas. No, he's not looking at you, for the very good reason that he's blind. It's only old Foley.

Rachel. O, Aunt Betsey! Ha, ha, ha! what blind devotion!

Betsey (*sitting in chair* R. *of table*). Well, I never! Rachel Allen, where's your dignity? Get up from that floor directly.

Chas. What's all this? Where have you been?

Rachel. Been shopping; and O, my, didn't we make a commotion! There's nothing but bare shelves and bare counters in every dry goods store from the Park to the Square.

Betsey. Goodness gracious! hear that child talk. And there's all my things a being ruined on this dirty floor.

Chas. (*picks up bundles, and places them on table*). Whose are these things?

Rachel. They're all mine, except the five largest; those are Aunt Betsey's.

Chas. And there's only six in the lot. That's a very modest way of letting me know that you've been loaded down with Aunt Betsey's purchases. Why not have them sent home?

Betsey. Young man, mind your business. When I go shopping I mean to have just what I buy, and nothing else. Them air counter chaps air dreadful spry and smilin, but they can't deceive Betsey Benton. Never!

Chas. But, Aunt Betsey, 'tis too much for Shellie's little arms.

Betsey. Young man, mind your business. When I was a gal I had to work, and I mean everybody round me shall, if I can make work for 'em.

Chas. Now look here, Aunt Betsey; you and I will have a falling out one of these days, if you don't treat Shellie better.

Betsey. Highty-tity, young man! Mind your business. She ain't a goin to be brought up to a life of idleness, I tell you.

Rachel. O, now, don't quarrel about me. Why, there's brother Matt. (*Crosses, R., and puts her hand on his shoulder.*) Well, brother Money Grub, how's trade?

Mat. Ah, Sunshine! The Elmyra's come. Trade is looking up.

Rachel. O, I'm so glad. I wish I was a man. It must be so grand to make money.

Chas. Why, you're avaricious, Shellie.

Rachel. No, I'm not, Charley. I want the money with which to buy richer treasures — the poor man's blessing and the sufferer's smile.

Mat. Ah, Shellie, if we could only think so after we acquire riches! But where have you been?

Rachel. Been shopping; and, don't you think, Aunt Betsey was nearly run over. O, such fun!

Betsey. Fun! fun! Well, I never! I'm most dead with fright, and that young one calls it fun!

Rachel. Yes, we were just crossing the main street, when somebody called out, " Look out, there! " And of course we looked out, and there was a running horse almost upon us. I gave one leap and landed on the sidewalk, but Aunt Betsey she just stood in the street, and flourished her parasol, when a ragged individual rushed between her and the horse, caught her up in his arms, and placed her on the sidewalk. O, she did look so funny, with her arms flying about like a windmill, and screaming like a locomotive.

Betsey. Well, I never! And you stood on the sidewalk and laughed — absolutely laughed. I never was so mortified in my life.

Rachel. Ha, ha, ha! I couldn't help it, you did look so in the arms of your preserver.

Betsey. Rachel Allen, I'm petrified! Where on airth is your dignity!

Mat. 'Twas a very serious matter. And who was the brave man who rescued you?

Betsey. How should I know? While I was looking for a dollar to give him, he slipped off.

Chas. I should think he would. A dollar for saving your life. (*Aside.*) O, it's too much.

Betsey. Where's your father?

Chas. In his office, Aunt Betsey.

Betsey. Well, Rachel, you pick up the bundles. I'll just speak to him, and then we must be getting home. (*Exit,* L.)

Rachel. Why, how queer you're dressed, Charley! Is that your working suit?

Chas. Well, no — yes, it is *one* of my working suits.

Rachel. What does the letter G stand for?

Rich. Stands for Goose, Shellie.

Rachel. Ha, ha, ha! How very appropriate!

Mat. 'Tis very appropriate, Shellie, but it doesn't stand for goose. It's the initial of Great, and, placed where it now is, it fitly represents the great heart beneath it. Charley wears that dress at this time, Shellie, because he has just saved a little girl from drowning at the risk of his own life.

Rachel. That's just like him. He's always doing something brave. (*Goes up and takes his hand.*) O, Charley, I shall love you just as long as I live.

Chas. Will you, though, Shellie? Then let me tell you that I shall ask that — I am — that you are —

Rachel. Why, what's the matter, Charley?

Chas. Well — I was going to say — that I — that I am —

Enter BETSEY, L.

Betsey. Now, Rachel, get your bundles, and we'll go.

Chas. Once for all, Aunt Betsey, I tell you I will not have it. She shall not carry those bundles.

Betsey. I say she shall. Young man, mind your business.

Chas. So I will; and it's my business to relieve the weaker sex of their cares when I can. I'll just take possession of the bundles, and bring them up to-night.

Betsey. Young man, I insist —

Chas. Now, look here, Aunt Betsey; don't get me mad; for when I get angry I always run and jump off the wharf — and I don't go alone.

Betsey. Good gracious! Do you mean to say you would throw me overboard?

Chas. I'm afraid I should if I got mad.

Betsey. Come, Rachel, let's go. That youth is on the broad road going to destruction. Come. (*Exit*, R.)

Rachel. Good by. I'm coming back with Grace when she comes for her father. O, Charley, for shame! Threatening to throw Aunt Betsey overboard! (*Exit*, R.)

Chas. Of all the aggravating creatures, Aunt Betsey is a little ahead. Why don't she get married? She's old enough. She's no earthly use in our house, except to fret and worry, and interfere in all my little arrangements. (*Enter* SCRAPS, R.) Hullo! you back again?

Scraps. Hey? yes. I've a little business with your father. I say, Master Charley, who's that lady I just met?

Chas. Lady? The young one or the old one?

Scraps. The tall, fine-looking lady. (*Pointing*, R.) There, that one.

Chas. Fine looking! (*Aside.*) Scraps is smitten. (*Aloud.*) That's Aunt Betsey, father's sister. Did you ever see her before?

Scraps. Hey? No — yes — yes — once.

Chas. You did! Where?

Scraps. Now, now, Charley, none of that. You're on the wrong side.

Chas. (*aside*). He's smitten, red hot! By Jove, an idea. Scraps is rich. Why can't I make a match between them? Dress him up, and start him courting Aunt Betsey. That's one way to get rid of her. (*Aloud*.). Ah, Scraps, you sly dog, I thought you'd met before. She often speaks of you.

Scraps. Often speaks of me?

Chas. Yes, thinks you are not what you seem. Nobility beneath the ragged covering, soul shines through his shaggy eyebrows, and all that sort of thing. O, she's romantic.

Scraps. Often speaks of me? Well, that's singular.

Chas. Now's your chance, Scraps. Dress up; put on a bold air; you've got the money. "Woo her as the lion woos his bride;" and she'll fall into your arms.

Scraps. Yes. Well, I'll think about it; I'll think about it.

Enter Mr. Benton, L.

Mr. B. This note, Richard, must be in Captain Baxter's hands at once.

Rich. Yes, sir. I'll despatch a messenger immediately. (*Exit*, R.)

Mr. B. Matthew, the Spooner Mills are short of stock. We can get our own price for the Elmyra's cargo.

Mat. Then I'd better run up in the morning.

Mr. B. I think you had. Take the first train. You

can return in the evening. By the way, who sleeps here to-night?

Mat. 'Tis my watch, sir.

Mr. B. That's bad. You cannot catch the early train.

Mat. O, yes, if Charley can come down at six.

Mr. B. No; I'll relieve you myself.

Mat. All right, sir; I'll make my arrangements accordingly. (*Exit*, R.)

Mr. B. Charles, go into my office. I've a few words for you.

Chas. Yes, sir. (*Aside.*) Words that burn — red hot! (*Exit*, L.)

Mr. B. Well, Job, old friend, how wags the world with you?

Scraps. Hey? O, well, Abel; well. I pick up enough to keep soul and body together, and now and then a dollar for a rainy day.

Mr. B. Why will you persist in this vagabond life? You would be a valuable man to me in the warehouse. I have often urged you to take a place here.

Scraps. I know it, Abel; but I like to be my own master. Here I should be cramped. Regular hours and regular work — Not for me, Abel; not for me.

Mr. B. I don't like to see an old friend creeping about the streets, picking rags from the gutter like a vagrant. Look at me. The old life is almost blotted out of memory. I have made my way to a respectable position, while you, who started in life with me, still cling to the old existence. It's too bad, Job.

Scraps. No, Abel, not too bad, for it's the life I love.

You were ambitious to rise in the world; to get money.
You have been successful, and your old friend rejoices in
your prosperity. But all your wealth requires much
care. You are anxious, uneasy. There are hard lines
in your face. The failure of one of your speculations
would go near to break your heart. While I manage to
scrape, " here a little, and there a little," roam about,
look and laugh at the follies of the world, watch the
struggles and triumphs of busy men, and speculate, without risk, on the rise and fall of stocks.

Mr. B. That's very ragged philosophy, Job.

Scraps. Hey? Philosophy? No, that's freedom, and
freedom gives one so much time for observation to acquire knowledge. Why, Abel, I know more about your
business than you do. With all your wealth, you are at
the mercy of your clerks.

Mr. B. My clerks are models of industry, energy,
and honesty.

Scraps. All of them?

Mr. B. Yes; I would not have in my employ one hour
a young man whom I could not trust fully.

Scraps. Blind, Abel, blind. I know better. I've
seen one of your clerks at the gaming-table night after
night. I have seen him enter places where no honest
man should go. I have seen this, Abel. I'm a little dull
of ear, but I've a sharp eye.

Mr. B. One of my clerks, Job? Which one?

Scraps. Hey?—Now, you're on the wrong side.
Abel Benton, find out yourself. I will watch, but you
must trap the game.

Mr. B. Is it my son? I tremble while I ask it.

Scraps. What, Charley? No, no; he's the soul of honor.

Mr. B. Is it —

Scraps. No, no; fair play, Abel. I've set you on the track. I shall do no more.

Mr. B. Very well, I will watch, and if I have the faintest suspicion I will act. My clerks! Job, if I did not know you so well, I should doubt you, and not them.

Scraps. O, I'm all right. Now for a little business. I had a scare last night, Abel. Somebody broke into my room, seized me by the throat, and demanded money; but I had strength enough to throw him off, and rouse my neighbors. He escaped; my money was safe; but it must be put in a safer place. (*Produces small bag.*) Here is a hundred dollars, all in gold. You, Abel, must take care of it.

Mr. B. Certainly. (*Takes bag, goes to table, c., sits and writes.*) I shall not count it; your word is enough. It shall be well taken care of. Here's your receipt. (*Gives receipt.*) The money shall go in here. (*Opens the drawer in table where he has placed the badge, and locks it.*)

Scraps. What! Leave my money there after what I told you?

Mr. B. For that very reason. You have directed suspicion to one of my clerks. Your money should be the bait to catch the rogue. Hush! No more. Here is my daughter.

Enter GRACE, R.

Grace (c.). Good afternoon, father. Are you ready to escort me home?

Mr. B. (L.). In a few moments, Grace. This is an old friend of mine, Job Layton.

Grace. One I have longed to see. (*Crosses to* SCRAPS, R., *and takes his hand.* — SCRAPS *confused.*) My father often speaks of you, his old friend. Why don't you come and see us? You shall be heartily welcome, and I will do my best to entertain you.

Scraps. Lord bless you, pretty one, your father and I parted company years ago — he to go up, I to stick in the mud. I go to your house? Why, your servants would slam the door in my face.

Grace. No, no, Mr. Layton, nobody is driven from our door. There's our easy-chair waiting for you, and if you will come you shall find yourself with true friends. Now promise me you will come.

Scraps. Yes, yes, some time I will come. (*Turns to door,* R.) Good by. (*Aside.*) She's a darling. Ah, Abel may well be proud of such a daughter. And I, — I might have had a daughter to hang about my neck, to brighten my home, instead of being a lonely, ragged scavenger. O, Job, Job, I begin to doubt you. Freedom is all very well, but the chain which a loving child throws about a father makes slavery worth enduring. Bah, Job! You a philosopher! More likely an old fool — an old fool. (*Exit,* R.)

Mr. B. Grace, if that man survives me, look to it that he never suffers. When I was poor he was my best friend. Many a time in our rag-picking days he has robbed his basket to fill mine. Under that old coat there's a true heart. He must never suffer.

Grace. Never, if I can help it, father. Charley is very fond of him. Where is Charley, father?

Mr. B. In disgrace. Waiting in my room for the lecture he so richly deserves.

Grace. Why, what has he been doing?

Mr. B. Jumping overboard to save a drowning child. I could forgive that, but he's rigged himself in that outlawed sporting suit, for which he shall be well lectured.

Enter DICK, R.

Rich. Good afternoon, Miss Benton. (*Bows, and crosses to desk,* L.)

Grace. Good afternoon, Mr. Carnes.

Enter MATTHEW, R.

Mat. Ah, Miss Grace! You are early.

Grace. Matthew, I'm glad to meet you. (*Shakes hands with him.*) Yes, I've come to carry father off.

Enter RACHEL, R.

Rachel. There, I've torn my dress with one of those dirty bales. I declare, I can't see the use of having so many rags about.

Mr. B. To turn into money, Shellie.

Rachel. Hallo, Uncle Abe! Out of your den? Come, get your hat. We've come to lead you home.

Mr. B. I'll be ready soon. By the by, young gentlemen, I have placed a hundred dollars in gold in the upper drawer of that table for safe keeping. It belongs to Job Layton.

Mat. A hundred dollars? Isn't that an unsafe place for so large a sum?

Mr. B. Not while I have honest clerks. I shall be

very glad to see you at my home to-morrow evening. You will return in ample time, Matthew. You will meet there my partner.

All. Your partner!

Mr. B. Yes, I am getting old, and have decided to take a partner — a young and active man. You will have an opportunity to make his acquaintance before he enters upon his duties. (*Exit*, L.)

Grace. Now he's going to scold Charley. But not if I can help it. I've prevented it before, and I'll try it again. (*Exit*, L.)

Mat. (*sits at his desk*). A partner! A young and active man! Who can it be?

Rachel (*comes down and leans over his chair*). What's the matter, brother?

Mat. Thinking, Sunshine, thinking. We must all do that, you know.

Rachel. Well, then, tell me your thoughts. My brother should have no secrets from his keeper. That's the bargain, Matthew.

Mat. A new master is to step in here, Shellie — here, where, for seven years, we have worked so well together — the old master and his clerks. A man with new ideas, perhaps tyrannical, to upset the old smooth order of things. What says my keeper to that?

Rachel. She says, Think on, brother. Think of the good old man who laid his hand on your shoulder so kindly when you were a stranger in a strange land; who has been your steadfast friend from that hour to this, and say, Let new masters come; while the old master lives I have faith that he will never doubt me.

Mat. Right, my keeper, right. Do what he may I will believe he loves and trusts me.

Enter CHARLEY, L.

Chas. Well, I'm out on that. After roosting on a high stool for nearly half an hour, anxiously expecting a storm, that dear sister of mine drops in just as the clouds begin to gather, and all's sunshine. Hallo, Shellie! You here again?

Rachel. Yes, Charley. Come, pick up the bundles, and start the caravan.

Chas. But we must wait for Grace.

Rachel. Then let's take a stroll down the wharf. I want to see the place where you walked overboard.

Chas. Yes, where I put my foot in it. I can lead you to it. It's a delightful spot, so cool and retired. Come along. (*Exit,* R.)

Rich. Well, Matt.

Mat. Well, Dick.

Rich. What are you going to do about it — the new partner?

Mat. Accept the new order of things, and work as diligently as ever.

Rich. Matt Allen, you're a fool! There should be no partner in this concern except you or me. The head centre cannot want capital. Perhaps this is a surprise for one of us.

Mat. Surprise? That's not his way of doing business, Dick. Think of our staid, sober old master perpetrating a joke! I couldn't imagine it. No, it's an outsider, — who, I cannot guess.

Rich. I have a strong suspicion, Mat, that you are the man. You have a strong friend beside the throne.

Mat. A strong friend? Who do you mean?

Rich. Grace Benton. It needs no very sharp eyes to see that she looks upon you with favor. Always a smile, a pleasant word, for *you*. She listens as though you were an oracle when you speak, and blushes when your step is heard. All sure signs. Don't be a fool, Mat. She's a rich catch. Be bold, and she is yours.

Mat. (*rising, indignantly*). Silence, Dick Carnes! Another word and I shall forget that we are friends, and chastise you for your insolence. Do you think me so base as to take advantage of the kindness that seeks to make me forget my humble position? so mean as to betray the trust reposed in me by my employer? Grace Benton is too high in social position for me to dare approach her as a suppliant for her hand or heart. Dick, I believe I am an honest man. I look upon a fortune-hunter as no better than a thief snatching at the treasures of another; and rather than have this imputation cast at me I'd leave this place forever.

Rich. But, Mat, if she loves —

Mat. Silence! Another word and we are enemies. (*Sits,* R.)

Rich. (*aside*). High and mighty! Chastise me for my insolence! Well, two can play at that game. An honest man, indeed! He's too honest. He has no suspicion that the new partner is himself. I have. And he's to step above me. I'd like to thwart the head centre. If he could be made to suspect Mat! But how?

Ah, the drawer! Scraps's hundred dollars! The head centre has the key, but it's not the only key that opens. The key of Mat's desk fits that lock. I know, for I've tried it. It's his watch to-night. I've an idea. (*Rises, puts on his hat, and crosses,* R.) Mat, don't get angry. You deserve the partnership, and you deserve the girl. It's a pity you can't have both. Good night. — (*Aside, at door,* R.) An honest man! I've known a fortune to be lost in a single night, and why not a character. Mat Allen, this night I'll play for yours. (*Exit,* R.)

Mat. She looks upon me with favor. She, the bright being that I have worshipped afar off, as men look upon treasures far beyond their reach. What could he mean? Have I betrayed myself? Does he know how madly I love her? No, no; never by word, look, or act have I betrayed my secret. Ah, Grace, Grace! glorious, unattainable; the idol of a cultivated circle, with a throng of admirers about you, your fortune is a safeguard against the approach of the humble worshipper — (GRACE *enters, advances across stage, and leans on his chair, listening*) — who would die to show his devotion. Year by year this love has grown upon me, and now 'tis almost too strong to prison in my heart. But I will be strong. I know 'tis an honest love, that could boldly speak were all the barriers of wealth and station removed. But this can never be; so to my heart alone, as to a sacred shrine, I'll go to worship you, my glorious Grace.

Grace. Dreaming the happy hours away, Matthew?

Mat. (*rises in confusion*). What — Grace — why — how — what — I beg your pardon. Did you speak?

Grace. Why, bless me, Matthew, what's the matter?

Have I interrupted some desperate plot, or some dream of love? You really look frightened.

Mat. Do I? Well, it's very natural. — No, I don't mean that. Does your father want me?

Grace. No; but I do. Now, compose yourself, and we will talk business. Do you know what day to-morrow is?

Mat. Why, it's Wednesday — isn't it?

Grace. Isn't it! What a bright business man. To-morrow is the anniversary of a very important event.

Mat. Your birthday?

Grace. O, that's not important. To-morrow is the anniversary of the entrance of Matthew Allen into business life.

Mat. And you remember this?

Grace. Indeed I do, for 'twas the beginning of a very happy life for all of us. 'Twas then I formed a dear friendship, which has continued until this day.

Mat. Ah, Grace, it is so kind of you to say it, — you, who are so exalted in society, to confess friendship for a poor man.

Grace. Poor man! I confess no such thing. The friendship, I admit, is with a brave fellow, who has battled night and day to serve the man who once befriended him; rich in honest worth, noble in every manly accomplishment; a man with a strong arm and a quick brain, who has the right to seek and claim the highest station, or woo and win the highest lady in the land.

Mat. Grace, Grace! This to me?

Grace. To you, Matthew, for you are the man. To-morrow my father makes choice of a partner. Who it is

I do not know. He has kept his secret even from me. I know not what changes may be made, but you, Matthew, must leave this place.

Mat. I leave this place? You know not what you say. I cannot do it.

Grace. Not do it? Why not?

Mat. Because I love you, Grace. I have hidden it so deep that I thought 'twould never escape me. But I must speak. I love you, Grace, dearly, madly, I know. Let me stay here. I will still be diligent in business. I care not who may come to lord it here; only let me be near you.

Grace. No, Matthew, you must go. Do you think I will allow you, my friend, to be supplanted in this place by a stranger. No, Matthew, you have energy and talent. Build for yourself. Imitate the example of your master, and take a partner.

Mat. A partner, Grace? You know not what you say. Where could I find a partner with capital, for that is what I should need?

Grace. O, I'll find one for you, never fear; one who will join you in any enterprise — strong, brave, true.

Mat. Where will you find me such a partner?

Grace. Here, Matthew, here, with a capital of earnest, true love. I will be your partner.

Mat. Am I dreaming? You, Grace, you?

Grace. Yes, I; the woman you have loved so long. Ah, Matthew! we cannot hide it. Try all we may, it speaks in the flush of the cheek, the gleam of the eye, the trembling speech. You have told me that you loved me, and I — I — Well, I am your partner, you know, Matthew.

Mat. Dear, dear Grace! My partner for life?

Grace. For life, Matthew.

Mat. Then on this hand —

Grace. No, no, Matthew. The head of the new house should have higher aspirations.

Mat. Grace, you're an angel! (*Puts his arm about her waist, and kisses her lips. — Enter,* L., BENTON, *with his hat and cane;* R., CHARLEY *and* RACHEL. — GRACE *and* MATTHEW *separate, look down, confused.*)

Mr. B. (*aside*). So, so; signed, sealed, and delivered. Good, good.

Rachel. It's a match, Charley. Did you hear that smack?

Chas. Do you think I'm deaf. 'Twas red hot, Shellie, red hot!

CURTAIN.

ACT 2. SCENE. — *Same as in Act 1. Dark. Candle burning on table,* C. MATTHEW *seated at* L. *of it, his hand on* RACHEL'S *shoulder. She sits on a box at his feet, her arm resting upon his knee.*

Mat. And so, Shellie, you have stolen away from your cheerful home, with me to keep vigil in this gloomy place.

Rachel. Yes, brother. Uncle Abe was busy at his books, Charley had gone out, and Aunt Betsey was nodding over her knitting, so I just put on my hat and shawl, scampered off, and here I am, to spend an hour with you.

Mat. Ever thoughtful, Sunshine. You well knew your bright face would light up the old counting-room, as it has every dark scene in my life. Ah, sister mine, how dreary the last seven years would have been without you to comfort and console.

Rachel. Seven years! Why so it is, and to-morrow, to-morrow is the day we celebrate. I declare, I'd almost forgotten it. It seems but yesterday that we stood beside the death-bed of our mother. Poor mother! how she must rejoice at our prosperity, for I feel her presence always.

Mat. Yes, sister; ever near us. Dark was the life journey of the best of mothers. Heaven guard us from thought or act that might disturb her peace or sully the brightness of her pure spirit.

Rachel. Amen to that, brother. Dear mother! Can I ever forget her last night upon earth. I was alone with her. She called me to her. The light fast fading from her eyes, her face white as the pillow on which she rested, her thin, white hand feebly sought to grasp mine; but still the sweet, patient smile was there. "Shellie," she said, — dear, dear mother! — "I am going — going to sleep. No more toil, no more trouble for me. 'Twill be a long, refreshing sleep. I must not repine, yet 'tis hard to leave you to battle with the world. And the other, — my boy, your brother, — O, Shellie, temptations will be around him. He must work for you both. Let him always feel the sunshine of a sister's love. Be his helper, his counsellor, his keeper. Sacrifice the dearest wish of your heart, if you can save him from the cold world's cruel snares." — Dear, dear mother! (*Weeps.*)

Mat. Nay, nay, sister, do not weep. She is an angel now. Nobly have you fulfilled her last request. Ever near me, ever thoughtful of my comfort, ever consoler of my dark hours, how much I owe to you. Ah, Sunshine, 'tis the strong arm that clears the path, but 'tis the gentle hand that points the way, revives the failing strength, and heals the stinging wounds. You have indeed been my keeper. Now dry your eyes, for I want your advice. You know we are to have no secrets from each other.

Rachel. That's the compact. Have you a secret?

Mat. Yes, indeed; an important one. I'm in love.

Rachel. O, that's no secret.

Mat. Indeed, sharp eyes! Well, I've another, then. I'm engaged. Wish me joy, sister. Grace Benton, the rich, beautiful, charming Grace Benton, has promised to be my wife.

Rachel. Well, I declare! And I suppose you want my consent.

Mat. Your consent?

Rachel. Certainly, sir. Am I not your guardian? Very well, sir; you shall have it. Bring her to me, and I will place my hand on your heads, and "bless you, my children," in the most approved manner. O, I'm so glad! But, stop! she has a father.

Mat. I am aware of that. Now what shall I do? Go to him, confess my love, and ask his consent, or run away with her?

Rachel. Both, of course — that is, one at a time. Ask his consent. If he declines the honor of an alliance, elope. (*Knock outside,* R.) Good gracious! What's that?

Mat. It sounded very much like a knock. Perhaps a message; perhaps some one for you. (*Knock repeated.*) At any rate, I'll soon find out. (*Rises; takes the candle.*) Keep quiet, Sunshine. I'll be back in a minute. (*Exit*, R.)

Rachel (*sits in chair* L. *of table*). No secrets from each other, and I haven't told him mine. Come here on purpose too. For I'm in love — engaged. Charley Benton has promised to be my wife — no, my husband. Shall I ask his father's consent, or run away with him. Dear Charley! he's such a queer fellow. I wonder if a young lady ever had a proposal from a man with his arms full of dry goods before. It all happened as we were going home to-night. "Shellie," said he, "dear Shellie!" And then he squeezed my arm, and dropped a bundle. "Plague take these bundles. — Shellie, I love you!" Another squeeze, and away went another bundle. I thought I should have died with laughter.

Enter MATTHEW, R.

Mat. (*places candle on table*). A note for me, Shellie.

Rachel. A note? From whom?

Mat. That's just what I'm going to find out. (*Opens note.*) Hallo! from Charley!

Rachel. From Charley Benton?

Mat. Yes. (*Reads.*) " Dear Mat : I'm in trouble. If you don't want me locked up for the night, come to Murphy's billiard-hall and rescue the subscriber, Charley Benton." What does this mean?

Rachel. Charley in trouble? O, Mat, go at once!

Mat. I cannot, Shellie. 'Twould cost me my situation. I am placed here in trust. Mr. Benton would never forgive me should I desert my post. Foolish fellow! he's always getting into a scrape.

Rachel. You must get him out of this. Think, Mat, 'tis his own son. He must not be locked up.

Mat. I dare not go, Shellie. To leave this place would be ruin to me.

Rachel. To be locked up in a cell would be ruin to him. Think of the disgrace. O, for my sake, brother, do go.

Mat. Your sake, Shellie?

Rachel. Yes, mine. I am his promised wife.

Mat. Shellie! And you have kept this from me?

Rachel. I came here to-night to tell you; but your happiness, of course, took precedence, and I must wait to tell mine. You will save him — won't you, Mat?

Mat. But there's no one to leave here.

Rachel. Yes, I am here, and you know I'm a famous keeper. I'll guard everything while you're away. Now go, that's a good brother. Here's your hat. (*Gives him hat.*)

Mat. Well, I'll go, Shellie, for your sake. I don't like to leave you here alone. Keep quiet, and do not leave the room. (*Exit, R.*)

Rachel (*sits L. of table. Speaks slowly*). Charley in trouble! Won't I pull his ears for him! What can he have done? Nothing wrong. — He's such a rash fellow! — What's that? How lonesome it is here! What can I do to amuse myself? (*Takes book from table.*) "Promissory Notes," — that's not very promising reading. (*Takes up another.*) "Bills Payable," — O, that won't pay. What's that? There's somebody at the door. I hear a key in the lock. Can Mat have returned so soon? Hark! Steps! and coming this way! 'Tis not his tread; 'tis stealthy, creeping! What shall I do? It may be a burglar. O, heavens! I'll blow out the light. (*Blows out light.*) Who can it be? O, I wish Mat was here! What will become of me? I'm shivering with fear. Let me hide somewhere. (*Crouches at end of lounge*, L.) Nearer, nearer! I can hear my heart beat.

Enter RICHARD, *stealthily*, R.

Rich. So, so! I've tricked the faithful watchman. The bait took, and he's off on a bootless errand. Well planned, my boy. Now for the key. (*Creeps to desk*, R.)

Rachel. Somebody's creeping about the room! Heaven protect me!

Rich. (*takes key from lock*). All right. Now for the gold. (*Passes to table*, C.) Here's the drawer. The key fits. Open sesame! (*Opens drawer.*) Here's Scrap's shiners. (*Takes out bag, locks drawer, creeps back to desk*, R., *and places key as before.*) Successful burglary! The gold is in my possession. Mat Allen will be suspected, and the partnership blown sky high for the present. (*At door*, R.) I must be off. He'll see the trick, and be back — but too late, too late! The treasure's flown. (*Exit*, R.)

Rachel (*comes forward*). Gone! 'Twas a burglar. The drawer has been robbed, — robbed in Mat's absence, — and I, who should have protected it with my life, skulked in a corner like a coward. What shall I do? O, brother, did I counsel you wrong? I'll pursue him until help appears, then have him secured. Yes, 'tis the only course left. (*Creeps to door*, R.) Hark! Gracious heavens, he is returning for more booty! Shall I raise an alarm? No, no; who could hear me? 'Twould be but the signal for my own destruction. O, Mat, Mat, why don't you come? (*Creeps back to hiding-place*, L.)

Enter CHARLEY, R., *with arms outstretched. Walks against table*, C.

Chas. O, crackee! (*Creeps down*, R. *Walks against desk*, R.) O, Gemini! Well, this is a hard road to travel! I never could have believed it, never. Our Mat deserting his post — for it must have been him I saw leaving the warehouse. Now where can he have gone? It's very lucky I had my key, or my little plot to secure the pitcher's badge would have been a dead failure. Ah, ha, my good father, I do hate to thwart your plans, but what's a fellow to do that has to present a badge, and has no badge to present? So I'm going to avail myself of your key, which I quite accidentally found in your pocket, to open your drawer and secure the badge. I wish Mat was here, for I could very easily have defended my action; but this looks very like burglary. However, the renowned pitcher must not be disappointed. So here goes. (*Goes to table*, C., *unlocks drawer, takes out badge, locks drawer*.) There you are, my beauty, to make glad the heart of Bob Dyke. Now for the Goosenecks. (*Crosses to* R. *of table*.) Might as well have a smoke as I go down. (*Puts cigar in his mouth*.) Wonder if I can find a match. (*Searches pockets*.)

Rachel. What is he doing now? O, if I could but

secure the villain! If I could but get a look at his face, that I might know him again! (*Creeps up to table, back* L. *corner, leans forward anxiously.*)

Chas. I've found one. (*Draws match across table.*)

Rachel. Ah, he strikes a light. Courage, Shellie, courage.

Chas. All right. (*When the match is well lighted, brings it up to his cigar. It illumines his face.*)

Rachel. Gracious heavens! Charley Benton! (*Falls on lounge.*)

Chas. What's that? Rats! rats! (*Flings book,* L.) " Dead for a ducat."

QUICK CURTAIN.

ACT 3. SCENE. — *Parlor in* ABEL BENTON'S *house. Lounge,* L. H. *corner. Table,* C., *back. Arm-chair on rollers* R. *of table. Arm-chair on rollers,* R. C. *Chair against wall, near* R. *entrance.* RACHEL *discovered lying on lounge with her face buried in her handkerchief.*

Rachel (*raising her head and throwing her handkerchief across the room*). There, I'm just going to put an end to this business. All day long I've been lying round, making myself wretched, and crying until my eyes ache for a miserable — I was just going to say thief. Well, he is a thief. He robbed his father's drawer, that's certain. I saw him myself. Charley Benton — my Charley! — O, dear! where's my handkerchief? No, I won't drop another tear. He isn't worth it. And I, like a little fool, instead of telling Mat all about it, must needs lie to shield him. I hadn't the heart to tell my brother, when he asked me if anything had happened, — for he hadn't found Charley, — that Charley had been there. My Charley! — Where's my handkerchief? No, I won't cry. I will keep his secret, but I won't shed another tear. I wonder what he took. Uncle Abe is awful sober, but he says nothing about a robbery, and Charley — I've taken precious good care to keep out of his way — I'll have nothing to say to him. It's most time for Mat to be back. I dread the meeting. How can I look him in the face after deceiving him so?

Enter CHARLEY, R.

Chas. Ah, Shellie, I've caught you at last. Now, you coquettish puss, explain the meaning of this avoidance of me for a whole day.

Rachel (*rising*). Mr. Benton.

Chas. Hallo! That's not my name. It's plain Charley.

Rachel. Then, plain Charley, you will oblige me by keeping your distance, by calling me Miss Allen, and by avoiding me, as I shall endeavor to avoid you, in future.

Chas. Why, Shellie, what's the matter? Last night you told me that you loved me.

Rachel. Last night I thought you worthy of any woman's love. I have found out my mistake.

Chas. But, Shellie, I am all in the dark.

Rachel. I was; but a ray of light, just the gleam of a match, has wonderfully dispelled the darkness in which

I was enveloped. You understand — a match. Henceforth we are strangers. (*Exit*, L.)

Chas. A match. It's the worst match ever I took a hand in. What does she mean? Does she mean the match we made last night? Is she going to throw it off without a trial? I don't like this, for I love her dearly. For her sake, last night, after the presentation, I withdrew from the Gooseneck Nine. I must know the cause of this sudden change. It's some of Aunt Betsey's work, perhaps. But I'll know. She's too dear a girl to give up without a struggle.

Enter SCRAPS, R., *in full evening dress, with his basket under his arm.*

Scraps. Here I am, Charley, in full regimentals.

Chas. Scraps, old fellow! — I beg your pardon, — Job Layton, Esq. Well, well, it's astonishing what good clothes can accomplish. But you don't want that basket.

Scraps. Hey?

Chas. You don't want that basket. It's out of place.

Scraps. Well, I don't know about that. There's nothing like having an eye to business. (*Picks up* RACHEL'S *handkerchief, and puts it in the basket.*)

Chas. Put it in the hall. Sink the shop here.

Scraps. Just as you say. (*Exit*, R.)

Chas. He's a splendid old chap. Now if we could only make Aunt Betsey believe so! He's just the man to make her a good husband. I think if we could take her by surprise she might accept Scraps, for I don't believe she ever had an offer. There's nothing like being quick in these matters; so I'll bring them together at once.

Enter SCRAPS, R.

Scraps. There, I've put it up stairs with my old togs. Now, what next?

Chas. Scraps, you have often said that any favor I might ask of you would be freely granted.

Scraps. To be sure I have; and I say it again.

Chas. All right. Then I ask you to marry.

Scraps. Hey? You're on the wrong side.

Chas. You're on the wrong side of matrimony, and the sooner you change your position the better. I've found a wife for you. Follow my instructions and you will be a happy man.

Scraps. Marry! I? O, come, Charley, none of your jokes. Who'd marry me — an old rag-picker?

Chas. A poor old rag-picker — with forty thousand dollars.

Scraps. Hush! Do you want to ruin me?

Chas. I know where you deposit.

Scraps. Well, don't tell all you know. Who's the lady?

Chas. Aunt Betsey, the lady you saw at the office. O, Scraps, you'd make a splendid uncle.

Scraps. O, but this is all nonsense. She doesn't know me; I've never met her; we're total strangers; it's absurd, ridiculous. I'm going home.

Chas. No, you're not; you're going to meet Aunt Betsey to-night; and take my advice, Scraps, propose at once. There's nothing pleases a woman so well as an energetic lover.

4

Scraps. But, Charley, I don't know how.

Chas. It's easy enough. Tell her you've long admired her; you have heard of her sweet disposition, her amiable qualities.

Scraps. But I can't, Charley. I should be sure to make a mess of it.

Chas. O, it's easy enough. Here's the programme: I introduce you — "Miss Benton, Mr. Layton, a gentleman who has called on particular business." I leave you alone. You bow; offer her a chair; take one yourself. A short pause. You speak. "Madam, 'tis a beautiful evening." She answers, "Delightful, sir." Then you, with a sigh, — don't forget that, — "But this trait of Nature is not confined to the weather alone. *Some* women" — emphasize the *some* — "resemble it." She sighs, blushes, and says, "Ah me." You speak quick. "You have unconsciously spoken my thoughts. 'Tis you, indeed," — clasp your hands, — "on whom my thoughts are fixed. Why have you so long remained single? Your attractive appearance, your graceful carriage, your classic face, your coal-black hair —"

Scraps. Hold on, Charley. That's too much. The beautiful evening, and ah me, and the sighs, are all very well, but the carriages, the coals, and all that, are too much.

Chas. O, these are merely complimentary epithets. You can number them: one, attractive appearance; two, graceful carriage; three, classic face; four, coal-black hair; five, amiable temper.

Scraps (*counting his fingers*). One, attractive appearance; two, graceful carriage, — all right, I'll keep tally on my fingers. What next?

Chas. The rest you must leave to inspiration, for here she comes. Tell her you adore her, and throw yourself on your knees, beg her to bestow her hand — Here she is.

Scraps. But, Charley, I shall make a mess, I know I shall.

Enter BETSEY, R.

Betsey. Well, I never. There's that front door standing wide open, and the coal bin just as full as it can be, too, and Abel away at this time of night, and Mr. Johnson standin in his front yard a smokin a nasty pipe. If there's anything I detest, it's a pipe. When Abel had them gas pipes put in, I told him jest how it would be, though what that's got to do with smokin tobacco the Lord only knows. Why, here's Charley, and a strange man, too. Wonder if he wiped his feet.

Chas. Good evening, Aunt Betsey. This is my friend, my *wealthy* friend. Miss Benton, Mr. Job Layton.

Betsey. How do you do, Mr. Job Layton? 'Pears to me I've heard one of them names afore. Layton! Why, bless me, there was a family of Laytons lived right opposite us — poor as puddock, too. Any relation of that tribe?

Chas. O, no; Mr. Layton is descended from a very aristocratic family, of very ancient origin.

Betsey. Biblical, pr'aps. There was a Layton in my family Bible. — No, 'twan't, nuther; 'twas Job, the man who had so many blisters. Pr'aps he was one of your family.

Chas. Aunt Betsey, Mr. Layton has a very delicate

matter to bring to your attention. He wishes to consult you on a subject that lies near his heart.

Betsey. What's the matter with him? Hope 'tain't neurology or rheumatics. That's always fatal when it affects the heart. What's his symptoms?

Chas. I'll leave him to explain. Treat him kindly, for he is one of the best of men.

Betsey. Is he? Well, so are they all, till they're found out. There was Judith Higborn's husband. Why, folks thought butter wouldn't melt in his mouth, he was so meek, till Judith sent him one day to the milliner for her bunnet, and that was the last ever seen of the husband, or the milliner, or the bunnet. Spring bunnet, too, wuth ten dollars.

Chas. Well, listen to his complaint, and remember he has my recommendation as an excellent husband. (*Exit*, R.)

Betsey (*aside*). Husband? Whose, I wonder? He don't look very bright. Well, Mr. Layton, what's your symptoms? (SCRAPS *bows, wheels chair down from* C., *and bows, motioning* BETSEY *to be seated.*) Thank you. (*Sits.*) Well, he's perlite, anyhow. (SCRAPS *goes to* R., *wheels down chair* R. *of* BETSEY.) What a draft from that door! Guess I'll take the other chair. (*Moves into chair placed by* SCRAPS.)

Scraps. Hey? She's on the wrong side. That won't do. I can't hear a word. (*Passes behind* BETSEY, *takes the chair at her* L., *and wheels it round to her* R.)

Betsey. Law sakes, you needn't have troubled yourself. (*Moves to the other chair.*) That was just as comfortable, just as comfortable.

Scraps (looking at her). It's no use. I can't hear a word there. (*Is about to move the vacant chair, as before.*)

Betsey. What ails the man? Stop! stop! Sit down. (SCRAPS *looks at her, then sits.*) Something the matter with his heart? I should think 'twas his head. Now, then, what's the symptoms?

Scraps. I can't hear a word. (*A short pause.— They look at each other.*) Madam, it's a delightful evening.

Betsey. Delightful evening! The man's a lunatic: I know it. Why, it's raining cats and dogs. The mud is twelve inches deep. It's horrid, horrid!

Scraps (aside). Don't hear a word. (*Aloud.*) But this freak of nature is not confined to the weather alone; *some* women are just like it.

Betsey. Now, what does he mean by that? *Some* women are horrid! Does he mean me?

Scraps (aside). She spoke, but I heard nothing. (*Aloud.*) Yes, you have unconsciously spoken my thought. 'Tis you, indeed.

Betsey. What? O, the man's a lunatic; he certainly is. He ought to be put in a strait thimajig at once.

Scraps (aside). What comes next? Single, single. (*Aloud.*) No wonder you have remained single so long.

Betsey. The sarcastic wretch.

Scraps (aside). So far, so good. Now then. (*Counts his fingers.*) One, appearance— (*Aloud.*) Your venerable appearance—

Betsey. O, the wretch! And he old enough to be my father.

Scraps (*counts his fingers.* — *Aside*). Two, form — (*Aloud.*) Your *antique* form —

Betsey. O, I'd like to strangle him!

Scraps (*counting.* — *Aside*). Three, face — (*Aloud.*) Your coal-black face —

Betsey. O, Charley Benton, you shall pay for this.

Scraps (*counting.* — *Aside*). Four, hair — (*Aloud.*) Your more antique hair —

Betsey. The man's a fool.

Scraps (*counting.* — *Aside*). Five, temper — (*Aloud.*) Your versatile temper —

Betsey. Stop, stop, I say! You've said quite enough. (*Rises.*)

Scraps. Hey? (*Aside.*) What next? (*Aloud.*) You are dying for me, or I am for you, it don't make much difference. (*Falls on his knees.*) Behold me at your feet. Bestow upon me your hand. — " If ever I cease to love — "

Betsey. I will; there. (*Boxes his ears, first right, then left.*) There! You're a fool, or a lunatic. If you ever show your face here again I'll scratch your eyes out, you mean, contemptible old ragamuffin. You jest make yourself scarce, or I'll have the police after you. Come here again, and I'll have a boiler of hot water ready, and use it, too. Venerable, indeed! You old idiot! (*Exit,* R.)

Scraps. Evidently not a success. Well, I'm glad of it. I've made a fool of myself to please the boy. I don't know what she said, but I'm on the wrong side. (*Rises.*)

Enter Mr. Benton, R.

Mr. B. Ah, Job, you're the very man I wanted. But how's this? Here in my house, and dressed so fine! What is the meaning of this?

Scraps. O, it's one of Charley's jokes. He wanted to bring me out in society. (*Aside.*) And he has, with a vengeance.

Mr. B. Well, I'm glad to see you. But listen. Your money is gone.

Scraps. Has it? Well, I'm not surprised.

Mr. B. You will be when you learn who took it. 'Twas Matthew Allen.

Scraps. You're mistaken. 'Twas the other.

Mr. B. What other?

Scraps. Richard Carnes.

Mr. B. No, Job, 'twas Matthew. Of that I am sure. He was left in charge of the office. He was seen in Murphy's billiard-room at nine o'clock. I'm sure. When I found the money gone this morning, I put a detective upon his track. There can be no mistake. It is Matthew Allen.

Scraps. I don't believe it. If forty detectives were on his track, if a thousand circumstances conspired to point out Matthew Allen as the thief, I would doubt all but his honesty.

Mr. B. Bah! Job, you're too credulous. He has been false to his trust. Against my express orders, he left my store last night; and should he ever return, I will discharge him from my employ.

Scraps. Don't be hasty, Abel. Give the lad a chance.

He has served you well. Even if he were guilty, you should be merciful.

Mr. B. Merciful to a thief? How do I know but what he has robbed me before? No, he shall be punished.

Scraps. Bah! You'll have to beg his pardon for suspecting him. Abel, keep cool. Wait till the real thief shows his hand.

Mr. B. He has shown it now. No, no, Job, you like the lad, and would save him if you could; but depend upon it (*Enter* RACHEL, R.) the thief who stole your money was Matthew Allen. (*Exit*, L.)

Rachel. O, what do I hear? Matthew suspected! No, no, it cannot be. Mr. Layton (*comes down* R. *of* SCRAPS), what did he say? What did he say? Whom does he suspect?

Scraps (*aside*). His sister! 'Twould break her heart. (*Aloud.*) Hey? You're on the wrong side. (*Crosses to* R.) I'll go and change this toggery, for I don't feel easy. (*Exit*, R.)

Rachel. Brother Mat suspected! O, I never thought of that. But I can clear him, I can clear him. But how? By denouncing Charley, my Charley, that I love so dearly? O, I can never do that. Perhaps he wanted the money for some special service. Perhaps — O, why should I try to excuse so base a deed? O, would that I were dead! If I betray Charley, his father will drive him from the house, and I should never see him again. And, spite of his crime, I love him so dearly! But my brother! He must not suffer for the crime of another, nor will he, for they have no proof. And Charley; he would curse me should I betray him. O, what shall I do! (*Falls on her knees by sofa.*) O, mother, sainted mother! if you watch over your child, guide her in this dark hour. (*Buries her head in sofa, weeping.*)

Enter RICHARD, R.

Rich. Ah, Shellie! at your devotions. (RACHEL *rises suddenly.*) Don't let me disturb you. Where are all the good people?

Rachel. Good evening, Mr. Carnes. Take a seat. Grace and my aunt will soon appear.

Rich. Thank you. (*Sits* L. *of table.* RACHEL *on lounge.*) Has Mat returned yet?

Rachel. No, we are expecting him every moment. I am sorry he could not arrive sooner.

Rich. (*aside*). So am I. I expected to find his coat hanging in the hall. Old Scraps's money-bag is heavy in my pocket and on my conscience. I must get it disposed of somewhere about Mat's wardrobe. (*Aloud.*) Where's Charley, Shellie?

Rachel. I don't know.

Enter CHARLEY, R.

Chas. Nor does she care, Dick. I'm glad to see you. Do you feel better, Shellie?

Rachel (*turns her back*). No, I don't feel better.

Chas. Then we must get Aunt Betsey to prescribe for you. (*Enter* BETSEY.) Here, Aunt Betsey, is another patient for you. Come, Shellie, tell her your symptoms.

Betsey. Symptoms! Well, if they're anything like

those of the last patient you found for me, I prescribe a lunatic asylum at once. How do you do, Mr. Carnes?

Rich. Good evening, Miss Benton. How becomingly you are dressed this evening! Your stately person —

Betsey. Now don't *you* be a fool. I've heard enough allusion to my personal appearance this evening already to make me sick. (*Sits* R. *of table.*)

Chas. (*aside*). Hullo! Scraps must have made a failure. (*Aloud.*) Did you comfort my friend, Mr. Layton, Aunt Betsey?

Betsey. You just bring him here again, that's all.

Enter GRACE, L.

Grace. Shellie, Shellie, Matthew's come. I heard his step on the walk — and I should know it. (*Stops confused.*) Why, I didn't know we had company. Good evening, Mr. Carnes.

Rich. Good evening, Miss Benton.

Grace (*aside*). Tiresome thing! Just spoiled my meeting Matthew in the hall. (*Aloud.*) Shellie, why don't you run and meet Matthew?

Rachel. My head aches fearfully. (*Aside.*) How can I meet him?

Betsey. Land sakes! He knows the way from cellar to garret.

Enter MATTHEW, R., *with coat on his arm, which he throws across chair,* R.

Mat. Ah, here you all are. Home again, as you see.

Grace (*running to him*). Matthew, welcome!

Mat. Thank you, my dear (*pause*), dear friend. (*Takes her hand.*)

Grace. Well, what success?

Mat. The best of success. The cargo of the Elmyra is sold. (*Enter* Mr. BENTON, L.) Good evening, Mr. Benton. I was just telling your daughter my mission was successful. The cargo of the Elmyra has been taken.

Mr. B. Indeed. Do you know of anything else that has been taken, *Mr.* Allen?

Mat (*surprised*). Mr. Allen? To what do you allude, Mr. Benton?

Mr. B. Matthew Allen, as you well know, I am a man of very few words. Last night you were left in charge of my warehouse. During the night a bag of gold, placed in a drawer for safe keeping, was abstracted. Where is it?

Mat. A bag of gold, belonging to Job Layton, stolen? I know nothing about it.

Rachel (*aside*). Why don't Charley speak? (CHARLEY *is in conversation with* AUNT BETSEY.)

Mr. B. This is strange. You were left in charge of the warehouse. Did you leave it during the night?

Mat. I did.

Mr. B. Where did you go?

Mat. That, sir, I cannot tell. I received a note late in the evening from a friend, calling upon me as a friend to assist him. That is all I can say. It remains for him to clear the mystery.

Rachel (*aside*). O, why don't Charley speak? One word from him, and Matthew is clear.

Mr. B. So, sir, *you* cannot clear the mystery; but I can. You left that place to go to Murphy's billiard-room. You were seen there. This money was left in your charge. You alone were responsible for it; and I charge you with the theft.

Mat. Mr. Benton!

Grace. Father!

Rachel (aside). And there Charley sits as cool as a villain. Why don't he speak?

Mr. B. Yes, Matthew Allen, I have trusted you fully. I have believed in your truth and honesty; but the very fact that you quitted that store is proof positive of your guilt.

Mat. Mr. Benton, all I have in the world I owe to you. I believe I have not been ungrateful for your kindness. Had I done the base deed of which you accuse me, I could not look you in the face, as I do now, and pronounce your charge false.

Rachel (jumping up.) Charley Benton, do you hear? Why don't you speak?

Chas. I beg your pardon, Shellie. What's broke? I've been having a talk with Aunt Betsey.

Rachel. Mat, my brother Matthew, is accused of theft — by your father, too.

Chas. That's a serious matter. I say, father, what is it?

Mr. B. Nothing that should be made public. Matthew Allen is about to quit my service disgraced.

Mat. Disgraced?

Mr. B. Yes, disgraced! Everything is against you — your absence from the store, the empty drawer, the missing money-bag —

Chas. (aside). Drawer, store, money-bag! *(Aloud.)* I say, Shellie, what's all this?

Rachel. And you ask me? Shame, shame, Charley Benton.

Chas. Well, confound it! If you won't tell me what it's all about, you'll excuse me if I don't interfere. (*Retires up.*)

Mr. B. (*to* MATTHEW). There is not one circumstance in your favor.

Grace. Father, you are wrong. There are a thousand: his good, true life; his zeal in your service; his care for his sister; — all stand out to shield him from suspicion.

Mr. B. You, Grace, defend him?

Grace. With my life, if need be. I know him to be so good, so true, so noble, that when you turn him from your door, my arm shall be around him, and my voice shall whisper in his ear, "Whither thou goest I go."

Mat. Dear, dear Grace!

Rachel (*aside*). Must I learn my duty from her.

Mr. B. Never! No daughter of mine shall link her fate with a felon — a thief!

Grace. A thief? 'Tis false!

Rachel. Ay, false, false! And I can prove it.

All. You, Shellie? (AUNT BETSEY *comes down,* L. *Situations:* MATTHEW, R., GRACE, R. C., RACHEL, C., MR. BENTON, L. C., AUNT BETSEY, L., CHARLEY *and* RICHARD *back by the table, looking on.*)

Rachel. Yes, I; for I was in the counting-room when that money was taken. My brother is guiltless. He was called to help a friend, as he tells you. I was left alone. I heard a step; blew out the candle. The thief entered, opened the drawer in the table, moved away, and then returned and made a second attempt. I was so frightened that I did not tell my brother.

Mat. That was wrong, Shellie.

Rachel. I know it, brother. I have deceived you, and am no more worthy to be called your keeper. But you shall be cleared. (*With feeling.*) Uncle Abe, suppose a young girl had a brother, whom she loved very dearly; a brother, whom she had told her dying mother, should never suffer, when any sacrifice could be made on her part. Suppose she also had a lover, whom she loved very dearly, — very, very dearly, — and she were called upon to sacrifice one or the other, who had committed a crime, what should you advise to do?

Mr. B. Save the innocent — if it broke her heart.

Rachel. Right, Uncle Abe; you are right, sir. Listen, then. Last night, when that thief came in for the second time, I was on the alert. After he had accomplished his purpose, he struck a match, and as he held it up to light a cigar, I saw his face.

Mat. His face, Shellie? Did you know him?

Rachel. Know him? (*Throws herself into his arms.*) Too well, too well. 'Twas him. (*Pointing.*) Charley Benton.

All. Charley Benton! (*All fall back, showing* CHARLEY *coolly seated on the table with his arms folded.*)

Chas. Well, what of it? I was in the store last night, did open the the drawer, and take from it —

Mr. B. The bag of gold?

Chas. (*coming down.*) No, sir, the pitcher's badge, which you so unceremoniously locked up for me.

Mr. B. But the money?

Chas. I know nothing about it. There was none there when I took the badge, that's certain.

Mat. So, Charley, your note to me was a blind to get me from the store.

Chas. What note? I sent no note. Hang it, what a mysterious time you are having here! Who's the robber, anyhow?

Mat. I received a note signed with the name of Charley Benton. Here it is. I thought it my duty to leave the store, as I had left my sister in charge.

Chas. And Shellie caught the thief?

Rachel. Stop, Charley. Did you take the badge the first or second time you entered the room?

Chas. Hang it, Shellie, are you beginning to be suspicious? I entered the store but once.

Rachel. And found nothing in the drawer but the badge?

Chas. Not a thing.

Rachel. Then there was another.

Rich. (*aside*). I wish I was well rid of this bag. There's Mat's coat in the chair. I can easily slip it into the pocket, and then I'm safe.

Mr. B. Yes, there was another; and that other your brother.

Grace. Still suspicious, father.

Mr. B. Still suspicious; and, until the thief is found, you, Matthew Allen, are suspended from service.

Mat. This is very hard, Mr. Benton.

Mr. B. You should not have left that store had fifty notes been sent you. Had the building been in flames you should not have disobeyed my orders.

Rich. (*who has crept over to chair,* R. *Aside*). Now, then, to fasten his guilt.

Mat. Very well, sir. I have tried to do my duty. If I have failed, my heart, my conscience acquits me of blame or guilt.

Rich. (*takes money-bag from his breast pocket. Aside*). All right. Now, then. (*About to place it in* MATTHEW'S *coat pocket.* SCRAPS *enters suddenly,* R., *in his old costume, his basket in both hands.*)

Scraps. Hey? (*Holds out basket.* RICHARD *starts back, and drops the bag into basket.*) You're on the wrong side, Mr. Carnes, the wrong side.

Mr. B. Job Layton, what are you doing?

Scraps. Recovering my money. Here it is. (*Comes down,* C.) Here is the money (*showing basket*), and here the thief. (*Seizing* RICHARD *by wrist.*)

Mr. B. Richard Carnes? You are mistaken, Job.

Scraps. Now don't be a fool, Abel. I knew when I placed that money in your hands it would be found in the possession of Richard Carnes. He's a notorious gambler; that I know. He frequents Murphy's billiard-rooms; he was there last night; wrote a note to Matthew Allen, and sent it to the store last night; then entered the store with a false key — O, I know him! I've proof enough that he committed this theft to put him in prison, and he knows it. Hey, Mr. Carnes?

Mr. B. Richard Carnes, what have you to say?

Rich. Nothing: if you take the word of that ragamuffin, I am a thief; but this little affair was arranged for an entirely different purpose. It has failed, and I am the loser. I am a gentleman's son; my father will make all losses good. As for the business, I have grown tired of it, and want a change; so, with your permission, I will throw up my situation. If I am wanted, you will find me at home. I shall not run away. Good evening, Mr. Benton; good evening, all. (*At door*, R.) A cursed stupid mess I've made of it. (*Exit*, R.)

Scraps. Well, that's cool.

Chas. Decidedly. Shall I stop him, father?

Mr. B. No; let him go. If he feels one half the shame I feel for my share in this business, he is sufficiently punished. (*Crosses to* MATTHEW.) Matthew, I beg your pardon. I have been hasty. Knowing your worth, I should have cut my tongue out ere I made the charge I did.

Mat. Let it pass, Mr. Benton. Circumstances were against me. I should not have left your store; and the fear of compromising your son kept me silent.

Mr. B. And you (*to* CHARLEY), what have you to say for your share in this?

Chas. Me? Well, I like that! It strikes me I'm the martyr — suspected of being a thief, and by Shellie, too.

Rachel. O Charley, forgive me. I thought I was right. It was my brother —

Chas. O, well, if a brother is to stand between you and me, the sooner I claim the privileges of a husband the better.

Betsey. Shellie, that man in the ragged coat! Bless my soul, it's him — the man that saved me from the runaway horse.

Rachel. Why, so it is. Strange I should not have recognized him.

Betsey. Who is he? What's his name?

4

Chas. Why, don't you know? That's Job Layton, Esq.

Betsey. What, the lunatic? Well, if I'd have known he was my preserver — Mr. Layton, Mr. Layton?

Scraps. Hey? You're on the wrong side. (*Turns his back to her.*)

Chas. It's no use, Aunt Betsey. You've lost your chance.

Grace. And now, father, where is the new partner you were to present this evening?

Mr. B. He is here. (*Places his hand on* MATTHEW's *shoulder.*) Matthew Allen, for your long service, for your true, earnest zeal, for your honesty and value, I offer you a partnership.

Mat. Me? O, Mr. Benton, you are my best friend, but I cannot accept.

Mr. B. Not accept?

Mat. No, sir, for I have already formed a partnership with another — this dear girl.

Grace. Yes, father, we have formed a partnership for life.

Mr. B. I see; and, though I have not been asked, I will give my consent. Have your partner, but he must also be mine, under the firm of Abel Benton & Son.

Chas. Well, it strikes me I shall be left out in the cold.

Mr. B. Your turn shall come next, with Matthew's consent.

Mat. Anything you wish, sir.

Rachel. But what's to become of me?

Chas. Now don't you fret about that, Shellie. Grace

is going into the new firm. Let's you and I form an opposition.

Rachel. And so Miss Grace is to usurp my place. Well, I suppose I must bear it.

Scraps. Shellie, that scamp of a Charley wants a keeper. I know him. He's a rascal — jumps into the water, you know. Marry him, and watch him.

Rachel. What do you say, Uncle Abe?

Mr. B. You have my full consent.

Rachel. And you, brother Mat?

Mat. I know no one more worthy of my dear sister than Charley Benton.

Rachel. There's my hand, Charley. And as I have tried to be true to my brother, so may I be true to you. If I have failed in my duty there, it was for love of you.

Mat. Nay, nay, Sunshine; you have been ever true. The happiness of this hour I owe to you alone.

Rachel. Say, rather, to our dear, trusty, watchful old rag-picker.

Scraps. Hey? You're on the wrong side. Earthly friends may do much to guide and guard each other, but Justice, Love, and Truth are servants of a higher Power, who, in the darkest hour, is ever the sure, safe, reliant keeper.

Disposition of Characters.

R.		C.		L.
		SCRAPS.		
	GRACE.		CHARLEY.	
	MATTHEW.		RACHEL.	
MR. BENTON.				BETSEY.

THE REVOLT OF THE BEES.

AN ALLEGORY.

FOR FEMALE CHARACTERS ONLY.

CHARACTERS.

REGINA, Queen of the Bees.
THRIFTIE, GAYLIE, Leaders of the Working Bees.
TRUSTA, WARNA, Guardians of the Hive.
GOLDWING, BRIGHTHUE, VARIA, SPOTILA, Butterflies.

This allegory is particularly designed for school exhibitions. Choruses should be seated on the platform, R. and L. An open stage should be left between the speakers.

SCENE.—*Exterior of the Hive. Bank,* C.

(*Invisible Chorus. Air,* " *Up! Away!* ")

Ho, Awake! Ho, Awake! Ho, Awake! All ye dwellers in the hive,
Away let us speed, for the day is alive.
How freely the flowers are opening their cups,
How glisten the dewdrops each greedily sups!

The fairest and brightest yield sweets as we strive
With treasures of honey to fill up the hive.
Labor gives high delight, delight beyond all measure,
Our hive we love so well we'll fill with sweetest treasure;
Labor gives high delight, delight beyond all measure;
O, high delight, the hive we love to fill.

Enter, L., WARNA, R., TRUSTA.

Warna. Hark to those welcome sounds: our vigils o'er,
The hum of labor stirs the hive once more;
Sweet sister Trusta, in your nightly round,
Hath ought suspicious or uncouth been found?

Trusta. Nay, nay, good Warna, 'twas a quiet night;
Nought but the moon hath crossed my weary sight.
Ah me! 'tis very hard to keep awake
While our companions of sweet sleep partake.
What should we fear? What need of guarding thus?
Who'd care or dare to interfere with us?

Warna. 'Tis an old custom, Trusta, a bee law,
In which our tribe has never found a flaw;
Our code of government is very wise,
And ancient as the orbs that rule the skies;
One rules — our gracious queen; the rest obey;
Some forth in search of honey daily stray,
Some mould the cells within our tasty hive,
Some store our treasure, some with burdens strive,
While others guard with jealous care the way,
That no unbidden guest may hither stray.
Each has a task, and all together strive
With fruits of " Industry " to store the hive,
And keep its motto bright above the door.
No laggards here, where all should work and store.

Trusta. To work and store. For what? When all's
    complete,
Rough-handed men assail our calm retreat,
Disturb our labors, and our workers slay,
Rifle our cells, our treasures bear away.
If this is Industry's reward for toil,
Surely *our* labor's not repaid by spoil.
    Warna. Trusta, your long night vigil makes you wild.
Why, this is treason, rank rebellion, child.
Should your bold words but reach the royal ear,
You'd be disgraced by punishment severe.
I marvel at this rude, complaining mood
In one who hitherto so fair hath stood.
    Trusta. Well, marvels never cease, the wise ones say.
I marvel, Warna, that we never play
Among the flowers, as yonder sportive flies,
Bent to no tasks, on airy pinions rise;
Dance, race, and flutter, in the summer air,
Making a pastime where we find a care.
    Warna. Hush, foolish Trusta; hither comes our
    queen;
Meet her with welcome voice and face serene;
Let not the idle fancies of your brain
Lead you in word or act to give her pain.

    (*Chorus.* Air, " Up! Away! " as before.)

    Enter, R., THRIFTIE *and* REGINA.

Regina. Once more a brilliant morning gilds our hive;
The woods with early songsters are alive;
The grateful incense of a thousand flowers,
Borne on the gentle breeze in unseen showers,

Invites our happy tribe, with quickening zest,
To favor gayly labor's just behest.
Forth to your tasks, my subjects; boldly beat
The choicest flower for its hidden sweet.
You, Thriftie, our most tried and trusty guide,
Shall lead your column to yon mountain side,
The fabled home of many a wondrous flower,
Endowed with sweets of pungency and power;
You, Warna, still stand guardian at the door;
You, Trusta, hold your station as before.
Anon we'll change the guards; till then beware
None enter here, to trap us unaware.

   Thriftie. Thanks, thanks, my queen: with confidence
      elate,
My swift-winged followers, all-impatient, wait
The call to duty. Gladly to obey
Thy lightest wish, we eager haste away.
Proud of thy favor, ere the sun's retreat,
We'll lay the choicest treasures at thy feet.   [*Exit*, R.

   Queen. Ay, zealous Thriftie, thy true, loyal heart
Can life and grace to any task impart.
Loving strong labor for the good it brings,
All toils are light where cheerfulness lends wings.

      Enter, R., GAYLIE, *slowly.*

What! laggards here? Gaylie, this sluggish pace
Befits no leader of our active race.

   Gaylie. I'm weary, gracious queen, of so much
      work,
And long *this* day's accustomed task to shirk:
From morn till night 'tis work. I fain would rest

A little while within my cosy nest,
Or, parted from the toilers of to-day,
Lightly for pleasure o'er the meadows stray.

 Queen. Gaylie, no more: you know not what you ask.
Pleasure alone comes with a finished task;
Rank idleness is but a torturing pest,
Goading to sin, the mockery of rest;
Crush out at once the feverish desire,
And to some more exalted state aspire.
This be your task: o'er yonder field of clover,
With those you lead, upon the instant hover;
Gather the sweets that there in richness lie,
And with your burdens to our mansion hie;
No more complaining, and no more delay,
Arrange your force at once. Away! Away!
         [*Exit* GAYLIE, R.
Now, guardians of the hive, be wise and wary,
Pass none within save those who burdens carry. [*Exit*, R.

 Warna. Trusta, you see that Gaylie's idle mien
Hath found no favor with our gracious queen.

 Trusta. Yet, I confess, her weakness hath a charm
My pulse to quicken and my bosom warm.

    (*Invisible Chorus.* " *Boating Song.*")

    Gayly our pinions swift bear us along,
    O'er the green meadows our flight we prolong.
    Freely and lightly we skim the still air,
    Realm of the butterflies, heart free from care.
    Brightly are gleaming our wings as we fly,
    Gay is the life of the free butterfly;
    Brightly are gleaming our wings as we fly,
    Gay is the life of the free butterfly.

Trusta. Listen; the butterflies are on the wing;
They have no task to check life's joyous spring. [*Exit*, R.

Warna. An idle tribe, who all unthrifty roam,
The gypsies of the field, no care, no home.   [*Exit*, L.

(*Chorus.* "*Boating Song*" *repeated, during which enter,*
   R., Goldwing *and* Varia, L., Brighthue *and*
   Spotila.)

Gold. Good morning, sisters of the sportive wing.
What gay report of frolic do you bring?

Bright. Goldwing, kind Nature ne'er made morn like
      this.
My early flight was one full draught of bliss;
O'er waving corn, through fields of new-mown hay,
Up flowery banks, triumphant was my way;
Light as the fleecy clouds, as free from care,
I sped, a careless rover of the air.

Spotila. My flight was on the bosom of the stream,
Sparkling with diamonds from the sun's first beam.
Forward and backward did I dancing go,
Chasing my shadow in the depths below.

Varia. I sailed on easy wing to yonder peak,
The god of day's first welcome kiss to seek;
There danced I in the splendor of his rays,
Amid the trees with golden tints ablaze.

Gold. A morn of pure delight you well have told.
Listen while I my wanderings unfold;
Hiding awhile beneath a dewy rose
Which in yon garden gloriously grows,
A fair-haired child, with merry, dancing eyes,
Peered in upon me in a glad surprise;

With wily hand, to covetous embrace
He sought to snatch me from my hiding-place.
But all in vain; my airy wings outspread,
Awhile I hovered o'er his golden head,
Then led him on a merry, dancing race
To many a nook and corner of the place,
Till quite o'erpowered, and mourning at his loss,
He sank to sleep upon a bed of moss.
  Bright. Goldwing, you are a wicked, teasing sprite.
  Varia. To tempt and tease was always her delight.
  Spot. This new adventure gives me no surprise;
Mischief has built its nest in Goldwing's eyes.
  Gold. Right, right, fair Spotila; to frolic free
In field or woodland is the life for me.
Hearken, sweet Brighthue; here, amid the trees,
There is a busy hive of honey bees,
Who earnest labor through the livelong day,
Spending no time in frolic or in play;
Grant me your aid, and from the weary task,
I'll lure them to the fields wherein we bask,
Teach them to sport and flutter in the breeze,
To race and chase amid the flowers and trees,
Disclose the glorious powers which we enjoy,
Pleasure and sunshine with no base alloy.
  Bright. I'm with you, heart and hand, my joyous
      sprite;
'Twill to our pleasures add a new delight.
  Varia. 'Twill cause a hubbub in the busy hive,
Should you succeed in that for which you strive.
  Gold. For that we care not; only lend your aid
Till of the leader I've a captive made.

The rest will follow to the fields anon.
Silence! stand close; the bees are moving on.
       [*They retire to* L.

(*Chorus.* " *Hunting Song,*" *during which enter* THRIFTIE *and her Attendants*, R.)

    On airy wing, with busy hum,
    Blithely to work we come,
    For sweets to store the home.
    The worker loves to roam
    Where birds are singing,
    So far, so near. So far, so near,
    Where flowers bright upspringing
    Bestow their treasures dear.

 Gold. Whither so fast, fair friends?
 Thriftie.   To yonder hill,
Seeking for treasures our fair hive to fill.
 Gold. The day is warm; the labor hard to wrest
The honey sweets from out the thorny breast.
Leave toil and care awhile, and freely stroll,
Light-winged, across yon green and grassy knoll.
 Bright. I challenge thee to try thy pinions' flight
In a wild race to yonder crownéd height.
 Spot. I dare you to a race o'er yonder plain.
 Varia. Thy speed 'gainst mine, yon silvery stream to
  gain.
 Thriftie. Nay, nay, good friends; my queen our task
  has set,
And at my call my train have early met.
With grateful thanks, we must decline to play,
When duty calls for work another way.

Gold. Nay, not so fast; lay by your toil and care,
And freely all our promised frolic share.
There Labor waits its weary power to press,
Here Pleasure beckons with a warm caress.   [*Points*, L.

(*Distant Chorus. Repeat* "*Boating Song*," *during which* THRIFTIE *steps back*, C., GOLDWING, BRIGHT-HUE, *cross stage, take two Attendants, place their arms about their waists, and pass slowly across stage to* L. VARIA *and* SPOTILA *cross, and have their arms about the waists of the other Attendants, facing* C. *as the song closes.*)

Thriftie (*loud*).   Halt.

(*Stands* C., *with hand raised. Two Attendants pass quickly to* THRIFTIE, *stand just behind her on each side, with hand lightly resting on her waist; the other two fall on one knee,* R. *and* L. *of* THRIFTIE, *with hands raised to her waist. The Butterflies* R. L.)

TABLEAU. *Music should be soft until the attention of the audience is fixed.*

                        Base pleasure-seekers, vain
Are your arts to tempt my faithful train.
True are their hearts when Thriftie leads the way;
With love they labor and with trust obey.
Off to your frolics; we have staid too long;
We move to duty; list our cheery song.

(*Chorus.* "*Hunting Song*" *repeated, during which* THRIFTIE *and Attendants march off,* R.)

Bright. Goldwing, your plot has failed.

Gold.   Nay, pause a while;
I'll find a way these grubbers to beguile;
The zealous Thriftie is the model bee;
None so industrious in the hive as she;
Anon we'll meet some more congenial soul,
Who'll gladly frolic on yon grassy knoll.
And here comes one with whom I gossip daily,
The grumbler of the hive.

         Enter GAYLIE, *and three Attendants*, R.

                     Good morrow, Gaylie.
     Gay. Ah, neighbor Goldwing, you're a merry elf;
You have no care; you never toil for pelf.

         (*They sit together on bank*, C.)

And yet no sister of our thrifty race
Wears gayer garb, or shows such cheerful face.

(*One of the Attendants moves up, stands behind* GAYLIE, R., *with hand on her shoulder.* BRIGHTHUE *does the same with* GOLDWING, L.)

     Gold. Ay, free from care am I; at will to roam
O'er hill and meadow, everywhere at home.
Come, Gaylie, join us in a sportive race;
'Twill smooth the wrinkles from your troubled face.

(*Another Attendant sinks at* GAYLIE'S *feet*, R., *with her left arm resting in her lap, looking into her face.* VARIA *does the same*, L.)

     Gay. Nay, neighbor Goldwing, I must now away;
Our gracious queen will brook no more delay;

O, for one hour of your gay, careless mirth!
'Twere brighter than the sunshine to the earth.

(*Another* Attendant *kneels* on the side of bank, R., *her elbow on bank,* head resting *on* her hand. VARIA *does the same,* L.)

Gold. Then shall the gayest revel be prepared,
And with you, neighbor Gaylie, freely shared.
O'er yonder mead we'll frolic light and free.
And you the empress of our sports shall be.
Your presence will our gayety enhance.
List, Gaylie, to the music of the dance.

(TABLEAU. *As arranged,* GAYLIE *and the Attendants look,* L., *with a pleased, eager, listening expression. The Butterflies watch* GAYLIE *attentively.* TRUSTA *steals in,* L., WARNA, R., *with fingers on their lips; stop in entrance, and, leaning forward, appear to be listening. Soft music until all is still, then distant chorus.* "*In light tripping measure.*")

"In light tripping music, surrounded by pleasure,
  We count the gay hours that too hastily fly;
  Hence, care and sorrow! daren't come nigh," &c.

Gay. What joyous sounds! O, how I long to share
Such merry pastime, free from toil and care!
Gold. Then come with us, leave toil and care behind;
Come where the Butterflies enjoyment find;
Spread wings, sail free; the happiest are they
Who make of life a frolic and a play.
Gay. (*starting up; all rise*). I will, I will; no more a toiling bee,
Your free and roving life delighteth me.
Off to your sports; I'll follow with my train.

Warna (comes forward). Hold, hold! rash Gaylie,
   on your life refrain.
  Gay. Warna, what right have you to interfere?
  Warna. As guardian of the hive we hold dear.
I warn you, Gaylie, that a dire disgrace
Falls on the luckless member of our race
Who disobeys our Queen's supreme decree.
Beware, O Gaylie, lest it fall on thee.
  Gay. Warna, thou art a despot's willing slave.
Away! your warning and her frown I brave.
With these gay rovers to the dance I fly.
  1st Att. I'll follow, Gaylie.
  2d Att.   So will I.
  3d Att.   And I.
  Gold. Ho! bravely said; away on nimble wing,
For pleasure beckons as we merrily sing.

(*Chorus repeated,* " *In light tripping measure,*" *during
which* GAYLIE *and* GOLDWING, SPOTILA *and Attendant,* BRIGHTHUE *and Attendant,* VARIA *and Attendant, march in pairs around stage to* L.)

  Gold. I've conquered; now my joy is all complete.
Gaylie once banished from her sweet retreat,
The bees demoralized will warring strive,
In factions, for possession of the hive.
Mischief, thou trusty friend, in power arise,
And seal the triumph of the Butterflies.
  Warna. O Gaylie, by the glories of our race,
I charge thee, pause, and shun this dire disgrace.
  Trusta. Nay, Warna, you're too strict. Let Gaylie go,

An hour's sweet pastime in the air to know;
I'll keep her secret, wait her safe return;
The absence of the truant none shall learn.

Warna. False guardian, cease, at duty's high decree,
Friendship can have no power to silence me;
Regina must upon the instant know
This base attempt her sway to overthrow.
O Gaylie, Gaylie, by the love we bear,
I pray you this unwelcome duty spare;
Think of the thrifty name our hive has borne,
Think of our sisters, who your loss will mourn.
Homeward ere now they cheerful move along,
Easing their burdens with a happy song.

(*Chorus.* " *Summer Evening,*" *during which enter,* R.,
    THRIFTIE *and Attendants.*)

    Bees with light wings move sprightly
        Home to the welcome nest,
    Bearing their burdens so lightly,
        Of treasure the sweetest and best.
    As we give songs, give songs of rejoicing,
        The hive we love is near;
    Let us give praise, give praise and glad voicing,
        The home we love is here.

Thriftie. Ah, sister Gaylie, 'twas a luscious treat
Yon rich and flowery mountain side to beat.
Such loads and loads of sweets, 'twill well repay
The labors of our tribe for many a day.

Gay. And what is this to me? You drudging bees
May pluck and store its richness, if you please.
With these gay friends I mean to sport in air,
And, free from labor, all their pleasures share.

Warna. O Thriftie! In some wild and wicked snare
Our once good Gaylie's fallen unaware;
Mocks at the orders of our gracious queen,
And rails at duty with a traitorous mien.
  Thriftie. Gaylie, forbear; a dangerous path you tread:
By no deceitful counsellors be led.
  Gold. Be bold, fair Gaylie; freedom is the stake.
We are your friends; you will not us forsake.
  Gay. Never! Thriftie, I will toil no more.

Enter QUEEN, *unperceived,* R., *stands* C. *back.*

Slave to no sovereign whose despotic power,
Some task gigantic finds for every hour,
Henceforth I'll freely rove, myself a queen,
With will as mighty, and with air serene,
As she whom you obey. Now off I fly.
Who dares to check my progress?
  Queen (stepping forward). I.
  All. The Queen!
  Queen. Ay, loyal subjects, here
Your Queen appears. 'Tis time to interfere.
Vile discontent, the curse of happy hives,
To raise a fierce revolt insanely tries.
Unseen, unknown, I've witnessed all its course,
And now to check it bring a last resource.
Gaylie, thou traitress, leader of a host
Of all my subjects loved and trusted most,
These wily Butterflies, so debonair,
Have of thy weak complainings made a snare.
Their life they picture as so bright and gay,
Is short and vapid, lasts but for a day;

While we, by labor, energy, and worth,
Long live and prosper; and o'er all the earth
Our busy traffic, with its proud renown,
Sets brightest ornaments in labor's crown.
Thou hast rebelled against our righteous laws,
And cast a foul reproach upon our cause.
Away! Thou wouldst be free. I here renounce
All claims, and doom of banishment pronounce.

Gay. (*falls at her feet*). No, no, not that;
O, gracious Queen, forbear,
Here, at your feet, I do implore you spare.
'Twas folly's promptings, pleasure's wild desire,
That, all unchecked, rebellion did inspire.

Gold. Gaylie, forbear; let not those drudging bees
Behold our chosen empress on her knees.

Gay. Tempter, away; thy flattery is base;
Too late I read thy falsehood in thy face.
O, gracious Queen, withdraw thy fell decree;
Let me a toiler with my sisters be;
No wild desire, no feverish unrest,
Shall tempt me from the haven of our rest.

Queen. It cannot be.

Thriftie. My prayers I lend,
Trusting, O, gracious Queen, thy will to bend.
Place Gaylie in my charge; I'll stake my life
My teachings will o'ercome all thoughts of strife.

Queen. I do relent. Gaylie, thy place no more
Can be a leader's. Henceforth, as of yore,
Within the ranks of those who burdens bear,
Thou must their service and their duties share.
This be thy punishment. But by the love
We bear thee, Gaylie, thy repentance prove.

Gay. Thanks, gracious mistress; let my actions speak;
Your favor to regain will Gaylie seek.

Gold. Gaylie, thou false one, pleasure calls. Farewell!
Think of our pastimes in thy gloomy cell.

[*Exeunt*, L., GOLDWING, BRIGHTHUE, VARIA, *and* SPOTILA.

Queen. Idlers, away! disturb no more our drove,
But to your gay and senseless follies move;
And now to work; Gaylie's revolt is o'er;
Into our hive your choicest treasures pour;
And as you strive our products to increase,
With industry, the germ of joy and peace,
Remember not alone in garnered show
Of wealth does she her bounteous harvests know,
But that true hearts may find, in every task,
Pleasure more lasting than the tongue can ask;
Its busy hum is music's gayest measure,
And love of labor is its richest treasure.

(*Chorus.* "*A Wish for the Mountains.*")

> Where the flowers are hills adorning
> Where the clover beds unfold,
> Where the early rays of morning
> Rim the leaves of green with gold,
> Where the brightest roses grow,
> Thither, thither will we go,
> Thither, thither will we go.

(*Repeat chorus; then march off*, WARNA *and* TRUSTA, QUEEN, THRIFTIE, *and* GAYLIE, *their Attendants*, L.)

NOTE. — The tunes used in this allegory may all be found in "The Grammar School Chorus," used in Boston schools. It can be obtained of the publishers, Lee & Shepard. Price $1.00.

A TENDER ATTACHMENT.

CHARACTERS.

MR. CLAPBOARD. Proprietor of "Bachelors' Paradise."
EBENEZER CROTCHET, a retired manufacturer.
HORACE CROTCHET, his son.
PETER PICKET, a soldier.
OBED OAKUM, a sailor.
TIMOTHY TINPAN, a tinker.
LOUIS LOOPSTITCH, a **tailor**.

COSTUMES.

CLAPBOARD, gray wig, brown coat, dark pants.

EBENEZER, gray wig, blue coat with brass buttons, dark pants, hat, **and cane**.

HORACE, modern suit, **neat and tasty**.

PETER, United States **army overcoat, fatigue cap, red wig**, red side whiskers.

OBED, light Yankee wig, pea-jacket, **tarpaulin hat**, wide sailor trousers, blue shirt.

TIMOTHY, black **crop** wig, smutty face, overalls, and woollen jacket.

LOUIS, tight black pants, with short legs, slippers, white stockings, black **coat**, with short arms, buttoned to the throat, black **cravat**, without collar.

SCENE.—*Apartment in* MR. CLAPBOARD's *home. Lounge* C., *back. Black velvet breakfast-jacket and smoking-cap lying across the corner. Small table,* R. *Chairs,* R. *and* L. *Entrances,* R. *and* L.

Enter MR. CLAPBOARD, R., *followed by* EBENEZER CROTCHET.

Clapboard. This is the room, sir.

Ebenezer. O, it is! This is the mysterious abode of my runaway son. Well, I don't see anything very inviting here; a few miserable chairs, a rickety lounge, a mean little table —

Clap. Come, come, sir; don't abuse my furniture.

Eben. O, pooh, pooh! What business have you harboring a runaway scamp who ought to be at home, you old, gray-headed ruffian?

Clap. Come, come, sir; once for all, I won't be abused in my own house. If your son chooses to hire a room in my house, to pay handsomely for the same, and to behave himself in a gentlemanly manner, here he stops just as long as he pays, you old heathen.

Eben. Old heathen! Confound you, do you know who you are talking to, Mr. Claptrap?

Clap. Clapboard, sir; Clapboard is my name.

Eben. Do you know who you are talking to?

Clap. I've a pretty good idea. Some fiery old lunatic just escaped from Bedlam.

Eben. Fire and fury! I'll break this cane over your head, insolent!

Clap. Do; and then I'll throw you and the pieces down those stairs, catamount!

Eben. (*Aside.*) O, this won't do. (*Aloud.*) I beg your pardon, Mr. Claptrap.

Clap. Clapboard, sir.

Eben. Mr. Clapboard, I was a little hasty. You must attribute it to the anxiety of a devoted parent. I have a son.

Clap. So I understand.

Eben. A week ago he left the parental mansion, for the purpose, as he said, of recruiting himself at a quiet place in the country. All very well, of course. I could bring nothing to say against that; but yesterday I received an anonymous note, mailed at this place, bidding me look out for my son, who, the note said, had formed a tender attachment. Do you hear? — a tender attachment!

Clap. Well, what of it?

Eben. What of it? Hear the man! Sir! Mr. Claptrap!

Clap. Clapboard, sir.

Eben. Mr. Clapboard. Ten years ago I retired from the soap and candle business with a fortune. This boy is my only son; young, impulsive, thoughtless, he has come to the country; his susceptible heart is a target, at which a thousand loving glances will be thrown by the eyes of rural beauties —

Clap. Humbug! There isn't a female within three miles of the place. This is called "Bachelors' Paradise." There's Jobson's house, Seymour's, and mine; specially erected for the convenience of artists, fishermen, and such like gentry, who want a quiet place in the country.

Eben. Is it possible! Then my son's tender attachment —

Clap. It's some trick played to frighten you.

Eben. Perhaps it is, but I have my doubts. Who lodges in this house besides my son?

Clap. Well, sir, on the floor below, there's Mr. Timothy Tinpan, a nice, gentlemanly — tinker.

Eben. A tinker? — (*Aside.*) Bachelors' Paradise! (*Aloud.*) Gentlemanly humbug! Who else?

Clap. The next floor above is occupied by Mr. Peter Picket, a military gentleman, who served his country in the great rebellion.

Eben. A soldier! (*Noise outside.*) What's that?

Clap. That's him. He's always going through his tactics. He dropped his gun.

Eben. Did he! Then Mr. Peter Picket had better *pick it* up. Well, who else?

Clap. Next above him is Mr. Oakum, a well-mannered mariner, engaged in the lumber trade.

Eben. Is that all?

Clap. No, sir; the floor above him, next the roof, is occupied by Mr. Loopstitch, a tailor, a native of France.

Eben. Soldier, sailor, tinker, and tailor! Here's nice company for my boy.

Clap. O, they're a nice, gentlemanly set, I assure you; very quiet. Mr. Picket is apt to be a little restless nights; walks in his sleep; and sometimes wanders about the house with a loaded musket. Mr. Oakum is of rather a musical turn, and has his "bark upon the sea" a little too often. Mr. Tinpan is very fond of rehearsing his war-cry, "Old kettles to mend;" and Mr. Loopstitch is making frantic efforts to master the trombone. But generally they are quiet, gentlemanly, respectable individuals.

Eben. I should say so. And my son abandons his luxurious home, his highly respectable connections, for such society as this?

Clap. Lord bless you, young gentlemen have their little freaks, you know.

Eben. And so have old gentlemen too. I have a very sudden one myself. For how long has my son engaged this room?

Clap. Let me see; he has paid me for it up to six o'clock to-night.

Eben. And after that I suppose it will be to let.

Clap. Of course. Though probably he'll keep it himself.

Eben. Hark you, Mr. Claptrap.

Clap. Clapboard, sir.

Eben. Mr. Clapboard, I want to hire this room myself. What does my son pay you?

Clap. Six dollars a week. Cheap enough.

Eben. All right. I'll engage it for a week myself, for which I will pay you twelve.

Clap. But, sir, he has the first choice.

Eben. No, he hasn't; he's not of age. I am his guardian, and I want it myself; so here's your money. At six o'clock I shall come and take possession.

Clap. But, Mr. Crotchet —

Eben. No more words are necessary. You keep a house for the entertainment of gentlemen who wish a quiet place in the country. You certainly cannot refuse so handsome an offer as I have made you.

Clap. But your son —

Eben. Has comfortable quarters at home, where he belongs. You can inform him of my appearance here, and of the bargain I have made. Tell him to go home and amuse himself; that I shall positively take up my quarters here at six o'clock. (*Aside.*) There's something wrong here; " a tender attachment," I'll be bound, and I'm determined to find it out. (*Aloud.*) Good day, Mr. Claptrap. [*Exit*, R.

Clap. Clapboard, sir — Now here's a nice mess! What will Mr. Horace say to this, after he has got everything comfortably arranged for his purpose, to be flustered in this manner. It's too bad!

Enter HORACE, R.

Horace. I say, Clapboard, why don't you light up your stairs? I nearly tumbled over an old chap just now, who was going down.

Clap. Old chap, indeed! Do you know who it was?

Hor. Haven't the least idea.

Clap. Well, sir, it was your father.

Hor. My father? Whew! Then the old gentleman has found me out!

Clap. He certainly has; but he's laboring under a terrible mistake. Some one has sent him an anonymous note, bidding him look after you, for you had formed a tender attachment.

Hor. A tender attachment? That's some mischief of the fellows at Jobson's. Well, what does he propose to do?

Clap. He's engaged this room.

Hor. Engaged this room? Why, Clapboard, it's mine — isn't it?

Clap. Until six o'clock. If you'll remember, that was the time for which you took it.

Hor. But I want it a week longer.

Clap. You're too late. He's engaged it, and paid for it; and will be here at six o'clock to take possession.

Hor. Clapboard, you've played me a shabby trick!

Clap. I couldn't help it, sir; he thrust the money into my hands; said he was your legal guardian, and told me to send you home.

Hor. I'll not go until my work is finished. Well, Clapboard, let him come; his stay shall be short.

Clap. What will you do?

Hor. That's a question for consideration. Six months ago my father and myself differed with regard to my choice of a profession. He wished me to be a lawyer. I determined to be a painter. He was immovable in his choice. I was stubborn and sullen in mine. By mutual consent we dropped the discussion, agreeing not to renew it for a year. I was at once filled with the desire to produce something that would induce him to agree with me, believing that if I could show that I had talent, he would let me have my way. I immediately threw myself into the society of artists, and by that means gained an inkling of the rudiments of the profession, and I found I had some talent. But how to convince my father? I hit upon the idea of attempting a painting; something remarkable — a great allegorical national picture, "The Crowning of Liberty," a magnificent idea! To carry it out, I required a studio and living models. I read your advertisement of "Bachelors' Paradise;" came down, engaged a room, fitted it up, and looked around for models. But, alas! it was indeed a "bachelors' paradise!" Not a female figure within three miles! Of course I was obliged to put up with the stock on hand; and with a soldier, a sailor, a tinker, and a tailor, as the only models to be obtained, I have been obliged to draw upon fancy to an alarming extent; and now it seems I am to be deprived of them by my meddling, inquisitive, good old daddy.

Clap. It's too bad, Mr. Horace. I wish I could help you out of the scrape.

Hor. I wish you could. But as you can't, suppose you go and hunt up my models, and let me get to work.

Clap. Certainly, sir; I'll send them in at once.

[*Exit*, R.

(HORACE *takes off his coat and puts on breakfast jacket and smoking-cap, then goes off,* L., *and returns with an easel, which he sets up,* L., *then goes off,* L., *and brings in canvas, brushes, and palette; arranges the canvas on easel to face* L., *places chair* L.

Clap. (*Outside,* R., *while* HORACE *is arranging his picture.*) Hallo, down there, Tinpan!

Timothy. (*Outside, as if down stairs.*) Faith, now, what's wanting, sure?

Clap. You're wanted here.

Tim. All right. Be aisy, honey, till I mind the nose uv this tay-kittle.

Clap. Hallo, Picket!

Picket. (*As if up stairs.*) Yaw, mine fren.

Clap. You're wanted in the studio.

Pic. Yaw, dat ish goot. I'll come right avay pefore soon.

Clap. Hallo, Oakum!

Oakum. (*Up stairs.*) Hallo, yerself!

Clap. Come down for a pose.

Oak. Ay, ay, Clapboard; in a jiffy.

Clap. Hallo, Loopstitch!

Loopstitch. (*In the distance.*) Oui, oui, monsieur.

Clap. You're wanted for a posish.

Loop. Vat you mean by dat, eh? Vot you call posish? I no comprehend.

Clap. Well, come and find out.

Hor. The models are aroused. Now for a season of inspiration!

Enter PICKET, R., *with a musket.*

Pic. Ah, Meester Horace, how you vas? Berty mooch?

Hor. Ah, Picket, you're right on haud.

Pic. Yaw, yaw; I ish coomed right along, by donder, mit mine gun upon mine pack.

Hor. Like a true hero, and with the martial spirit inspiring your bosom — hey?

Pic. Yaw, I shpose vat you mean, but I don't know.

Enter OAKUM, R.

Oak. Hallo! Heow are yeou anyheow? Goin' at the picter ag'in?

Hor. Yes; I believe I can make my brush fly this afternoon.

Oak. Wal, yeou painter chaps dew beat all creation; that's a fact. I s'pose yeou know what yeou're abaout; but darn me if I can see into it. What's the use er wastin' yer time a flingin' away paint on that air diminutive quiltin'-frame. Would do more good ef yeou'd give old Clapboard's house a coat; it wants it bad enough!

Enter LOOPSTITCH, R.

Loop. Sacre! vat for you want — hey? I have break off mine thread right in de meedle of ze pantaloons.

Hor. You remember our bargain. You were to be at my service when wanted.

Loop. Service? Sacre, zis is too much all ze time. Monsieur Fusee have no pantaloons; he make ze trouble, ze fuss; he raise vat you call ze storm, if he no have ze pantaloons.

Oak. Well, let him sweat, Frenchy. I'll lend him a pair.

Enter TIMOTHY, R.

Tim. Arrah, b'ys, how are yees, ouyhow? It's the tip uv the morning till yees, Misther Horace.

Oak. Hallo, Tim! How's trade?

Tim. Thrade, is it? Bad luck to its! There's none at all at all. It's loike the nose of Paddy Flinn's pig — it's away down in the mud.

Oak. Well, here's hoping that, like Paddy Flinn's pig, it may pick up a bit.

Tim. That's thrue for ye, Misther Oakum.

Hor. Now, then, let's to work. Tinpan, you and Loopstitch don your habiliments, and we'll go to work.

Tim. Don — which is it?

Loop. Sacre! I no comprehend.

Oak. Darn it, Tim, jump into the Goddess of Liberty's clos; and, Loopstitch, put on that air gown of Victory's.

Tim. Begorra! that's a sinsible way of putting things.
[*Exit*, L.

Loop. Victory! Oui, oui; I comprehend victory.
[*Exit,* L.

Oak. Sich a set of darned stupid 'furriners I never did see.

Pic. Yaw; dey ish very hard of hearing, by donder!

Oak. Well, Picket, you managed to give us a pretty good scare last night, walking round with that old blunderbuss! Ef yeou ain't keerful, yeou'll let fly at some on us, and then there'll be a purty case of manslaughter.

Pic. Yaw; manslaughter ish goot. I like him mooch ven I fights mit Sigel. By donder! I tink of dat ebery night in mine shleep, and I no shleep at all.

Oak. Well, consarn yeour picter! deon't yeou come up my way; if yer du, I'll souse yer head in a bucket of tar!

Pic. Yaw; I no like dat purty well.

Enter TIMOTHY, L., *dressed as the Goddess of Liberty; red skirt, mail waist, blue drapery about shoulders.*

Tim. Begorra! how's that for a famale woman? What would Judy O'Flanagan say to that? Tim Tinpan in a red petticoat? Whoo! kittles to mind, kittles to mind!

Enter LOOPSTITCH, *in a long white gown, with a green wreath in his hand.*

Loop. Sacre! I feel all over like vat you call ze goost.

Oak. And darn me if you don't look like one!

Loop. Vat you mean by dat — hey, Monsieur Oakum?

Hor. Come, now take your places.

Tim. All right; away wid yees. (*Takes position in centre of stage; left hand against his breast, right hand pointing up.*)

Hor. That's right; now Victory. (LOOPSTITCH *gets upon a stool behind* TIMOTHY, *and holds wreath over his head.*) Very well. Now, then, for the army and navy. (PICKET *stands* R. *of* TIMOTHY, *leaning upon his musket;* OAKUM *stands* L., *his arms folded.*) Good, good! Positions are all right. Now, then, for the expressions.

Tim. Hould on a minute; there's something crawling up my back.

Hor. Never mind, never mind!

Tim. But I do mind. It's biting me, the ugly thief! Here, Frenchy, give me a dig in the back.

Loop. Sacre! vare vill I find vat you call de spade?

Oak. Here; I'll fix you. (*Gives* TIMOTHY *a thump on the back.*)

Tim. Murder and Irish! you've broke my ribs!

Hor. Come, come, Tim; put a smiling expression upon your face.

Tim. Smile, is it, with a hornet crawling up my back!

Hor. We're wasting time. Smile, I tell you.

Tim. Well, then, here goes. (*A horrible smile.*)

Hor. Now, Loopstitch, triumph in *your* face.

Loop. Oui, oui. Vive la triomphe!

Hor. That's very good. Now, Picket, let a martial spirit glow in your face.

Pic. Yaw, yaw. (*Starts,* R.)

Hor. Where are you going?

Pic. For mine lager, mit de spirit up stairs.

Hor. No, no; you don't understand me. Look as you looked when you met the rebels, fierce for the fight.

Pic. Ven I fight mit Sigel?

Hor. Yes; as you did then, do now.

Pic. Yaw; den I'll go right up stairs.

Hor. What do you mean?

Pic. Ven I fight mit Sigel, ven de repels coom, ve runned away.

Oak. What a darned sneaking coward!

Tim. Easy, now, Mr. Horace; my hand's getting tired.

Hor. Let me see what I can do. (*Goes to easel, and takes brush.*) Now, steady, all.

Tim. Och, murder! the crayture's crawling up my back again!

Pic. I am ash dry ash never vas.

Hor. Steady, steady!

Tim. Ow, my back! Give me a dig, Frenchy.

Oak. Confound you, I will! (*Hits* TIMOTHY *in the stomach, who doubles up.*)

Tim. Ow, murther, murther! (*Backs into* LOOP-STITCH, *who tumbles over.* TIMOTHY *runs up and down stage howling.*)

Loop. Sacre! you have broke me all to pieces.

Hor. Order, order! How do you suppose I can paint with such confusion? You have spoiled everything.

Tim. Faith, it's not myself that's to blame.

Oak. Darn him! he's got a nest of hornets under his jacket!

7

Hor. We can do nothing to-day. It's now nearly six o'clock. An individual will be here at six to take possession of my room; he has hired it, and I must vacate.

Oak. What, hired the room over your head?

Hor. Yes; it's a little plot of my father's to get me home again. If he stays here, I must give up my painting; and of course you will be wanted no more as models.

Loop. Sacre! zat is too bad! ver mooch too bad!

Tim. Faith! must I lose my sitivation?

Pic. Yaw; we can't come here some more!

Hor. That's exactly the state of the case. Of course, as he's my father, it will not do for me to take any measures to cause him to leave. With you it is different. If you can manage to make him sick of his bargain to-night, we shall resume operations to-morrow, as usual.

Oak. Darn him, we'll pitch him out of the winder!

Hor. No, no; no violence!

Tim. No, b'ys; no voilence. We'll break his head intirely! That's all.

Hor. He's very particular to have everything about him quiet. I offer no suggestions. If you can manage to scare him a little, I've no objections.

Tim. Faith, lave us alone for that.

Oak. Come to my room, boys; we'll fix the old skinflint! Come along.

Tim. Yaw; flint ish goot ven I fight mit Sigel.

Oak. O, never mind Seagull. Come along.

Loop. Sacre! Vat you fix his flint with? I no comprehend.

Oak. I'll fix everything all right. Leave it to me. Come along. [*Exit*, R.

Tim. I'm wid yees. If there's to be a shindy, count me in. [*Exit,* R.

Loop. Monsieur, I be vat you call in ze dark ver much all over.

Pic. Yaw, it pe all covered mit de dark like de moonshine. [*Exit* LOOPSTITCH *and* PICKET, R.

Hor. What a set of stupid donkeys! If they manage to circumvent my respected parent, I'll forgive them. (*Exchanges jacket for coat, and puts on hat. Stage dark.*) How dark it is!

Clap. (*Outside,* R.) You're very prompt, sir.

Eben. (*Outside,* R.) I am always prompt. Is the room ready?

Clap. (*Outside,* R.) Yes, sir; walk this way.

Hor. There he is, right on time. There's sure to be a rumpus, and I'm bound to see the fun. [*Exit,* L.

Enter CLAPBOARD, *with a lighted candle, which he places on table, followed by* EBENEZER.

Eben. Now, sir, I've caught you at your tricks! Why, he's gone!

Clap. Why, you certainly didn't expect to find him here.

Eben. I certainly did. Where is he?

Clap. He's probably at Jobson's, over the way. But he'll be back soon. He'll be delighted to see you.

Eben. Clapboard, you lie! you know he won't.

Clap. Come, come, Mr. Crotchet, don't insult a man in his own room.

Eben. 'Tis false! it's my room; and you may take yourself out of it just as soon as you can!

2

Clap. You don't mean to stay here!

Eben. Yes, I do. I've had another note from my unknown correspondent. The object of his tender attachment visits him every evening, and I'm bound to see her.

Clap. O, pshaw, Mr. Crotchet! you've been humbugged!

Eben. I know it; but I'll be humbugged no longer; so here I'll stay to unmask the hypocrite!

Clap. Well, stay, then; but if you're made uncomfortable, don't blame me.

Eben. What do you mean?

Clap. No matter; I've cautioned you. Keep your eyes open, and don't blame me. Remember you have been cautioned. Good night. [*Exit*, R.

Eben. Clapboard, Clapboard — What does he mean? Can there be any danger? I'm an old fool! What business have I down in this unfrequented place, all alone? I'll go back. No, I won't! Horace would laugh and chuckle! He shan't do that! Who's afraid? I'll make myself comfortable on that lounge; and when he comes, he shall learn how terrible is the vengeance of an enraged and injured parent. (*Reclines upon lounge. Noise overhead; jumps up.*) What's that? It's that infernal soldier! Clapboard said he walks in his sleep. Suppose he should come here — with a loaded musket too! Gracious! (*Trombone heard outside.*) There's the tailor practising. What a confounded din!

Oak. (*Sings, outside, very loud.*) "My bark is on the sea."

Eben. There's that sailor going it!

Tim. (*Outside, sings.*) " Ould kittles to mind! Ould kittles to mind!"

Eben. And there's the tinker. (*Trombone,* " *ould kittles,*" *and* " *bark upon the sea,*" *all together.*) What a confounded din! I wish I was well out of it.

Enter PICKET, *with musket, slowly, on tiptoe.*

Pic. Who goes dare?

Eben. O, heavens! There's that insane old grenadier! What will become of me?

Pic. Sh—! By donder, I see some noise! Sh—! Who goes dare? Sh—! Somepody mit a gun. Advance pefore you speak, and say something. Sh—! (*Creeps about the room on tiptoe.*)

Eben. (*On lounge.*) If he discovers me, I am a lost man!

Pic. By donder, if dare ish nopody here, vy don't you speak? You vant your coat-tails shot through mit a pullet. (*Creeps back to door,* R.) I fight mit Sigel. Sh—! By donder! I never hear so mooch silence pefore! [*Exit,* R.

Eben. He's gone. I breathe again. O, Lord, what's that? (LOOPSTITCH *in the white robe passes slowly across stage, from* R. *to* L., *with his arm outstretched, hand pointing straight before him. Exit,* L.) An apparition! What infernal place have I got into? I'll go home at once. (*Goes to* R. *The door is locked.* LOOPSTITCH, *without the robe, creeps in,* L., *and gets behind lounge.*)

Loop. Sacre! I vill give him a touch of my needles!

Eben. What an old donkey I am, to get into such a

scrape! What shall I do? I can't get out. Suppose I alarm the neighborhood! That won't do; I should have the whole set upon me. I'll try to sleep. (*Lies upon lounge.* LOOPSTITCH *leans over and runs a needle into his arm.*) O, murder! What's that? Confound this infernal place! (LOOPSTITCH *sticks another needle.*) O, my arm, my arm! (*Jumps up.*) I can't stand this! Here! Help, help, help, help!

Enter OAKUM, R. *Creeps in very mysteriously; takes* EBENEZER *by the wrist, and leads him down to the front of the stage.*

Oak. Silence! Sh—!

Eben. O, take me out of this! I'm a poor old man.

Oak. Silence! Sh—! Listen to me. You received a note from somebody—

Eben. Yes, I did. Confound somebody!

Oak. Silence! Sh—! "Tender attachment!" It's all true, by jiminy!

Eben. I knew it.

Oak. Your son — has a tender attachment. The object of it is approaching. It will soon be here.

Eben. You don't say so!

Oak. Old man, you have a son; that son has a tender attachment; the object of that tender attachment — sh—! — will soon be here.

Eben. Confound you, you said that before!

Oak. Be wise, be cautious, and you shall triumph. Silence! It comes! the — object — comes! (*Creeps off,* R.)

Eben. Well, that's the queerest customer that ever I met. Hallo! who's this?

Enter TIMOTHY, *dressed as the Goddess of Liberty, with a veil thrown over his face.*

'Tis she, at last! Now to unmask the villain!

Tim. Idol of me sowl!

Eben. Irish, as I'm alive!

Tim. Och, yees illigent darlint! and did yees think yer own Kathleen, accushla, would deny yees the comfort of her prisence?

Eben. So, madam, you are found out! Know, to your sorrow, that you stand in the presence of the father of the unhappy young man you came to meet?

Tim. It's the ould man — is it? Faith, ould chap, how is yes, onyhow?

Eben. Insolent!

Tim. It's a foine-looking ould fellow yees are; and is that yer own hair, or is it a wig, I'd like to know.

Eben. Young woman, no more of this. I came to snatch my son from your society.

Tim. My society! Faix, yes might do better. It's a comfort I am to him anyhow. You would be afther parting us at all at all!

Eben. Hold your tongue, and leave the room!

Tim. Hould yees blarney yerself, or I'll — I'll pull the hair from your head!

Eben. Leave this room, instantly, or I'll put you out!

Tim. You put me out, is it? Begorra! the sooner yees commince that same, the better's to the liking of Tim Tinpan.

Eben. (*Taking hold of him.*) Leave the room, I say!

Tim. Off wid yees, or I'll break ivery bone in yees body!

Eben. You will — will you? (*Takes hold of him.*)

Tim. (*Throws off veil.*) Arrah, boys, here's a shindy! Come on, old gint! (*Flourishes his fist.*)

Eben. Here! Help, help, help! (TIMOTHY *clinches him.*) Leave the room!

Enter HORACE, L., OAKUM, CLAPBOARD, *and* PICKET, R. LOOPSTITCH *crawls from behind lounge.*

Hor. Why, father! what's the matter?

Eben. O, you villain! you scamp! you renegade! You have come just in time to save your father from a terrible fate! But I've found you out! Your "tender attachment" is known to me. Look upon her! Can you look upon your father's face, and confess a tender attachment to such a thing as that?

Hor. Not a tender attachment, father; but I will confess I am under great obligations to that individual, Timothy Tinpan, the tinker.

Eben. What! is that woman a man?

Tim. Troth, and a foine ould Irish gintleman!

Hor. Yes, father, he is one of my models.

Tim. Faith, a model Irishman, by yer lave!

Eben. Models! What do you mean?

Hor. That I have been endeavoring to overcome your repugnance to my becoming a painter, by attempting the execution of a painting which you see upon that easel. These individuals have been my models. Timothy Tinpan, the tinker.

Tim. That's me, sure.

Hor. Obed Oakum, the sailor.

Oak. Ay, ay; second mate of the Harriet Jones.

Hor. Louis Loopstitch, the tailor.

Loop. Oui, oui; sal I make you a pair of pantaloons, monsieur?

Hor. And Peter Picket, the soldier.

Pic. Yaw, dat ish me, mit my gun upon mine pack.

Eben. What, and the note I received —

Hor. Is one of Harry Jones's jokes. He confessed it to me an hour ago.

Eben. Clapboard, we've been making donkeys of ourselves!

Clap. Speak for yourself, Mr. Crotchet, I can't join you in that.

Eben. Horace, I'm a meddling old fool. I should have trusted you. I'll go home. You may go on with your picture; and if out of the material which I find here you can produce anything satisfactory, I'll give my consent to anything you ask.

Hor. Thank you, father. I'm rather discouraged at present; but if these individuals can cure you of " a tender attachment," they may be of use to me; and if they can help me to achieve my purpose, you will be obliged to admit that there are worse companions than a soldier —

Pic. Yaw, what fight mit Sigel.

Hor. A sailor —

Oak. Tarnal cute, when his bark's on the sea.

Hor. A tinker —

Tim. A broth of a boy for minding the broken nose of a tay-kittle.

Hor. And a tailor —

Loop. Oui, oui ; vith vat you call ze tender attachment for ze needle.

Disposition of Characters at fall of the Curtain.

R.   L.
  Loop.   Pick.
      Tim.   Oak.
          Hor.   Clap.
              Eben.

AMONG THE BREAKERS.

A DRAMA IN TWO ACTS.

CHARACTERS.

DAVID MURRAY, Keeper of Fairpoint Light.
LARRY DIVINE, his Assistant.
HON. BRUCE HUNTER.
CLARENCE HUNTER, his Ward.
PETER PARAGRAPH, a Newspaper Reporter.
SCUD, Hunter's colored Servant.
MISS MINNIE DAZE, Hunter's Niece.
BESS STARBRIGHT, "Cast up by the Waves."
"MOTHER CAREY," a reputed Fortune-Teller.
BIDDY BEAN, an Irish Girl.

COSTUMES.

MURRAY (age 45). Full black beard, iron-gray wig, dark pants, red or blue sailor's shirt, with black necktie, pea-jacket, and tarpaulin hat.

LARRY (age 25). Red crop wig, pea-jacket, dark pants, red or blue sailor's shirt, and tarpaulin hat.

HUNTER (age 45). Dark English side whiskers, iron-gray wig, dark, fashionable suit.

CLARENCE (age 21). Janty yachtman's suit.

PARAGRAPH (age 30). Black crop wig, large red mustache, gray pants, white vest, black velvet coat, light hat, umbrella.

SCUD (age 40). Gray woolly wig, black face, green plaid pants, gaiters, white vest, ruffled shirt front, standing collar, blue coat with brass buttons.

MISS DAZE (age 20). Fashionable dress of summer fabric, Florida hat, white crape shawl, parasol.

BESS (age 18). Short red dress, muslin waist, neat polka jacket, flowing hair, janty sailor hat.

"MOTHER CAREY" (age 40). Disguise of an old fortune-teller. Long, white hair, wig, dress of dark stuff, red shawl draped about her shoulders, crutch-cane. She hobbles, and has the appearance of a woman of seventy.

BIDDY BEAN. Neat calico dress, apron.

[In the storm scene, thunder, lightning, and rain are effective. Thunder is produced by shaking a large sheet of iron, holding it by one corner, lightning by blowing powdered rosin into the flame of a candle through a common "pea-shooter." A "rain"-box is made by driving pegs of wood into the bottom of a box about eighteen inches long, six wide, and six high. Into the box throw a handful of dried peas, fasten on the cover, and copious showers can be produced by letting the peas slowly rattle along the box from end to end.]

ACT I.—SCENE. *Room in the Light-keeper's house. Table,* C., *set for supper. Long box or bench,* L. *Rocking-chair,* R. *Stool,* R. *Door,* C., *leading to the beach, the lighthouse, &c. Door,* R., *leading to the kitchen. Door,* L., *leading to* MURRAY's *sleeping room.*

LARRY *and* BIDDY *discovered,* R. *and* L. *of table, eating.*

Biddy. Faith, now, Misther Larry, it's joking ye's are.

Larry. Niver a once. There's not a live man widdin tin miles, savin' the masther, Misther Murray, mysilf, owld Mother Carey, and Bess Starbright, the famale life praserver, who can bate the worrld wid the pull uv her oars, and the light in the tower beyant wid the glame of her bright eyes. It's mysilf would like to be drownded, for the sake of being pulled from a wathery grave by that same darlint. And that's the extint uv fashionable society at Fairpoint.

Biddy. Ye don't mane it. O, musha! why did I lave the city for this wilderness of rocks and say?

Larry. Why, d'ye ask? Because yer own thrue Irish heart towld ye's that here would be found a broth uv a b'y pinin' for famale society. O, Biddy Bane, yer a jewel, so ye are, and I dying wid the love I've had for ye's a twilvemonth, though I niver set eyes on ye afore the day.

Biddy. O, blarney, Misther Larry! It's a smooth tongue ye's have, onyhow. But till me, is the masther kind?

Larry. Well, the laste said about him the betther. He's the gloom upon him, and sometimes I think there's something gnawin' at his conscience. Well, well, I mustn't talk. You've only been here a day. Say for yesilf.

Biddy. Have ye lived here long, Misther Larry?

Larry. A matther of five or six years; owld Murray fifteen. The last kaper of the light was found dead one morning afther a stormy night, when the lamps were not lit, and a ship drifted into the breakers and wint to paces. Not a sowl saved except Bess Starbright, whom the waves tossed up to Mother Carey's door.

Biddy. An' who's Mother Carey — I donno?

Larry. An' it's will ye don't, for to my mind she's the very — you know what I mane. She lives on the bache, and picks up a livin' by tellin' fates, and fortunes, an' sich like. It's a famous resort for the city folks in their yachts, and she picks up many a silver bit from the loikes of 'em.

Biddy. A witch is it? O, musha! I'll pack up my thrunk, and lave to onct.

Larry. O, no you won't, Biddy, darlint. She's no trouble to such a dacent, nate, bawitchin' little sowl as ye are; and, besides, here's a warm heart and a sthrong arm to love and protict ye's — d'ye mind?

Biddy. O, be aisy wid yer jokin'! Ye bring the faver to me cheeks.

Larry (*rising, and coming to side of* Biddy). It's no joke at all, at all. Ye've come, like the darlint that ye are, to cheer my solitude, and swaten the cup uv life wid the honey of yer prisence (*puts his arm around her waist*), and I love ye, Biddy Bane, so I do, intirely.

Biddy. Away wid ye's nonsense — don't I tell ye.

Enter MOTHER CAREY, C. — BIDDY *jumps up; runs,* L.

Biddy (L.). O, murther! who's that?

Larry (L.). Aisy, Biddy; it's only Mother Carey.

Mother Carey (*comes down*). Man, why sit you idle here? See you not the black storm clouds gathering in the west? Hear you not the whistling of the winds that creep across the sea? the roar of the breakers on the rocks? the seething of the waves along the beach? The storm fiend is abroad, and no warning light in yonder tower. Away! away! ere 'tis too late.

Larry. By me sowl, you're right. A storm comin', and the lights not lit! O, Biddy, Biddy! it's all your work! [*Exit,* C.

Mother C. (*to* BIDDY). Ah, a new face in the old lighthouse. Fresh and fair, buxom form, and strong arm. Who are you?

Biddy. If you plase, marm — misses — Carey, I'm nobody — yes, I mane I'm Biddy Bane; come down from the city to do housework for Misther Murray.

Mother C. But you tremble. Is it with fear?

Biddy. Yes, marm — no, marm!

Mother C. You need not fear me, Biddy. I'm a poor old woman, with little strength, and no power to harm you.

Biddy. Yes, marm; but Larry says you're a witch!

Mother C. He does! Ha, ha! a witch! Well, well, Larry's clever, but don't believe all he says, though he praises the brightness of your eyes and the tint of your cheeks. A witch, indeed! Larry's a fool!

Enter LARRY, C.

Larry. I'm obleeged to yer for the compliment, Mother Carey, long life to ye's. (*Comes down* L. *of* BIDDY.)

Mother C. What nonsense have you been telling this girl?

Larry. 'Pon me sowl, no nonsinse at all. I told her ye's towld fortunes and fates; but barrin' that little touch of owld Satan, I'll swear ye've a warm heart, to which same many a poor tar can tistify who's been hilped by yer when driven ashore.

Mother C. Where's the master to-night, Larry?

Larry. The masther, is it? Off on one uv his thramps. He takes a moighty dale uv ixircise for one wid a shmall appetite.

Mother C. (*to herself*). Restless as the sea; pacing the sands for hours; wandering among the rocks — a stern, gloomy, mysterious man; within, a storm of evil passions blinding his soul to all outward beauty; revenge flashing up among the dying embers of a fierce life, to be smothered by the ashes of remorse. Bad! bad! bad! (*Turns up stage.*)

Biddy. I say, Misther Larry, would ye be afther axing her to till my fortune jist?

Larry. To be sure I would. I say, Mother Carey, this is Biddy Bane. Would ye's be afther tilling her fortune?

Mother C. Give me your hand, child. (*Takes* BIDDY'S *hand.*) A fair, smooth hand.

Larry. Bedad, that's thrue, onyhow. That's what I said. Biddy, said I —

Biddy. Howld yer pate.

Mother C. Silence! A fair, young hand; the lines of fate but indistinct, yet foreshadowing good fortune — ah! I see a lover not far off.

Larry. Bedad, Biddy, he's close at yer elbow.

Biddy. Whist yer blarney! Ye'll sphoil the charm.

Mother C. I see a little home on the rocks.

Larry. " A cottage by the say " — d'ye mind, Biddy?

Mother C. Troops of children —

Larry. Young Larrys and Biddys, bedad, and a pig — d'ye say a pig?

Biddy. Be aisy, Masther Larry.

Larry. Look for the pig. Don't ye's hear him squalin'?

David (outside, c.). Hallo! Larry! Larry!

Larry. There's the masther. Ay, ay, sir! (*Going towards door.*) A lover, an' a cottage! — Mother Carey, jist find that pig in Biddy's hand, or there's no luck in the fortune, sure.

Biddy. The masther's coming, and the table not cleared! (*Rattles among the dishes at table.* — MOTHER CAREY *retires up,* R. C.)

Enter DAVID, C.

David. The boat's sawing her rope across the rock. Quick, or she'll be adrift!

Larry. Ay, ay, sir! [*Exit,* C.

David. There's a yacht beating around the point; no time to spare; yet she's quick, and I think will make it. That girl, Bess Starbright, has put off in her wherry, fearless of danger, to lend a helping hand. How is this, girl, the table not cleared?

8

Biddy. Indade, sir, I couldn't help it. Mother Carey here was tilling my fortune jist.

David. Ah, Mother Carey, still at your old tricks, deceiving the credulous with your boasted power. Out on you, silly old fool! Girl, bring a light!

Biddy. To be sure I will. [*Exit*, R.

Mother C. Better a fool than a knave, David Murray.

David. What's that?

Mother C. Boasted power! David Murray, you sneer, but I have the power to drive the flush from your cheek, to make your knees tremble, and your heart quake with fear, silly old fool that I am. I deceive! You say this! you, whose whole life is a deliberate lie!

David. What know you of me?

Mother C. Look. (*Takes cup from table.*) What see you here?

David. Pshaw! that's an old trick, Mother Carey.

Mother C. What see you here?

David. Nothing; an empty cup.

Mother C. You're right; an empty cup: yet as I look into it, David Murray, it fills with tiny clouds that float and roll together; now expand, divide, and vanish, disclosing a picture of the past. A room luxuriantly furnished. On a bed lies an old man, thin, pale, wasted with fever. His eyes are fastened upon a young man, who watches at his side. He is dying. See! a door opens; a figure appears, in form and features so like the old man, 'tis plain it is his son. He approaches the bed. The dying man's face flushes. He starts up, raises his hand, as though he would bless — No, no, that angry gesture! it is a curse, a bitter curse! and now he falls back dead — dead — dead.

David (*agitated*). Woman, or fiend! where learnt you this?

Mother C. (*still gazing into the cup*). Silence! The clouds gather again — thicker — thicker — thicker — and now they separate and vanish. There's the son again. A woman clings about his neck, begging, entreating, praying. Useless; there's an evil look in his eye, a wicked purpose in his heart. He pushes her away. Again — prayers, entreaties. Wretch! accursed wretch! She is his wife; but, with a horrid oath, he turns and fells her to the ground!

David (*agitated*). Ha, ha! paint away, old Mother Dragon! Your pictures begin, and end as they began, in smoke. Well, what next?

Mother C. Again they gather — thicker — thicker — thicker. Again they roll away and vanish. Ah, 'tis the other now — the young man who closed the eyes of the dying.

David (*aside*). Bruce Hunter!

Mother C. He sits beside a cradle. In it sleeps a child — a pretty little girl, rosy cheeks, long lashes, curly hair. How pretty she is! The man rises, listens, then leaves the room. Now a window opens; a man appears; his face is hidden by a veil. He stealthily approaches the cradle; raises the child in his arms. Heavens! where is the father? He moves towards the window. Now he stops, listens, then raises the veil. I see his face. Merciful Heaven! it is —

David (*dashing the cup from her hand*). Fool! no

more of your jugglery! Away! Home, and paint pictures in your own tea-cups. Spread them before *women* weak enough to listen to the ravings of a crazy old fool.

Mother C. Crazy. Right, David, I am crazy. My brain snapped one night, long, long ago, and so I'm crazy; ha, ha! You've read much, David, though you are but a poor lightkeeper. You remember the story of the old archer who went mad when the noble destroyed his daughter. They laughed at his ravings, but they found that when he bent his bow his arrow flew straight to the mark. Poor, old, crazy archer! I'm just like him, David, crazy, as you say, but my arrows always fly straight to the mark, straight to the mark. [*Exit*, C.

Enter BIDDY, R., *with a candle, which she places on table, and carries dishes off*, R., *leaving a pitcher of water and two tumblers on table.*

David (*pacing the stage*). Who is this woman? After fifteen years' silence, has an avenging Heaven put into the mouth of an old hag daggers to pierce my conscience? Is she a witch? My father's death-bed — my deserted wife — Hunter's child — she saw them all. They came at her call; faded at her bidding. Wretch that I am, I can conjure them, but they never disappear, — never. Yet I was right. The old man wronged me; cut me off from the possession of his wealth — mine by right. My wife offended me with her reproaches and entreaties; and Hunter, curse him, robbed me of a father's love; coiled his flattering tongue about the old man's heart, and, like a spaniel, licked his way to favor. What should have been mine became his. He, the pauper's son, slipped into my inheritance. But I was revenged. I snatched his darling from her cradle fifteen years ago, and since that time father and child have never met. Yonder breakers, with their angry voices, tell no tales; and yet I dare not face them, for on their crests I've seen amid the storm the features of a little child, with sad, sad eyes, come and go, come and go. O Heavens! if I could but shut out that sight, close those eyes that haunt me everywhere. Revenge is sweet, indeed, but remorse is terrible to bear. (*Sits on bench,* L., *and covers his face with his hands.* — *Knock at door,* C.; *a pause; knock again. The door opens, and* SCUD *sticks his head in.*)

Scud. Am anybody to home, hey? (*Enters, with a lunch-basket on his arm.*) Not a soul. Eberybody gone a fishin'. (*Sees* DAVID.) No, dar's an individle in solitary conflection. (*Steps up, and touches him on shoulder.* DAVID *looks up.*) Yes, sir, ax yer pardon, sir. Am de lady ob de house disumgaged?

David. The lady of the house? There is none.

Scud. Shoo! what dat? no lady? Well den, whar's de widderer?

David. The what?

Scud. De widderer, ob coorse; dar *was* a lady ob de house, — nebber heerd ob a house widout one, — and if she's gone, ob coorse she's left a widderer; one ob dem fellers wid a bumbezine round his stovepipe, moaning, in de words ob de sublime poet, —

> "She has left me here for to shed a tear,
> And play on de old jawbone."

David. There's no lady, no widower. I am the master here. Who are you? and what do you want?

Scud. Who are I? Shoo! don't you know me? Frought eberybody knew me. Why, I'm Scud, de capn's right bower.

David. Then spades are trumps. Well, who's the captain?

Scud. Who's de what? Bless my soul, whar you bin! Don't know de cap'n! Well, well, de igromance ob some people am surprisin'. Why, de cap'n ob de Pacer, de fastest yacht on de coast. You see, Mr. — Mr. — what might I call you?

David. You might call me Sir — that's respectful.

Scud. Yaas, exactly. Well, den, Mr. — Mr. — Sar — Mr. Sar, you see we was out in de bay, we was, me, and de capin, and Massa Clarence, and Miss Daze, and de yacht, when, by golly, afore we knowed it, up rolled de brack clouds, and de wind blowed four ways to once — north-east, sow-west, and — and — well I forgot de oder pints, — and so we let go de jib, and de formast, and de main truck, and de windlass, and de mizzen — mizzen — somethin', — let 'em all go, and den, by golly, dem ar winds jist took dat ar yacht and laid her clear up onto de beach down dar.

David. Ha! Remarkable gale.

Scud. Wan't it? Dat's jest what I tole de cap'n. Cap'n, says I —

David. No matter what you told the cap'n. What do you want here?

Scud. Hey? Jes want to stay here all night.

David. Well, stay, if you can sleep on the floor. That's all the accommodation you'll get here.

Scud. Shoo! sleep on de flo'! What, Massa Clarence, and Miss Daze, and de cap'n? Why, dey cotch dar def a cold.

David. You don't mean to say your whole boat load will quarter on me?

Scud. Dat's jes what I mean. Golly, you wouldn't go for to leab us all out onto de rocks to be devoured by de wild beasts ob de sea, and — and de skeeters — would yer? (*Knock at door,* C.) Here dey am. (*Throws open door.*) Walk right in, gemblems and ladies.

Enter CLARENCE, C., *with* MISS DAZE *leaning on his arm.* — *Seats her in chair,* L.

Clarence. You succeeded in finding shelter, Scud.

Scud. Yaas, sir; take a cheer, sir.

Enter HUNTER, C.

Hunter. Good. Any port in a storm.

David (*starting up.* — *Aside*). Bruce Hunter! and beneath my roof!

Scud. Yaas, sar; found a port, sure nuff. Dis am de master, Mr. — Mr. — Sar.

Hunter. I trust you will excuse this intrusion, my friend. The storm overtook us, and we were forced to land. This seems to be the only house on the point attached to the light.

David (*assuming a rough manner, and with his back to* HUNTER). Yes, cap'n, this is the lightkeeper's house, and I am the keeper. Not much of a place, as you see. You're welcome to what's here. There's no beds, nor nothing to eat, so make yourself comfortable. (*Turns up stage.*)

Hunter. Thank you, friend, we will do our best. Beds we can do without for one night; as for edibles, Scud is our commissary.

Scud. Dat's a fac, sure's yer born, cap'n. I toted de lunch-box along. We'll soon fix 'em all right. (*Goes to table, opens basket, and takes out plates, saucers, and food.*)

Hunter. Friend, will you eat with us?

David (*fiercely*). Eat with you? (*Changes.*) No, I'm obliged to you, I'm not hungry. I must look to my light. (*Goes to door,* C. — *Aside.*) Eat with him! Never! The food would choke me. [*Exit,* C.

Hunter. Our host seems anything but sociable.

Clar. A rough customer. Scud, what did you say to him? I'm afraid you were rough spoken.

Scud. Shoo! I? Why, Massa Clarence, I's a lamb. I jes axed him if de lady ob de house, or de widderer, was to home, and tole him we was comin' — dat's all.

Clar. Ah, Scud, you should polish up your manners. You'll never lose anything by politeness. You should have flattered him a little.

Scud. Flattered him? By golly, he'd a flattened me in a jiffy, I tole yer.

Clar. You don't understand. You should have praised his house, the neatness of this room, his appearance, before proffering your request. In such a situation as this a little tact goes a great way.

Scud. Yaas, sar. Some ob de hard tact in dis yer basket been goin' free or four voyages.

Hunter. Ha, ha! Clarence, your lesson will be thrown away upon Scud.

Clar. The squall has driven us into queer quarters, father.

Hunter. No matter, my boy, as long as we are not driven among the breakers, we should be thankful we have escaped the storm. (*Lightning.*) Ah, here it comes. (*Thunder.*)

Minnie (*with a drawl*). I declare, Uncle Chawles, this is positively delightful. So romantic! to be swept along by the fury of the blast, lashed by the heaving billows, tossed like a tiny chip at the will of the sportive winds, and at last left like shipwrecked mariners upon a desolate island.

Scud. Dat's a fac, an' a disolute lighthouse-keeper a growlin' into de bargain. (*Lightning, thunder, and rain.*)

Hunter. Not so bad as that, Minnie. We have seen at least one inhabitant. It's too bad to deprive you of a pleasant sail, and, what's worse, condemn you to pass the night in this desolate house.

Minnie. Now don't, Uncle Chawles. I do so love adventure. This is just for all the world like a novel. Let me see, what shall we call it — "The Castaway Yachters?"

Clar. Or "The Drenched Duck."

Hunter. With you as the heroine, Minnie.

Minnie. No, I escaped that. How can you, Uncle Chawles, break all my pretty bubbles of romance with your sarcasm.

Hunter. I beg your pardon, Minnie, if I broke anything. Let's all break fast; that will offend nobody. Ready, Scud?

Scud. Yes, sar; dar's biled chicken, biled ham,

biled tongue, hard biled eggs — eberyting but biled taters — and dar's —

Bess (outside, sings).

> "A wet sheet and a flowing sea,
> And a wind that follows fast,
> And fills the wide and rustling sail,
> And bends the gallant mast." *

There, mind your steps, messmate; here, give me your hand. Now, a long pull, and a strong pull, and a pull all together. Here we are, in port at last. (*Door opens,* c. — *Lighting upon* BESS *an instant in the doorway, then she enters, followed by* PARAGRAPH. — *Thunder and rain.*)

Paragraph (*shutting up his umbrella*). The heavens be praised!

Bess. Here, Mr. Murray, I've brought you — Hallo! strangers!

Hunter. Why, it's our old friend Paragraph.

Paragraph. What! the Hon. Bruce Hunter? Sir, yours respectfully. (*Shake hands.*) Master Clarence, yours truly. (*Shake hands.*) Miss Daze, one of the sweetest days of my life, yours devotedly. (*Shake hands.*) Scud, black cloud of the evening, how are you? (SCUD *grins.*)

Bess. Why, you seem to have fallen among friends.

Paragraph. Exactly. Allow me — Hon. Bruce Hunter, Miss Bess Starbright, the rover of the seas; Miss Minnie Daze, Miss Bess Starbright, the bright star of the bay; Mr. Clarence Hunter, Miss Bess Starbirght, the preserver of this Paragraph. (*All interchange greetings.*)

* Or any nautical song.

Scud (aside). Dat ar Paragraph ain't got no stop to it.

Paragraph. And now stop. Business before pleasure. *(Pulls out a note book, and writes.)* "The storm spirit abroad. Terrific peril of our own correspondent. Afloat in a leaky boat. A wrecked writer and a spunky heroine. Peril and privation. Rescue and relief." How's that for a heading?

Hunter. Heading for what, pray?

Paragraph. The news column of The Roaring Rampage, of which highly influential journal I am the duly accredited roving correspondent.

Minnie. Why, bless me, Mr. Paragraph, last week you were an artist.

Paragraph. Exactly, last week, as you say; this week, genius has taken a new flight. Literature is above art. Consequently I have dropped the brush, and taken up the pen. All day I have been in search of an item. This morning I heard of a prize fight, and hastened to report it. Reached the ground, placed myself in a capital position to witness the set-to, when I was ignominiously hustled from the ground by friends of the contending parties. Then rushed off to report a dog fight, but, alas! the dogs wouldn't fight, but flew among the spectators, and I hurriedly left. Then I took a boat to board an incoming steamer. Boat leaked, squall came on, boat upset; clung to the keel until succor, in the shape of that dear little girl with the tarpaulin hat, tore me from my frail support and landed me here, wet, hungry, and minus the news. Bless her, she's a trump. I was a foregone conclusion, a Paragraph cut short, but for her. Henceforth I am her slave.

Bess (*seating herself on box*, L. C.). Well, I never What a fuss about nothing.

Paragraph. Nothing? Hear her; hear the bold rover of the seas. To have saved the life of Peter Paragraph she calls nothing.

Bess. Why, bless you, Mr. What's-your-name, I have pulled twenty fellows out of the water in the last ten years. It's no trouble. I was found in the water. Ever since I could pull an oar, I've had a boat and lived on the water. I know every inch of the coast, every turn of the weather, the depth of every part of the bay, and when I see a boat in distress, what more natural than for me to put out. Pooh! there's no danger; it's just fun.

Hunter. Your hand, my brave girl. You have saved our friend, and, though you treat the matter lightly, 'tis a stout heart that would brave the storm in such a cockle shell as yours.

Paragraph. My sentiments exactly. Miss Starbright, such heroism as yours deserves reward. (*Kneeling.*) Here on my knees I offer you my hand.

Bess. Your hand? What for? I don't need it. I can climb trees like a squirrel, pull ten miles without rest — what do I want of your hand.

Paragraph. But you do not understand. I'm rich. I can place you in a situation where pulling and climbing are not necessary. I offer you my hand in marriage.

Bess. Marriage! Ha, ha, ha! that's too good. You marry me — Mother Carey's chicken?

Paragraph. Yes, were you Mother Carey's old rooster, I'd marry you.

Bess. Ha, ha, ha! O, take him away, somebody,

do! Ha, ha, ha! I shall die, I know I shall! Every man I pull out of the water wants to marry me; but as soon as their clothes are dry, off they go, and "never come back, never come back, they never come back to me." I say, Mr. Paragraph, don't let's talk of marriage. If you're my slave, find me something to eat. I'm awful hungry.

Hunter. Here's plenty. (HUNTER, CLARENCE, *and* PARAGRAPH *run to table,* **take plate of lunch, and crowd around** BESS.)

Hunter ⎱
Paragraph ⎰ *together.* ⎰ Allow me, a slice of tongue.
Clarence ⎱   ⎰ Allow me, a slice of ham.
                         ⎱ Allow me, a little cold chicken.

Bess. La! how polite! But I can't eat it all, you know. (*Looks at* CLARENCE. — *Aside.*) O, my! what a splendid fellow! (*Aloud, to* CLARENCE.) Thank you, I'm very fond of chicken. (*Takes plate from him.* — HUNTER *and* PARAGRAPH *return to table.* — CLARENCE *seats himself* **beside** BESS *on the box.*)

Minnie (*aside*). Heroism has won the day. They have quite forgotten poor me. (*Aloud.*) Ahem! *I* am very fond of cold chicken.

Paragraph (*going to her with plate*). Good gracious! has nobody thought of you? (HUNTER *sits at table, and eats.*)

Minnie. Thanks. 'Tis sweet to be remembered, even by a false one.

Paragraph. False one? (*Aside.*) What have I done? A year ago I offered her my hand, which she accepted, — and to-day, in her presence, I've gone and offered it to this sea nymph. It's bigamy — circumstantial bigamy. (*Aloud.*) My dear Minnie —

Minnie. No, I'm not your dear Minnie. You are false. We have plighted vows together, and you've broken them before my eyes.

Paragraph. No, no. I must show my gratitude to the preserver of my life, you know, and what more natural than to " offer her this hand of mine." She didn't take it, and I shan't offer it again. But you, you are the ideal of my soul, the loadstone of my existence, the object of my adoration! dearer to my heart than —

Scud (comes down with plate). Biled ham, Miss Daze?

Minnie. No, I thank you, Scud. (SCUD *retires up.*) O, Peter, you know my weakness for cultivated society. I thought you would take your place among noble artists. I find you have changed. You have taken to literary pursuits. At the first mention of new aspirations, my heart fluttered and I pictured a bright future for you among the noble wielders of the classic pen, but with one blow you have dashed my hopes, and I find you false as the fickle moon, as hard-hearted as —

Scud (coming down with plate). Biled eggs, Miss Daze?

Minnie. No, I thank you, Scud. (SCUD *returns to table.*)

Paragraph. Don't, Minnie, don't. You'll break my heart. Do not spurn me for a thoughtless jest. You alone are my own dear, loved, tender —

Scud (coming down with plate). Chicken, Massa Paragraph?

Paragraph. Confound it, no! Go away with your senseless bawbles.

Scud. Bawbles? Yes, I guess not, Massa Paragraph. It's chick'n; cook 'im myself. Have some, Miss Starbright?

Bess. No, I thank you, Mr. Scud. I'm very well settled.

Scud (*aside*). Misser Scud! Now der's a lady. Bress her bright eyes, and hansom' as a picter. Jes look at Massa Clarence! He's smashed, clean gone. Settled — golly, she's settled him sure nuff. (*Returns to table.*)

Clarence. But, Miss Starbright, 'tis but a rough life after all. Our ladies in the city find their enjoyment in the dance, the ride, the care of flowers, needlework, and other delicate and refining pastimes. Here you have no company save the rough sailors and fishermen of the coast. Here you are out of the world.

Bess. You think so? Why, this place is a world in itself. Before us is the wide ocean; behind, smooth plains; beyond that, the hills, with their wooded fronts; here around us, the bold headland, the jutting point, roaring breakers and rippling waves, jagged rocks and smooth beach; above, the heavens, now studded with stars, anon sombre and black, or cut by swift lightnings. All forms of nature centre here. There's much of the awful, and much of the sublime. Yet 'tis the dearest spot on earth, for 'tis my home. Rough is the life I lead, 'tis true, but here are no temptations to assail; and I've one true heart on which to lean — could I ask for more?

Clarence. Indeed, but 'tis a blessed spot, and, as you picture it, it seems like a magic realm, one of those fabled grottos, made to enclose a priceless gem, for whose possession princes strove. Here you are the gem. May I not be the prince?

Bess (aside). I never met such a splendid fellow. O, dear! and he'll go away to-morrow. (*Aloud.*) Hark! What's that?

Mother C. (outside). Bess! Bess! my child!

Bess (starting up). O, there's my mother! Here, mother, here.

Enter MOTHER CAREY, C. — BESS *runs into her arms.*

Mother C. Safe, safe, my child! 'Twas a rough gale. I feared for your safety.

Bess. Never fear for me, mother. My boat is tight, and my arms are strong. Come, let me introduce you to my new friends. (*Situation:* CLARENCE *seated on the bench,* L. MR. HUNTER *stands talking with him.* MISS DAZE, R. PARAGRAPH *talking with her.* SCUD *at table, putting away food.* BESS *and* MOTHER CAREY, C.) Mr. Hunter?

Hunter. Well, Miss Bess?

Bess. My mother.

Mother C. (grasping BESS, *and glaring at* HUNTER). No, no! not that name! Hunter! (*Aside.*) What does he here? Have the wolf and the lamb met at last.

Bess. Don't mind her, sir. The sight of a new face is very apt to agitate her.

Hunter. Very glad to meet you, madam, to tell you how much we owe your brave daughter.

Mother C. Yes, Bess is a good girl. A daughter to be proud of.

Bess. Now don't make me blush, mother. Mr. Hunter and his party were driven ashore. They are to pass the night here.

Mother C. Here beneath this roof? Better the cold sands for a bed, the heavens for a shelter, than this place.

Hunter. What mean you?

Mother C. Show me your hand.

Bess. Mother is a fortune-teller, Mr. Hunter. She is called, by the good people who visit here, a witch. I can assure you she sometimes makes wonderful prophecies.

Scud. A witch! O Lord! she takes de kink right out ob my har.

Hunter. My good woman, I have very little faith in predictions, yet here's my hand, if you wish.

Mother C. (*taking his hand*). A good hand. There's fortune here. Fame, too, — the lines straight, distinct, — but here's a dark line I like not — a vein of trouble among the fortunate lines. There's a lifelong pain at your heart. Am I not right?

Hunter. You are. Fifteen years ago I lost a daughter — stolen from her cradle.

Mother C. And never found?

Hunter. Never.

Mother C. And yet you know the thief?

Hunter. I do.

Mother C. An enemy?

Hunter. The only enemy I ever had; and he one whom I never wronged by deed or word.

Mother C. Have you ever searched for him?

Hunter. Every effort was made to find the child and the kidnapper, but all in vain, and at last I came to think that, out of his deep revenge, he had destroyed the child and himself.

Mother C. You're wrong. The child still lives; will be restored.

Hunter. Still lives? How know you this?

Mother C. I read it in your hand.

Hunter (snatching away his hand). Pshaw! An idle trick. Woman, 'tis wrong to trifle with tender emotions. But, 'tis your trade.

Mother C. My trade! Man, the knowledge I possess has been acquired by hard experience, and patient study of the ways of life. I tell you, he who so wronged you is travelling towards you, as you, all unwittingly, are nearing him. As sure as the sun shines, as the winds blow, as the waves beat upon yonder rocks, you will meet, and, in that meeting, I foretell happiness for you, defeat and destruction for him. Mark me, Mother Carey tells you this — and her prophecies never fail, never.

Clarence. Let me try my luck, father.

Mother C. Father? Who spoke then?

Clarence (coming, c.). 'Twas I, mother. Read my hand, and tell me my fate.

Mother C. (puts her arm over his shoulder, takes his hand, and leads him down). No, no, not the hand; let me read it in your face — fresh, open, honest; a face the mother should be proud to look upon. I can easily foretell your fortune — a bright, brave, happy life. Your mother —

Clarence. Alas! she died when I was very young.

Mother C. Too young to remember her?

Clarence. No, mother. There's just a glimpse of a loving face fastened upon my memory, which my father's praises of her goodness have fashioned into an indefinable presence, that is always with me, acting on my life, keeping me from wrong, and aiding me with high aspirations, a radiant image so pure and bright that in my heart I call it by the tender name of mother.

Mother C. (*with emotion*). Bless you, my boy. Doubt not, wherever she is, whether in this world or the unseen, her love still guides and guards your life. (CLARENCE *retires up stage.*)

Hunter (*comes down,* C. — *Aside*). Now to test her power. (*Aloud.*) Mother, the boy called me father.

Mother C. He was right. You have reared, protected, loved him — what though the tie of birth be wanting? — the boy is right.

Hunter (*aside*). She is a witch. (*Aloud.*) But, the mother?

Mother C. Ask me no more. My brain grows weary, and the thoughts of wrong and outrage make my soul sick. What I have told you will come to pass. Be content, and wait as I have waited. (*Goes to door,* C.) The wronger and the wronged shall meet, and when they do, remember Mother Carey's prophecy.
[*Exit,* C.

Scud. By golly, she's gone off on a broomstick.

Bess. Well, I must be getting home. (*Puts on hat.*)

Clarence. Let me accompany you.

Bess. I'm not a bit afraid; and besides, haven't I got a beau already. Here's Mr. Paragraph. He'd be mortally offended if I should slight him.

Clarence. O, no, he wouldn't mind it. You see he's very busy with Miss Daze. He's engaged to her.

Bess. What? Engaged to her? Why, he offered himself to me a little while ago. I'll put a stop to that. Ahem! Mr. Paragraph?

Paragraph (*turns to* C. *of stage*). Well, Miss Starbright?

Bess. A glass of water, if you please.

Clarence. Let me —

Bess. Stop! Mr. Paragraph is my admirer, I may say, my affianced husband, as he offered himself to me, and I did not refuse him. Mr. Para — ah! Peter — a glass of water.

Paragraph. Yes. O Lord! the little jade's in earnest. Yes, Miss Bess. Hot or cold?

Bess. Cold for me. (*Aside.*) Hot for you, I guess.

Paragraph. Yes, I go. (*Starts for table.*)

Minnie. Peter!

Paragraph. Well, dear? (*Returns to* MINNIE.)

Minnie. A glass of water for me first.

Paragraph. Certainly. (*Going to table.*)

Bess. Peter!

Paragraph (*returning*). Well, Miss Bess?

Bess. I shall expect to be served first.

Paragraph. Yes, marm. (*Goes to table; fills two glasses; comes down,* C.; *looks at* MINNIE, *then at* BESS; *stands irresolute a moment, then starts for* MINNIE.)

Bess. Peter!

Paragraph. O, yes, certainly! (*Turns to* BESS.)

Minnie. Peter!

Paragraph. Coming, dear. (*Turns to* MINNIE.)

Bess. I protest. (PARAGRAPH *starts for* BESS.)

Minnie. I insist. (PARAGRAPH *turns to* MINNIE.)

Minnie. }
Bess. } Peter!

Paragraph (*stands in* C. *of stage, falls on one knee, and stretches out his hands containing the glasses to* BESS, R., *to* MINNIE, L.) "Pity the sorrows of a poor young man." Ladies, help yourselves.

Minnie (*jumps up*). You're a false, deceitful man, and I'll never speak to you again. (*Goes up stage.*)

Bess (*jumps up*). Very well, Mr. Paragraph, I release you from your engagement. The next time you are shipwrecked, don't expect me to save you. Come, Mr. Clarence, as he who should be my protector has deserted me, I will permit you to see me home. Good night, all. (*At door,* C.) Peter!

Paragraph (*still on his knees*). Miss Bess!

Bess. "Henceforth I am your slave." Ha, ha, ha! You make a capital fountain. Good by. (*Exit,* C., *followed by* CLARENCE.)

Paragraph (*rising*). Betwixt two stools I fall to the ground. Here, Scud.

Scud. Yaas, Massa Paragraph.

Paragraph (*handing him a glass*). Join me in a toast. Here's to "woman's rights,"

"To torture and tease,
To do just as they please."

[*Drinks; retires up.*

Scud. Yaas, Massa Paragraph, ebery time. (*Drinks.*) (*Aside.*) By golly, dey jes cook his goose. (*Retires up.*)

Enter LARRY, R.

Larry. Beg yer pardin, ladies and gints. Would be afther takin' a look at the lighthouse? The rain's stopped, and it's only a stip.

Minnie. O, yes! Uncle Chawles, I should like to see the interior of a lighthouse.

Hunter. And so would I. What say you, Paragraph?

Paragraph. Lighthouse? Yes, there's a chance for an item there.

Larry. Thin follow me. (*Sees* SCUD.) Hullo, nagar!

Scud. Hallo, paddy!

Larry. Begorra, ye's so black and shiny, I thought 'twis the avil one!

Scud. By golly, yer fool! Does you tink I's a lookin'-glass?

Larry. Ugh! blarney! [*Exit*, C.

Scud. " Shoo, fly; don't bodder me! "

Hunter. Come, Minnie. (*Gives her his arm, and exit,* C.)

Paragraph. She turns her back upon me without a word, and goes off to the light, perhaps to make light of me. Peter, my boy, you've been a fool. Let this be a warning to you. Never make love to a woman when another's in sight. [*Exit*, C.

Scud. Shoo! Triborlat'n am a comin' sartin sure! Dar's a Hibernicum in de house, and de nat'ral antipidies ob de African persuas'n for dem ar fellers is a risin in de intestines ob dis yer buzzim! Who be he am? Hey? What? De brack blood ob forty-leben ginnyologies ob ancisters and ancisteresses cries, Away, white trash! Dar ain't no asswassiation to be fright ob. I'll jes tell de cap'n. Whar's de towel? Can't put away de plates widout wipin' um, and I ain't got no towel.

Enter BIDDY, L.

Biddy. Where's Misther Larry? (*Sees* SCUD.) O, my sowl and body, who's that?

Scud. I want — I want — Stop, Scud. Massa Clarence tole yer to be 'ticlarly polite. Dis am de gal what hab de towels. See me! now, see me! (*Lays his hand on his heart, bows several times, and approaches* BIDDY.) Sublimest ob your sexes!

Biddy. Howld yer blarney jist. It's ashamed I am uv the loikes uv yer.

Scud. When I look at yer, it seem jes as if chahorse am come agin.

Biddy. Sure, I don't know who's coom, at all, at all.

Scud. You hab de peach-blow on yer cheek —

Biddy. Will, I don't know what ye mane.

Scud. De wermillion hues ob de sunflower kermingle dar.

Biddy. Troth, I belave he's a gorrilla.

Scud. And de light ob affliction am in yer eye.

Biddy. O, away wid ye's! It's hathen Chinee yer talk'n, jist. Where's Misther Larry?

Scud. Sweetest ob de female persuasion, what you ax me?

Biddy. Where's Misther Larry, stupid?

Scud. Mister Larry Stupid am gone away. Listen to me. Gib me what I ax yer. (*Falls on both knees, facing audience.*) Gib me, angeliferous creture, O, gib me — (*Takes her hand.*)

Enter LARRY, C.

Biddy. Quit ahoult uv my hand!

Scud. Don't be skeered; it's only peliteness; and I ax yer, gib me, O, gib me — (LARRY *creeps up behind, takes him by the nape of the neck, and shakes him.*)

Larry. Ye thafe of the worrld. (*Shake.*) Ye black hathen! (*Shake.*)

Scud. Here, you up dar! Wha — wha — what yer 'bout dar?

Larry. Troth, ye'll soon find out. (*Shake.*) Ye blackguard!

Scud. Look hyar, Hibernicum; quit foolin', quit foolin'.

Larry. What d'ye mane by insultin' the swatest girl in Fairpoint?

Biddy. Och, it's blushin' I am, Masther Larry.

Scud. You jes lef dat ar coat alone, or I'll tell yer mudder.

Larry. I'll break ivery bone in yer augly carcass, so I will. (*Shake.*)

Scud. You jes lef me be, dat's all. Dis am a free country.

Larry. An' this is a fray fight. Now, nagar, ye'll ax the parthin uv Miss Biddy Bane — d'ye mind?

Scud. Well, I ax it. Lef me be, now.

Larry. An' say, I'm a black —

Scud. You're a brack —

Larry. What's that? You repate afther me. I'm a black —

Scud. Dat's what I said. You're a brack —

Larry (shaking him). Will yer mind what I say?

Scud. Quit, you fool! quit, you fool! I'm a brack —

Larry. Ogly, mischievous owld darkey! —

Scud. Ugly, Miss Cheever's old darkey! —

Larry. An' diserve a kickin', so I do! —

Scud. And deserve a kickin', so I do!

Larry. Now git up, an' if iver I find ye's demaning yerself afore this illigent crather, I'll break ivery bone in yer ogly, black carkiss, so I will.

Scud (rising). Look hyar, Hibernicum! De day ob triberlation am a comin'! You jes look out, dat's all. Mind what I say, de day ob triberlation am a comin', and Scud am a comin', too.

Larry. Howld yer pate, ye black son uv a gun.

Enter HUNTER, C., *with* MINNIE.

Hunter. Hallo! what's the matter here?

Scud. Nuffin, Massa Cap'n. I was axin de lady for a towel — dat's all.

Larry. An' he got a wipe uv anither kind — hey, Biddy?

Enter DAVID, C., *with blankets on his arm.*

David. I'll do the best I can for you, captain. Your friend I've already disposed of for the night in the lighthouse. There's a room above for the lady, a small room there for the boy; here's a bench and blanket for you. Your servant can go to the light with Larry. Sorry I can't do better.

Hunter. Say no more, friend. We shall get along very comfortably.

David. Biddy, show the lady to her room.

Biddy. To be sure I will, and make her comfortable, too. This way, my lady. [*Exit*, R.

Minnie. Good night, Uncle Chawles. Don't be anxious about me. I shall sleep soundly, never fear — it's so romantic. [*Exit*, R.

Hunter. Good night, Minnie. Well, Scud, you're assigned quarters in the light.

Larry. I'll take care of him, sir. Come along, Scud. I'll find a soft plank and a comfortable shake down for ye's.

Scud. Yes, I guess not. Had jes enough ob yer shake downs. By golly, my teeth am all droppin' out me.

Hunter. Go with him, Scud. He'll take good care of you.

Larry. That's thrue for ye, sir.

Scud. Well, lead on, Hibernicum. Dar's allus a clam afore de storm, but de day ob triberlation am a comin'. [*Exit* LARRY *and* SCUD, C.

David. The room in there is very small, so I advise you to give it to the boy, and keep this for yourself.

Hunter. All right, friend. Hope I'm not turning you out of your own quarters.

David. No; my duties keep me in the light all night.

Hunter. Rather a rough life you lead, friend.

David. Rather. Plenty of work, and poor pay.

Hunter. You look like a man who has seen better days.

David. Do I? Well, perhaps I have, and perhaps I haven't. That's my business. I can tell you this, cap'n, I've tried to do the fair thing wherever I've been placed. Love my friends, and hate my enemies. That's about the way of the world, and I'm no better or worse than the common run of mankind. You'll sleep here — will you?

Hunter. Yes, I'll stretch myself on that bench.

David. Don't lock the door, for I have to pass in and out during the night. You sleep sound?

Hunter. Very.

David. I'll try not to disturb you. Good night, and a *long*, refreshing sleep. [*Exit,* c.

Hunter. Good night, friend. That woman's words ring in my ears. My child still lives. O, would they were true. Where could she have learned so much. Paul Hunter and I meet again? Impossible. I wish I could drive such thoughts from my mind. They almost madden me. To feel the clasp of the dear one's arms about my neck, to hear her sweet voice speak the name of father, after so many years, would be a miracle. O, Paul Hunter, deep and terrible was your revenge upon an innocent head. Heaven forgive you, as I hope I do.

Enter CLARENCE, C.

Clarence. Well, father — back again, as you see.

Hunter. And the sea nymph — safe at home?

Clarence. Yes. O, father, she is the sweetest, brightest, dearest girl I ever met!

Hunter. Hallo, boy! Have you lost your heart?

Clarence. Entirely gone, father. Do you know, I'd like to win that girl; to make her my wife.

Hunter. And why not?

Clarence. Her station in life is very low. For myself I would not care, but you would hardly like to take as a daughter one so poor and —

Hunter. Tut, tut, boy! I'd rather see you woo this brave girl, poor as she is, believing, as I do, she has a noble heart, a pure soul, and a loving disposition, than have you bring home as a wife the belle of the gay circles of our city life.

Clarence. Do you mean this?

Hunter. I do, my boy. I was once so poor that I dragged my half-starved body to your grandfather's door, and begged of him a crust of bread. That good old man took me in, fed me, clothed me, treated me as his own son, and when he died, left me all his wealth.

Clarence. Treated you as his son? left you his wealth? 'Twas yours by right.

Hunter. No, Clarence, for I am not your father.

Clarence. Not — my — father? Mr. Hunter —

Hunter. Clarence, to-morrow you are of age. Then I shall make disclosures which will startle you. To-morrow I shall place in your possession the title deeds of a large property — yours by right. I did not mean to speak of this now. Ask me no questions. To-morrow you shall find that, though I am not your father, I have tried to be your friend.

Clarence. Friend! Heaven bless you for your kindness to me. You have indeed startled me. I know not what to think or say. But I will obey you, and be silent.

Hunter. That's right. Now let's to bed. There's a little room which you will occupy. I shall sleep on this bench. Good night.

Clarence. Good night, father. (*Goes,* L., *and opens door.*) Why, here's a comfortable room and a bed. I see here your fatherly care. You would give me a cosey nest, and take the hard couch for your bed.

Hunter. The light-keeper told me it was only a closet. Why should he deceive me so?

Clarence. Well, father, you take the bed, and I'll take the bench. Nay, I insist. I could not sleep here, knowing you were not as comfortably provided for.

Hunter. But, Clarence —

Clarence. Nay, let me have my way. 'Tis perhaps the last request I shall make while I can call you father. (*Takes candle from table.*) Here, take the candle. I shall not need it. Good night, father.

Hunter (*takes candle*). I do not like this, but you shall have your way. Good night, my boy. (*They shake hands.*) Heaven bless you. [*Exit,* L.

Clarence. Good night, kindest and best of friends. Not my father? Who is he, then? Who am I? This place seems the very abode of mystery. An unknown heroine, a witch, who startles even the cool, impenetrable Bruce Hunter, and then he with mysterious hints of secrets in my life. To-morrow I shall know all; be wealthy owner of a large estate, and lose my father. I cannot fathom it. I'll to bed, and try to sleep. (*Gropes his way to bench,* L., *on which are lying two blankets which*

DAVID *brought in; one he rolls up for a pillow, then lies down, covering himself with the other.*) That long walk has made me sleepy. (*Yawns.*) What a pleasant walk, and what a delightful girl — by no means ignorant. She's well read; Mother Carey has reared her well — and then so captivating. Ah, me, if she were only mine! I'll win her. Bess — Bess — what a pretty name. Bess Hunter — Mrs. Bess Hunter — (*Yawns.*) This sea air is a decided narcotic. Bess, — brave, lovely, captivating, — she's the treasure of the seas. Bess — Bess — Bess — (*Sleeps. Lightning, thunder, rain.*)

Enter SCUD, C., *with a blanket.*

Scud. Rainin' like de debble! Dat ar Hibernicum's a fo — fo — fool, dat's what he am. Gib me a soft plank on a stone floor! No, sar; not for Scud. I'll jes find a soft plank hyar onto de bench. (*Goes to bench.*) Hallo! By golly, dar's a lodger dar now. Shoo! it's Massa Clarence. Whar's a soft plank? (*Feels about the floor.*) Hyar's one — jes a shade softer dan a slab. I'll retire here. (*Lies down in front of the bench.*) Dar's nuffin like a good crop ob wool onto de cranium when de pillers am all gone to de wash. Hallo! what's dat? More lodgers? (*Lightning and thunder. Door,* C., *opens softly. Enter* DAVID, *with a long knife in his hand.*)

David. He sleeps! My enemy's at my mercy. 'Tis a cowardly act — a blow in the dark. But let me remember my wrongs. Bruce Carter, son of a pauper, living in luxury; I, the rightful owner of all he calls his own, living here like a dog. He must die. One sure blow, and we are quits. The breakers roar for prey.

Who so fit to feed them as he? All sleep well. This knife shall find his heart. One plunge, and his body is in the waves.

Scud. Dar's somebody in de house dat don't belong hyar, dat's sure enough. Wake up, Scud. Triberlat'n's a comin'; I feel 'em in dem remarkable organs, my heels. (*Sits up.*)

David (*in* C. *of stage*). Why do I falter? He is my enemy. Shall I spare him? If I lose this chance, with the light he will go, never to return. I must do it. (*Lightning and thunder.*)

Scud (*rising*). By golly, dar's a man in de middle ob de floor wid a meat-axe! Who's he comin' fur to go fur? (*Rises.*)

David (*creeping towards bench*). Curse the knife! How my hand trembles.

Scud. Triberlat'n am a comin'! I hyar 'im breave.

David. Now for it.

Scud (*seizing him by throat*). Nuffin hyar, butcher! nuffin hyar!

David. Confusion! (*They struggle.*)

Scud. Drop dat knife! Hyar, cap'n! Help! murder! Help! help! (*Wrests the knife from* DAVID, *and throws him to* R.)

Enter HUNTER, *with lighted candle in one hand, pistol in the other.* CLARENCE *sits up, rubbing his eyes.*

David. Curse that black fiend!

Hunter. What's the matter, Scud?

Scud. Murder — jes — almost — dat's what's de matter. Dat ar chap was gwine for Massa Clarence wid a knife, an' I went for dat chap, jes — dat's all.

Hunter. Murder — Clarence! Short work for murderers. (*Levels pistol at* DAVID. *Lightning.*)

Enter MOTHER CAREY, C.

Mother C. (C.). Hold, Bruce Hunter! The man who's life is in your hands must not die. Look well at him 'Tis Paul Hunter.

Hunter (*dropping pistol, and falling back*). Paul Hunter!

David (*dashes past* SCUD *towards* MOTHER CAREY). Woman! fiend! you lie!

Scud (*puts his arms through* DAVID'S, *and bends him over his knees*). Hold on, old man! Gib de old lady a chance, for triberlat'n's ar a comin'!

Mother C. Ha, ha! Remember Mother Carey's prophecy. The wronger and the wronged shall meet. Happiness to one; destruction to the other. Justice for both at last, — at last. (*Lightning and thunder.*)

QUICK CURTAIN.

ACT II. — SCENE. *Same as in Act* 1. *Table,* C. *Chairs* R. *and* L. *of table. Bench,* L. *Arm-chair,* R. L., *near entrance, barrel with cover, large enough to comfortably contain* SCUD.

Larry (*sings, outside,* C.).

  " When first I saw swate Peggy,
   'Twas on a market day,
  On a low-backed car she sat and rode,
   Upon a truss of hay," &c.
          [*Enters,* C.

AMONG THE BREAKERS.

Och, it's an illigant mornin', jist, an' it's dyin' I am for a sight uv the lovely girl that's made me pass a slapeless night dramin' uv her. Where's the masther — I donno? Not once the night has he put his head in the light. Will, it's his onaisy sphirit kapes him a walkin' an a walkin'. Ah, there's Biddy comin', as rosy as the clouds iv the mornin'. (*Enter* BIDDY, *with her hands full of dishes.*) The top uv the mornin' to ye's, Biddy, ye jewel.

Biddy. Ah, ha, Misther Larry, yer up betimes wid yer compliments an' flatterin' spaches.

Larry. To be sure I am. For it's little slape I have wid yer purty face forninst me an' the shlumbers of midnight. Och, Biddy, darlint, won't ye's come for to go for to be my widdy?

Biddy. Indade, an' I'll be nobody's widdy. If I'd not my hands full I'd box yer ears, so I would.

Larry. Och, be aisy! That's a dilicate way of axing ye's to be my wife. Hands full! By that same token, Biddy, darlint, I'm just going to stale a kiss from your purty lips.

Biddy. Indade, but yer not. Kape off, or I'll scratch ye's face, so I will.

Larry. Wid yer hands full? Troth, but I'll jist thry that same. (*Puts his arm round her waist.*)

Biddy (*struggling*). Away wid ye's!

Larry. Whin I've tasted the cherries uv yer lips. (*They struggle. She drops the dishes. He kisses her. Cover of barrel is raised, and* SCUD's *head appears.*)

Scud (*aside*). Dar's a smash. Stolen sweets, illustrated wid — wid — wid plates. (*Disappears in barrel.*)

10

Biddy. Now say what ye's done. Ye's broken the pace.

Larry. Niver mind the paces. I'll make it all right wid the masther.

Biddy (*picking up pieces in her apron*). The masther is it? Och, Misther Larry, there's been avil work here the night.

Larry (*picking up pieces*). Avil work? What d'ye mane, Biddy?

Biddy. Whist! I heard a hullabaloo, an' down here I cript, an' paked in at the door. An' there was the masther hild by the black cook, an' the cap'n wid a pisthol in his fist, an' owld Mother Carey a houldin' uv her broomstick, an' all talkin' an' talkin' togither somethin' about a murther; an' thin the owld lady scooted out uv the door, an' — an' they locked masther up in his room, an' — an' thin I jist crept off to bid. Och, but it's an avil place, jist!

Larry. A murther, an' the masther locked up? Bedad, I don't onderstand it at all, at all.

Biddy. No more do I; but I'll give warning the day, an' go back to my cousin, Bridget Blaney, so I will.

Larry. An' lave yer own thrue Larry, that's dyin' for the love uv ye's? Biddy, come wid me to the praste beyant, an' be my own thrue wife.

Biddy. Och, d'ye mane it, Misther Larry?

Larry. Mane it? Biddy, my darlint (*puts his arm about her waist*), I'm a lonely Irishman, widout the convaniences uv relations, a pinin' for the swates uv domestic life. Take me to ye's heart, for I'm cowld wid the hunger uv love that burns in my bosom.

Biddy. Troth, Misther **Larry**, yer a broth uv a boy, so ye are; an', wid the praste's blessin', I'll be your own thrue wife, Biddy Bane.

Larry (*embracing her*). Och, ye darlint, it's crazy I am wid the joy I fale. By the blissid St. Patrick, we'll be the happiest couple in the wide world.

Biddy. That we will. Now let me go. The brickfast's not riddy, an' the table's not laid. (*Goes,* R.)

Larry. I say, Biddy; like a thafe I stole a kiss (*approaching her*); like an honorable gintleman I put it back. (*Kisses her.* SCUD *raises cover.*)

Biddy. Be aisy, Misther **Larry**. [*Exit,* R.

Scud.

"De monkey marred de baboon's sister,
Smacked his lips, and den he kissed her."

Shoo! (*Disappears.*)

Larry. She's a darlin', so she is. The masther's locked up in his room. Begorra, I'll jist do meself the favor to lit him out, an' set him fray. He's my own masther, an' if he's in throuble, Larry Divine's not the b'y to show him his back, jist. (*Going,* L.)

Scud (*throwing off cover, and standing up in the barrel*). Stop dar, Hibernicum, stop dar! Dis am a private way; it am dangerous trabellin'.

Larry. Out uv that, ye hathen imp of blackness. Hould yer prate, or I'll break —

Scud (*pointing pistol*). What's dat? Who — who — who — who's a what? Quit, yer fool! quit, yer fool! Dis yer am a deranged rebolber; keeps goin' round an' goin' off, shootin' all de time. You can't go in dar.

Larry (retreating). Put up that pistol. It might go off.

Scud. Da's a fact, da's a fact. I tell yer, Hibernicum, triberlation am comin', sart'n sure. De tables am turned. Down on yer marrow bones dar, down on yer marrow bones!

Larry (kneeling). Scud, Masther Scud, ye jewel, be aisy wid the pisthol.

Scud. Now yer jest mind what I say. Ain't got dis chile by de scruff ob de neck dis time. Now, mister, say what I tole ye. I'm a red-headed, meddlin', pugniferous Hibernicum. Say it — by golly, can't hold dis yer pistol.

Larry. Yes, yes. I'm a rid-headed — by my sowl, I'll break —

Scud. De pistol am goin'.

Larry. I'm a rid-headed, middlin', pugnacious Mickey!

Scud. Da's a fact. Brack libbered, ugly — say it.

Larry. Niver, ye thafe.

Scud. It's goin', it's goin — can't hole him.

Larry. I'm a black-livered —

Scud. Da's a fact, da's a fact — scoundrel — say it.

Larry. Scoundrel. (*Aside.*) That ye are.

Scud. An' Massa Scud am a gentleman. Can't hole de pistol.

Larry. An' Masther Scud am a gintleman — (*Aside.*) Thafe.

Scud. Now den, Hibernicum, shake yer hoof, shake yer hoof, vamose. One — two — tree —

Larry (rising). Off it is, belave it, honey. (*Goes to*

door, C.) I'll be avin wid ye, ye black thafe of the worrld.

Scud. De pistol am a goin'; can't hole him, by golly, can't hole him. (*Exit* LARRY, C.) Golly, see um run. De day ob triberlation am come. Massa cap'n tole me to get under cober an' watch dat ar door. Dis yer am de only cober I kin find. Almos' stuffocate me. My knees am all out ob jint in de barrel, but dar ain't nobody goin' into dat ar door while I've got dis yer pistol. Hallo! somebody's comin'. Whar's de cober? It am clean gone. (*Drops into barrel.*)

Enter PARAGRAPH, C., *with note-book.*

Paragraph. What's this — a murder? The Irishman said that somebody had murdered somebody. His master locked up, and to use his expressive words, "Owld Nick broke loose." Peter, you're in luck. Here's an item. (*Writes.*) "Horrible outrage. Dastardly assassination. The banks of Fairpoint bathed in gore. High crime on the Lowlands. Testimony of an eye-witness. Our special correspondent on the spot." There's a heading for an extra. But where's the murderer, and where's the murdered? The light-keeper locked up! He must be the assassin. I'll interview him. What! Miss Daze, my adored Minnie, for whom I fished and lost? I'll try her with a fresh bait. (*Takes out his handkerchief.*)

Enter MINNIE, R.

Minnie. Mr. Paragraph! Sir, I thought we were to have no more of your society.

Paragraph (with affected emotion). Minnie, — ah, Miss Daze, — I am about to leave this place, hallowed by tender recollections, never to return. (*Wipes his eyes.*) After a sleepless night, I have come to my senses. Yes, Peter, who so madly loved you, adored, celestial, seraphic, ecstatic, unaffected divinity of loveliness, has come to a realizing sense of his inferiority. The said Peter now sees how high you are above him. Pardon this weakness. (*Weeps, and blows his nose.*) In an hour you will find said Peter, your once loved Peter, far away. You'll never hear of him again, save by report of his valor in the field.

Minnie. In the field? What mean you Peter — Mr. Paragraph?

Paragraph. To-morrow I enlist in the noble army of martyrs who serve our dearly beloved Uncle Samuel; to-morrow I don the habiliments of a soldier — the tightly-fitting pantaloons, the baggy coat of blue, and march away to battle against " Lo."

Minnie. Against who?

Paragraph. " Lo, the poor Indian," on the broad prairies of the West. Ah, the thought is a soothing balm to my lacerated bosom. It is an inspiration. I feel the glow of martial fire; the smoke of battle fills my nostrils. I see the red man of the forest; my hand grasps his top-knot; my gleaming knife encircles his head. Ah, ha! his scalp is at my belt.

Minnie. How romantic. O Peter! glorious Peter! you were born to be a soldier.

Paragraph. There's but one drawback to this glowing picture. To leave you, whom I so madly love, to leave you, fair type of civilization, to find companionship with the red squaws of the West. The thought is madness.

Minnie. And do you think I will submit to the parting? No, Peter. When you go forth as a soldier I will be by your side. I will carry your musket; I will share with you the burden of your knapsack, and, on the far distant prairies, cook for you the sportive buffalo, while you scalp the red man.

Paragraph. O, this is too much. Devotion, thy name is Woman. O Minnie Daze, I'm all ablaze with love and valor. Thus do I swear fidelity to you, my soldier bride. (*Kisses her.*)

Scud (*popping up his head*). Dat's de sojer's fust shot, all de world ober. (*Disappears.*)

Minnie. O, Peter, how could you? Pardon my blushes; 'twas so abrupt. Give me time to recover. Anon we'll meet, my gallant soldier. O, this is indeed romantic. [*Exit,* R.

Paragraph. Go for a soldier! Not much, my blooming Minnie. I've made peace with you without a battle, and I'll contrive to keep it without the help of the red man. Now, then, to interview the murderer. That's his room. (*Going,* L. SCUD *rises in the barrel.*)

Scud. Halt dar, Massa Paragruff.

Paragraph. Scud! What are you doing in that barrel?

Scud. Dis yer am de sentry-box, Massa Paragruff.

Paragraph. O, ho! I see. You are on guard.

Scud. Yaas, Massa Paragruff. I'm de brack guard ob de place.

Paragraph. Exactly. There has been a murder committed. Am I right?

Scud. Yaas, indeed. Almos' killed a man.

Paragraph. Good. Hold on a minute till I get my note-book. (*Takes out note-book.*) I'll interview you first.

Scud. Interwhich? Yaas, I guess not. Yer can't come inter dis yer barrel.

Paragraph. Now then, Scud, tell me all about it. You witnessed the deed?

Scud. Yaas, indeed, I was dar, chile, in de thickest ob de fry.

Paragraph. Yes. (*Writes.*) Scud, intelligent colored man — age, forty — occupation, servant — witnessed the deed.

Scud. See hyar, Massa Paragruff, what yer doin' dat for? What yer writin' my photography for? I didn't kill nuffin.

Paragraph. It's all right. Now, then, who was murdered?

Scud. Hey? Why, de wictim, ob course.

Paragraph. But who was the victim?

Scud. Why, de chap what was de wictim.

Paragraph. O, stuff! What was his name?

Scud. De back name, or de front name?

Paragraph. Both, you mule.

Scud. Young man, look hyar. If you go for to hurlin' obstreperous epigrams at dis yer chile, I'm done, dat's all.

Paragraph. I beg your pardon, Scud. Please give me the name of the victim.

Scud. Why, yer know him. 'Twas Massa Clarence.

Paragraph. Clarence murdered, and I asleep. (*Writes.*) **Victim,** Clarence Hunter — age, twenty-one — pride of his father — promising youth — cut off — flower of manhood. Go on. Who was the murderer?

Scud. De fellow wid de knife.

Paragraph. Deed committed with a knife. Well.

Scud. Well, you see, Massa Clarence was a sleepin' onto de bench down dar, an' I was a sleepin' onto de floor down dar, an' de fellow come into de door dar wid a knife; an' he stan' up in de floor jes dar, an' de lighten come, an' I seed him. Den he went for Massa Clarence, an' dis yer chile went for him, an' somefin dropped, dat's all. Den we locked him into dat yer room.

Paragraph. In that room? Enough. From the lips of the murderer I will hear the rest. O Peter, you're in luck. Here's matter for two columns of sensation. (*Going,* L.)

Scud. Hole on, Massa Paragruff. Whar are you goin'?

Paragraph. Into that room.

Scud. Can't do it, no sar. I am de cap'n ob dis yer — dis yer — barrel, an' dar ain't no passin' dis yer bulwark, no sar.

Paragraph. What, would you hamper the freedom of the press?

Scud. Don't know nuffin bout de press. Free list am suspended. No dead heads in dar. No, sar; can't go.

Paragraph. But I shall. My professional reputation is at stake. Stand back.

Scud (*presenting pistol*). Stand back yerself, or yer'll make a bifsteak.

Paragraph (*retreating*). Put up that pistol.

Scud. 'Tain't one ob dat kind. It keeps goin' round, an' goin' off, an —

Paragraph. Put it down. I'll tell your master, you scamp, and have you horsewhipped. Point a pistol at a gentleman, and a member of the press! You shall catch it. (*Hurries off*, c.)

Scud. Yaas, sar, do, sar, fotch de master, an' git me out ob dis yer barrel. Freedom ob de press! Ya, ya! dat am a mighty organ, but dis yer pistol am a sight more powerfuller. Hallo! dar's somebody else. Can't go into dat ar room, no, sar. (*Disappears in barrel.*)

Enter BESS, C.

Bess (*singing*).

> "Ever be happy, gay as a lark,
> Pride of the pirate's heart."

Rather early to make a call. But it's such a splendid morning, bright, clear, with a capital breeze, and just the morning for a sail; so, to be hospitable and polite, I've launched my boat, and sculled across the bay to invite my beau of last night to take a seat. O, wasn't he splendid — so tall, and such a noble style about him! Ah, me, Bess Starbright, it's well for you that he stays but a day.

Enter CLARENCE.

Clarence. Well, well, Miss Bess, here you are.

Bess. Yes, Mr. Clarence, here I am, to wish you a good morning.

Clarence. I've been to your house to make a morning call.

Bess. That's very kind of you. And I took my boat and rowed across the bay, and so missed meeting you on the sands. Come, it's a beautiful morning; give me your company for a sail.

Clarence. A sail? That's delightful. Shall I call the rest of our party?

Bess. Just as you please — but — but — but my boat will only carry two.

Clarence. Ah, that's a delightful boat! I thank you for your kind invitation, and will give you my company with pleasure. This is my birthday, Miss Bess.

Bess. Your birthday? Accept my congratulations.

Clarence. Thank you; but I shall ask you for something more. I am twenty-one to-day, Miss Starbright, and with my manhood comes the possession of a large property, and an income sufficient to satisfy the most lavish disposition.

Bess (*aside*). Rich! Ah, me! would he were as poor as I. (*Aloud.*) I'm very glad, sir.

Clarence. Yes, I have wealth. I also have a pair of strong arms, a healthy frame, a passably clear head, and, I hope, a warm heart. I'm rather an oddity, for I believe nothing in this world is of any good unless it is made useful; and unless I can make the wealth serve me as well as I have made the others, I shall think my birthday gift of fortune is a useless incumbrance.

Bess. Why, I declare, sir. You're quite a preacher, too.

Clarence. Am I? Do you know what text I should like to preach a sermon from?

Bess. I'm sure I don't.

Clarence. With you as the congregation, I as the preacher, " Love one another."

Bess. Sir — Mr. Clarence!

Clarence. Miss Starbright — Bess — listen to me. Last night, after you left me, I stood at your window. I heard the sound of a piano and your voice, sweeter than any which ever fell upon my ears. You have beauty, taste, talent. You are out of place here. I have met beautiful, cultivated women in society, but never before has my heart been moved by that mighty power which makes or mars all destinies. Bess, let my hand lead you to a station more fitting your noble, brave spirit. Be my wife, Bess, for I love you.

Bess. You love me? — you rich, I a poor girl?

Clarence. Nay, let's drop comparisons, or change names, for your brave acts would count in honorable wealth beyond my rich possessions.

Bess. O, Mr. Clarence! I know not what to say. I cannot but be pleased with your preference. I, too, have had my sweet dreams since you came here, but 'tis so strange. 'Tis better we should let it pass as a dream. To-day you will leave me; to-morrow you will look upon it as *but* a dream, and forget me.

Clarence. 'Tis a dream from which I hope never to awake then. No, Bess, I am determined you shall be my wife.

Enter HUNTER, C.

Hunter. And he's a most determined young scamp, Miss Bess.

Bess. What, Mr. Hunter, will you allow this?

Hunter. I cannot help myself. He is of age; and besides, I rather like his spirit.

Bess. But what will Mother Carey say?

Enter MOTHER CAREY, C.

Mother C. Be not too hasty. Time tries all. Wait. There are mysteries to be cleared, accounts to be settled, wrongs to be righted. Love can wait, as well as hate.

Clarence. Nay, Mother Carey, there's no time like the present. I love your daughter; would make her my wife. I believe I can gain her consent. Have I yours?

Mother C. Patience, boy, patience. An hour from now the tide will change. Who can tell what its flood may strew upon the beach, — perhaps treasures of hope and joy; perhaps fragments of wrecked hopes, and ghastly corses of despair. Wait, boy, wait. Come to me then, and what I have the right to bestow shall be yours.

Clarence. Thanks! I will await your pleasure. Come, Bess, I'm anxious for that sail.

Bess. Gracious! I forgot all about it. Come, you shall see how I manage a boat.

Clarence. And then you shall see how I manage a wife.

Bess. When you've caught her. Come along, sir.

[*Exit*, C.

Hunter. Hallo, Scud! (SCUD *rises from barrel.*)

Scud. Ay, ay, Massa Cap'n.

Hunter. What in the world are you doing there?

Scud. I's on guard, Massà Cap'n. Didn't ye tole me to watch de door dar? Spec I did — wid a pistle, too.

Hunter. Well, get out of that barrel — quick!

Scud (*tips the barrel down, and crawls out*). Relibe guard! Yaas, sar, spec I will. I, golly, got de rheumatiz in my heel. (*Hobbles to door*, C.) Here, cap'n, hyar's yer pistle. (HUNTER *takes it.*) I jes paid off dat ar Hibernicum! (*At door*, C., *a broom comes down upon his head.*)

Larry. Ye did, ye thafe uv the worrld!

Scud. By golly, stop, yer fool! Help! help! (*Runs across stage, followed by* LARRY *beating him.*)

Larry. I'll tache ye, ye black son of a gun. [*Exit*, R.

Hunter. And now we are alone, I thank you for the service you have performed in disclosing a villain. May I not ask you to clear this mystery?

Mother C. Bruce Hunter, or Carter, — it matters not, — you are a noble man. In all honorable ways, you have attained the love of friends, great wealth, a high name in the council halls, the good opinion of your fellows. One more effort, and happiness is yours.

Hunter. Still mysterious. What must I now do?

Mother C. Bring a sinner to repentance.

Hunter. I am still in the dark.

Mother C. Listen. Fifteen years ago, under my humble roof rested a woman weak and faint after a long journey. Her story was a bitter one. Young, the bloom of girlhood scarcely swept from her cheek, she was a wife and mother. Her husband was a reckless, dissipated man, whose father had disinherited him for marrying a poor girl, willing his property to an adopted son.

Hunter. Paul Hunter!

Mother C. And yourself. My characters are real. Fired with revenge, the disappointed man determined to rob his foster brother of his dearest treasure. The wife, with tears and supplication, attempted to persuade him from his purpose. He struck her to the earth, sought the home of his enemy, and accomplished his purpose.

Hunter. So far all's true. The rest is mystery.

Mother C. He fled; but not unwatched, for the wife stealthily followed.

Hunter. Wretched woman! She should have sought the unhappy father, disclosed the hiding-place of the villain —

Mother C. She was his wife. The two were one. His secrets were her secrets, to be kept sacredly. With the knowledge of his guilt she must cover her head, though the heavy burden crush her to the dust. She found his hiding-place; watched and waited for the hand of fate to lead the father to his child. For she had made a vow that while her husband lived her lips should be silent, unless that husband, on his bended knees, with remorse leading his guilty soul to repentance, should himself proclaim the truth, and sue for pardon.

Hunter. Where is that woman?

Mother C. Beyond your reach. Bruce Hunter, he who so wronged you is at your mercy. In your hands is the weapon that can take his life; in your heart is the power to lead him to repentance. Use either, and the mystery is cleared. You have your choice. But reflect. Revenge, speedy, quick, terrible, blots out a wretched life, to stain you with its blood; repentance washes a soul, brings it nearer to a merciful Father, and weaves into your spirit the rich reward of a noble act. (*At door*, C.) Bruce Hunter, I have done. When next we meet, the mystery is cleared. [*Exit*, C.

Hunter (*sinking into chair* R. *of table*). "You have your choice. The power is in your heart to bring him to repentance." 'Tis false. There's nought within this bosom but a fierce desire for revenge. When I remember these long years of separation from one who might have made my life so happy; when I remember the cruel wrong wrought by this inhuman monster, can I stop to parley with him, to turn him to repentance? No; this weapon shall right me quick, and thus restore my daughter. (*Rises.*) Daughter! Ah, but when I have her in my arms, will she not shrink from the embraces of a father whose hands are stained with blood? That woman is well skilled in her vocation. She sets fierce passions warring in my breast, and stakes her fortunes on the power that in life's battle oft for me has won the field. She's right. I cannot sully the fair record of the past with crime. Away the thought. Heaven help me to subdue this man. (*Goes* R., *unlocks door, and throws it open.*) Paul Hunter! You are wanted. (*Returns to seat* R. *of table.*)

David (*outside*, L.). Wanted, ha, ha! by the officers of justice. Well, I am ready. (*Enters*, L.) I am ready. How? — alone? Come, let's have no delay in this business. I am anxious to enjoy the quiet of grim walls, the solitude of the felon's cell. Bring in your men. You'll find no resistance. I'll walk as calmly to my fate as did the martyrs to the stake.

Hunter. There are no officers here. You are as free as I.

David. Free? Have you forgotten, that last night I attempted your life; that I would have killed you as I would a snake that bit me?

Hunter. O, no, I haven't forgotten it, Paul. But for the fidelity of a faithful friend some one would have been a corse this bright morning.

David. Faithful friend! Curse him.

Hunter. And he saved a life dearer than mine. Your little plot failed, Paul. 'Twas the boy whose life was endangered, not mine.

David. Bruce Carter, you have escaped me; but if you value your life, leave this place forever. There's a fiend in my bosom urging me to murder: there's a frenzied power creeping through my frame I cannot control. Begone — ere 'tis too late.

Hunter. 'Tis too late now, Paul Hunter; too late for you and I to separate, until that dark veil which covers the past is lifted. For fifteen years you have embittered my life; and now, when we meet, you bid me begone. Fool! you forget I am the avenger now. 'Tis my wrongs that cry aloud. Of what do you complain?

David. Complain? Nothing. Why should I? There was a rich old father in the past, whom I loved dearly, and who loved me; but another stepped in between, and robbed me of his love. But I must not complain. He died cursing me: 'twas the work of this other. But I must not complain. Those broad lands, elegant houses, stores of notes and gold yonder, mine by right, which this other enjoys. But I must not complain.

Hunter. You're wrong, — all wrong, Paul.

David. Silence! I know your smooth, oily tongue; I knew that from the moment you stepped into my father's door, your aim was to destroy my influence, and reign supreme. I knew this, and you succeeded. I couldn't beat you there, but I had a terrible revenge.

Hunter. You stole my daughter.

David. Ay, from her cradle. Yes, the smooth tongue was wanting, but a soft step, a subtle trick outfought you, Bruce Carter; and I bore her off in triumph.

Hunter. Where is she now?

David. Where you will never find her. I foiled your efforts to track us, for I knew whom you suspected. Ah, 'twas a glorious victory. One other would content me. To snatch you from my rich possessions, — mine, do you hear, Bruce Carter? — to get my hands about your throat, to drag you to the bank beyond, and hurl you into the breakers. That would content me. You hear me? We are alone, face to face. I'll struggle with you for a life, to end this mortal hate. (*Approaching him fiercely.*)

Hunter (*producing pistol*). Stop! There's a quicker way than that which you propose. 'Tis loaded, — works well, — is deadly sure. I'll place it here upon the table (*lays it on table*), within your reach. At any moment you can grasp it, and with it take my life. I only ask that you will patiently listen to what I shall say.

David (*quickly places his hand on pistol*). You're in my power. Yes, I'll listen.

Hunter. Paul, your life has been all a mistake; your estimate of me is all a mistake. I never tried to supplant you: was always your friend. You remember, you were dissipated, married against your father's command. Often I have stood your friend, but you would not believe me, so 'twould be useless to try to convince you of my friendship.

David. Bah! Rather weave ropes of sand.

Hunter. I never saw the girl you married. I think your father was mistaken in her.

David. Mistaken! She would have graced his noblest assemblies. She was too good for me.

Hunter. And so you deserted her?

David. Have a care, Hunter. I'm desperate.

Hunter. Your father, by a will, made me his heir.

David. Why torture me with that?

Hunter. To make plain what follows. One night I lost my daughter. You know how.

David. Indeed I do.

Hunter. The night following, a little boy, a bright little fellow, about six years of age, was brought to my home, with a note, running something like this: "This boy has been deserted by his father, who has wronged you. His mother cannot care for him, as a stern duty compels her to fly. You are rich, powerful, enjoying what might have been this boy's. Be a father to the son of Paul Hunter, and Heaven and a despairing mother will bless you." Signed, Mary.

David. My wife and son! "Mary!" My wife! O, how that name strikes upon my heart. Well, the boy —

Hunter. By the provisions of your father's will I

was required to take the family name. By his bounty and affection I was already in good practice as a lawyer. Of the property willed me, I kept a strict account, invested in the surest and safest manner, never used one dollar for my own advancement, so that now the property has trebled in value, and to-day, by my own free act, is transferred, with full title and possession, to one who is of age to-day — your son.

David (*aghast*). My son! My son!

Hunter. Yes, the boy who has been, and is as dear to me as the little girl I lost; the boy who has grown to be a noble man, with brains to conceive and energy to accomplish; the boy whose life you attempted last night — your son Clarence Hunter.

David. No, no, not that. Bruce Carter, spare me; spare a miserable wretch. Attempt the life of my own son? Open, earth, and hide me; fall, ye walls, and crush me. I am accursed! accursed! accursed! (*Crouches on stage.*)

Hunter. Come, Paul, I think you will believe me innocent of any design to ruin you. Let us bury the past. For that boy's sake be a man; shake off this desire of revenge. Come, I offer you my hand.

David. Your hand, Bruce, to such a wretch as — No, no, I see now my error. You are a noble man, Bruce. You have repaired wrong with blessing. Take your hand? Why, mine would stain it — Ah! the child! Hark! Do you hear the breakers? They come — dash — dash — creeping all about us. See — see that face! it comes again — the little girl — sad face, tearful eyes — on the crest of the breakers! Drive them back! shut those eyes! they burn into my soul.

Hunter. The child — my child, Paul?

David. Yes — O Bruce, if there's a spark of manhood in you, revenge your wrongs. There's the weapon at your hand. Blow out my brains. Here, on my knees, I beg for pardon, ere you fire: on my knees, Bruce. But do not spare me. I am a murderer, — the child is dead!

Hunter. Dead! dead! Then all's lost —

Enter MOTHER CAREY, C.

Mother C. No, all's well. The child lives.

Hunter. Do not deceive me.

Mother C. That repentant man at your feet bore her to the shore, — 'twas the night of the wreck, — plunged her into the waves, thinking no questions would be asked were she found with the dead passengers of the wreck. But the waves cast her up, high up upon the beach, and she was cradled in a mother's arms. She lives! (*Enter* BESS STARBRIGHT, C.) Bruce Hunter, behold your daughter.

Hunter. She my daughter? The proof — who are you?

Mother C. The woman of the silent tongue, the protector of your child, the deserted wife — (*throws off wig and cloak, appearing in dark dress*) — Mary Hunter.

David. Mary, my wife, what does this mean? (*Sits on bench, and covers his face.*)

Mother C. Bess, the father I promised you, has come at last. Bruce Hunter, take your child. I have full proof.

Hunter. My daughter! (*Takes her in his arms.*) It must be true, it must be true. Bess, the name your mother gave you, your eyes so like hers — strange I should not have noticed them before.

Bess. Dear father, how glad I am to know you! Mother Carey has always told me that he would come to claim me. I never dreamed that he would be the father of Clarence.

Hunter. Clarence? He is not my child. One good turn deserves another. Mary Hunter, you have restored my daughter. I give you back your son, brave, noble, honorable. Clarence, I promised you astounding disclosures to-day. This lady is —

Mother C. Your mother, Clarence.

Clarence. My mother?

Hunter. She is right. I will explain.

Clarence. Dear, dear mother. (*Kneels at her feet.*)

Mother C. (*raising him in her arms*). Here, to my heart, my boy. Hard must be that duty which separates a mother from her child. This happiness repays all my pains.

Clarence. Mother, I know not what witchcraft you have practised here; I only know that Mr. Hunter never yet deceived me, and something in my heart tells me he is right now.

Enter PARAGRAPH *and* MINNIE, C. *Come down*, R.

Paragraph. Mr. Hunter, Miss Minnie and myself have just been calculating the exact hour of your departure.

Minnie. We are so impatient to be off.

Enter SCUD, C.

Scud. De yacht am all ready. Dar's a breeze sprung up from the sow — sow — north by west, an' —

"De ship it am ready, an' de sails dey are set,
So I must be off to sea, Phœbe Jane."

Hunter. Nay, there's no hurry, friends. The old fortune-teller has turned out to be a very dear friend, and we are in no hurry to leave this spot.

Clarence. Mr. Hunter, I'm in a very awkward predicament, for I love Miss Bess Hunter as dearly as I love Bess Starbright.

Hunter. My dear boy, don't give yourself any uneasiness. Bess, my child, you love Clarence?

Bess. I'm afraid I do, father.

Enter LARRY *and* BIDDY, R.

Hunter (joining their hands). Then be happy. Next to the happiness of calling you my daughter, is the joy of having the power to make my dear boy

"The happy bridegroom of so fair a bride."

Larry. D'ye hear that, Biddy. There's to be a weddin'.

Biddy. Och, bless their dear hearts.

Larry. If ye plase, Misther Hunter, Miss Biddy an' I am thinkin' uv pairin' off.

Scud (at door, C. *Sings).*

"De monkey marred de baboon's sister — "

Hunter. Silence, Scud!

Larry. Ah, ye hathen! An' if ye plase, sir, would the young couple want sarvants?

Biddy. Yis, sir, to tind the door and kape the home tidy.

Larry. An' tind the childer —

Biddy. Whist, Larry! it's spilin' the chance, ye are.

Hunter. I understand. We will remember you. (BESS *and* CLARENCE, *hand in hand, go up to* MOTHER CAREY. *She raises her hands, as though blessing them.* PARAGRAPH *and* MINNIE *come down,* R.)

Paragraph. Mr. Hunter, as you seem to be master of ceremonies, permit me to announce the early marriage of the beautiful Miss Minnie Daze and the versatile Peter Paragraph.

Minnie. Peter, how can you, before all these people?

Hunter. Accept my congratulations.

Paragraph. Thank you. Being about to enter the ministry, I find a wife will be a necessity.

Hunter. The ministry? Why, you change professions rapidly, Paragraph.

Paragraph. Do I? Well, I always did wish to be a pastor of a flock, it's so ennobling.

Minnie. And so romantic. (*They retire up stage, arm in arm.*)

Hunter. Chameleons, that change their hues, and live on air. (*Crosses to* R.) Ah, Paul Hunter, Clarence, I told you this was the great clearing-up day. There's another disclosure I must make. This man, whom you have known as the light-keeper —

David (*rising*). Is the light-keeper still. (*Aside to* HUNTER.) Not that name to him. He would hate me.

He knows I sought his life. Give me time. I would not blast his happiness now. Wait. (*Crosses*, C.) Mother Carey, before you quit this place, do a kindness to an old neighbor. (MOTHER CAREY *comes down*, C.) Before you quit your old vocation, tell me my fortune. Here's my hand. What read you?

Mother C. (*takes his hand*). Here, nothing; but in your heart I read the story of your future life. I see the dark stormy clouds of revenge slowly but surely drifting away from your life. Gleams of hope appear, brighter and brighter, as an old dream of love glows upon your memory; as she who was so faithful to you, forgetting all wrongs, with the fondness of earlier days creeping into her being, yearning to be nearer and dearer, forgives and pardons all.

David (*falling on his knees, and kissing her hand*). O Mary, Mary! bless you! bless you!

Mother C. Time washes away all sorrow. As we strive to brighten life with good deeds and true repentance, so will you strive, Paul, and the dark night shall pass away, and bright the morning come to bless our new espousal.

David (*rising*). True wife! may I never forget your goodness. 'Twas a dark night, indeed, that swept my soul. I will strive, and, with Heaven's blessing and your dear aid, win peace for my soul. Ah, wife, I have been like the unmanageable ship upon the waters, swept by the fierce winds of hate, battered by the cruel waves of remorse. They have cast me among the breakers, but noble hands (*takes* HUNTER'S *hand*, R.) have been stretched out towards me, and out of the darkness has gleamed the light of hope (*takes* MOTHER CAREY'S *hand*, L.), and on the open sea of repentance a strong and steady purpose shall waft this battered hulk to a haven of rest.

TABLEAU.

DAVID, C., *clasping the hand of* HUNTER, R. C.; *his left hand in* MOTHER CAREY'S; *her right hand on his shoulder.* PARAGRAPH *and* MINNIE, R. C., *arm in arm.* CLARENCE *and* BESS, L. C., *arm in arm.* SCUD *at door*, C. LARRY *and* BIDDY, R. C., *back.*

GENTLEMEN OF THE JURY.

A FARCE.

FOR MALE CHARACTERS ONLY.

CHARACTERS.

PELEG PRECISE, Foreman. JOB TIMOROUS, JACOB DOUBTFUL, ABEL STRONGFIST, JARVIS JOLLY, SOLOMON SNOWBALL, DENNIS O'ROURKE, NATHAN SHORT, ENOS PAUNCH, BRAZEN BLOWER, PETER PUNSTER, SIMEON SLOW, Jurors.

SCENE.— *A Jury Room. Table, c., with paper, pens, ink, &c. Twelve chairs around stage.*

Enter from R. *all the characters, in the order in which their names are written, single file, across Stage, and face Audience. Door at* R. *is slammed and locked.*

Timorous. Good gracious! we're locked in! (*Rushes across stage to* R.) Here, officer! officer!
Slow (*at extreme* R., *catching* TIMOROUS *by arm, and*

swinging him round). Stop that. It's all right, you know.

Timorous. No, I don't. I'm afraid of fire —

Punster (*swinging him round to next man*). What er that?

Timorous. And subject to fits —

Blower (*ditto*). You're no *fit* juror.

Timorous. I must have air —

Paunch (*ditto*). Where *air* you, now?

Timorous. Or smother —

Short (*ditto*). Take him to his mother.

Timorous. What do you call this treatment?

O'Rourke (*ditto*). The movement cure, bedad.

Timorous. It's outrageous —

Snowball (*ditto*). Da's a fac', da's a fac', honey.

Timorous. Diabolical —

Jolly (*ditto*). Ha, ha! now you go ag'in.

Timorous. Infamous!

Strongfist (*ditto*). Move on, stupid.

Timorous. I won't stand it.

Doubtful (*pushes him into chair*). Then sit down.

Precise (*at table*). Gentlemen, be seated. (*All sit.*) Before we discuss the case with which we have been intrusted, perhaps we had better take a vote.

Short. My idea exactly.

O'Rourke. Begorra; let's take something cowld.

Precise. We have been instructed to bring a verdict, "Guilty or not guilty." Please write your verdict. Here are slips of paper. (*Passes them round. All write, some on the table, some on chairs;* SNOWBALL *writes his against the wall.*)

O'Rourke (*approaches* Snowball). Whist! I say, d'ye write Guilty wid a G or a J?

Snowball. Ob course not. Write him wid a pencil — so.

O'Rourke. O, be jabbers! It's yerself's a heathen — you ignoramus.

Precise. Now, gentlemen, if you are ready. (*Collects votes, spreads them on table, and assorts.*)

Timorous. I want a glass of water — I'm faint.

Strongfist. Shut up. Don't disturb the meeting.

O'Rourke. Bedad, it's a glass eye ye'll be wantin' if yer do.

Punster. His eye waters at the thought.

Precise. Gentlemen, the vote stands, six "Guilty," six "Not guilty."

Jolly. Hallo, a clean cut!

Short. Six mules in the crowd, certain.

O'Rourke. A majority on both sides, d'ye mind.

Snowball. Major who? Major who? Dar ain't no sogers here, hey, I ax you?

Precise. Well, gentlemen, there's work before us; and, that we may know each other, I propose that those who voted "guilty" take seats on the right, those who voted "not guilty," on the left.

Short. Good. I'm for the right.

Jolly. I feel decidedly guilty.

Slow. And so do I.

Strongfist. Right face. March!

O'Rourke. Begorra, captain, I'll train in that company. (*They all pass to* R. *as they speak.* Doubtful, Timorous, Snowball, **Paunch**, Punster, *and* Blower *pass to* L.)

Punster. Though on the left, we're in the right.

Paunch. Well, look here, I'm getting hungry. Ain't we going to have our dinner?

Blower. You're always thinking of eating.

Snowball. By golly, da's a fac'. Dat ar Mr. Punch hab an appetite like an earthquake.

Paunch. Bah! what do you know about it? Well, wake me up when you're through. (*Tips his chair back against wall, throws his handkerchief over his face, and falls asleep.*)

Snowball. Dar, de old man gwine for Morphine.

Precise. My vote was "Guilty," and of course I belong with the party on the right.

O'Rourke. Thrue for yez, honey; and ye'll find it the party that's always right, jist.

Snowball. Hold yer hush, hold yer hush!

O'Rourke. Vat's that, ye heathen? I'd jist like to pound that thick pate till I had yer spachless — so I would. Begorra, ye'd cry Guilty then.

Timorous. O, come, let's have peace.

O'Rourke. Pace, is it? Ye've had a pace of my mind, onyhow.

Precise. No quarrelling, gentlemen. The quicker we decide this case the better. The government has charged one Peter Popgun with an attempt to defraud the revenue of the manufacturer's tax on gunpowder. Its secret agents, suspecting said Popgun, made a descent upon his establishment, which is a country store, seized certain articles, such as saltpetre, sulphur, and charcoal, which they found in a certain little back shop, said articles being, in their opinion, used by said Popgun in the manufacture of gunpowder. The said Popgun denies the manufacture of gunpowder, and sets up a defence that the said articles are used by him in concocting a certain patent medicine, known as the "Medical Dead Shot." Evidence has been produced on both sides. We have been charged to bring in a verdict on the evidence alone. I am quite convinced, by the testimony, that said Popgun did manufacture gunpowder, and evade the tax. Still, I should like to hear a free expression of opinion.

All (*jumping up*). Mr. Foreman.

Precise. Stop, stop. One at a time.

All. Yes, yes; one at a time, Mr. Foreman.

Precise. Stop, stop, I say. We can never settle it in this way.

Strongfist. Of course we can't. Let us six fight the other six. That will settle it.

O'Rourke. True for yez. A fray fight. I'm wid yer. (*About to remove his coat.*)

Precise. Silence. There can be no fighting here. You all want to speak. I will call upon each juror, giving both sides equal advantages of time and opportunity. Is not that fair?

All. Certainly. Of course. Go on. Go on.

Precise. Very well. I will first call upon Mr. Timorous.

Timorous (*rising*). Mr. Foreman, and gentlemen of the jury. (*Very low.*) I rise — I may say — yes, I rise —

O'Rourke. Louder.

Strongfist. Speak up like a man.

Timorous. I said — I rise — to say, if I may say — I rise to say —

O'Rourke. O, be jabbers, you're all out to say. (*The party on the* L., *with the exception of* PAUNCH, *rise indignantly.*) Mr. Foreman, Mr. Foreman!

Precise (*pounds on table*). Silence! Order, gentlemen, order.

Blower. Mr. Foreman, this attempt of the party on the right to intimidate the party on the left is unjust.

Punster. Far from being righteous or courteous.

Snowball. Am we jurors, or am we not jurors? I ax you?

Precise. The interruption shall not occur again. Go on, Mr. Timorous.

Timorous. If you please, Mr. Foreman, I only rose to say — that, if I might be allowed to say it — that — I've got nothing to say.

Party on right. Shame! Humbug! Put him out!

Precise. Order, gentlemen. — Have you no reason to give for your vote of "Not guilty"?

Timorous. O, yes; lots. I voted "Guilty," no, "Not guilty," because — well, because — Popgun don't look like a man who would concoct such a sanguinary mixture as powder. He hasn't the air of a ruffian. His thoughts don't run in that explosive channel. I'm something of a physiognomist.

Snowball. Mahogany! What's dat?

Timorous. A physiognomist. I judge by the face —

Party on right. O, humbug!

Blower. Mr. Foreman, I protest this attempt to stifle the voice of Justice is a high-handed crime.

Snowball. Yes, sar; it's bigamy, kleptomania, arson.
Precise. Order, gentlemen. — Go on, Mr. Timorous.
Timorous. But then I haven't any particular opinion in the matter; and if you want me to change —
Blower. Silence, traitor!
Snowball. Shut up yer tater trap.
Punster. Suppose you sit, for a change. (*Pulls him down to seat.*)
Timorous. Anything to oblige.
Precise. Mr. Jolly.
Jolly (*rising*). My turn, hey? Mr. Foreman, and gentlemen of the jury, —

> To make or not to make, that is the question.
> Whether 'tis better to let Popgun suffer
> The law's full penalty for mixing powder,
> Or to take arms against this awful tax,
> And by our verdict free him.

Gentlemen, **Popgun** is a dangerous man. I am for his annihilation. He is a second Guy Fawkes. Behind his shop are concealed those explosive materials destined to spread havoc and destruction in an innocent neighborhood. We might spare him if the possible destruction of a thousand or two of his immediate neighbors was the only consequence to be feared. But he's a sneak; he dodges the tax. That we must not suffer. The medicine story won't do; the dose is too heavy; it won't stay on the stomach. That gun recoils upon Popgun, who is too heavily charged by the evidence to be discharged by this jury. (*Sits.*)

Precise. Order, gentlemen. **Mr. Doubtful.**

Snowball. No, sar, no, sar. I move we lay him onto de table, *sinner die.*

O'Rourke. Die, is it, ye black sinner? Howld yer pate, or you'll die jist.

Doubtful (*rising*). Mr. Foreman, and gentlemen of the jury, there's one p'int in this evidence I want cleared up.

O'Rourke. Is it a pint of whiskey, I donno?

All. Order, order.

O'Rourke. That's what I'd like to do, and drink it, too.

Doubtful. If that air Popgun made gunpowder, why didn't somebody see him do it? Cause a man's got saltpetre in his house, and sulphur and charcoal, it doesn't foller that he's going to make gunpowder. I've got charcoal in my house — kindle the fire with it; sulphur to bleach with; saltpetre for curing purposes. But nobody ever said I made gunpowder. It's rediculous. Popgun's got eggs in his store. Why don't you say he hatched them? (*Sits.*)

Snowball. Da's a fac', da's a fac'. Second de motion.

All. Order, order.

Precise. Mr. Strongfist.

Strongfist. Well, you're a pretty set of sneaks over there, you are.

All. Order, order.

Strongfist. O, I know what I'm about. I'd like to get in among you. I believe in justice. I believe in any man's having his say in this world; but I don't believe in arguing about a matter that's as plain as the nose on your face. The man made gunpowder, and sold it, didn't pay the tax, and you fellows over there know it. You're a set of obstinate fools; and it's the duty of all loyal citizens to stand by the government and punish traitors. The government's been insulted by this contemptible Popgun, and you fellows on the left uphold him. Our duty is clear, to bring you to your senses. (*Takes off coat.*) So, come on. (*Squares off.*)

O'Rourke. I'm wid yez. Fag a ballah! Erin come unim.

All. Order, order.

Precise. Gentlemen, peace, I pray. Mr. Strongfist, your argument is very weak.

Strongfist. Is it? Well, my fist is strong; let me try that.

Precise. No, sir; you will please be seated. Mr. Paunch.

Snowball (*shaking him*). Here, Mr. Punch, Mr. Punch.

Paunch. Hey? O, yes. Mr. Foreman, I've got precious little to say. I'm hungry; I've had nothing to eat since morning. I was invited out to dinner at five o'clock with Alderman Cross. Fine leg of venison and native tomatoes, sliced, stewed, and broiled. The alderman is a capital eater, weighs three hundred and fifty, and has the best hogs —

Precise. Won't you confine yourself to the question, Mr. Paunch?

Paunch. O, yes. Hogshead of Madeira you ever tasted. It's capital. Then his cheeses! Good gracious! they're mighty —

Precise. Mr. Paunch, Mr. Paunch!

Paunch. They're mighty fine. What did you say, sir?

Precise. Will you give your reasons for voting "Not guilty"?

Paunch. Certainly. Stop. Did I vote "Not guilty"? I don't remember. It don't make any difference. Settle it as you please, only remember I must dine with Alderman Cross at five. (*Sits and goes to sleep again.*)

Snowball. Question, question! We'll all dine with Cross, hey! I ax you.

Precise. Mr. Slow, you next.

Slow. Hey? Yes. Well, I don't know. Popgun did make gunpowder, I guess, cause he had a little shop. (*Pauses.*)

Precise. Well, go on, Mr. Slow.

Slow. Yes. Well, he had a little shop, Popgun had, and he made somethin' in that shop; and if he didn't make gunpowder, he made somethin' in that little shop that he didn't pay no tax onto. And so he's guilty er somethin' or other in that little shop. So long's he's caught, what's the odds, as long as you're happy. (*Sits.*)

Snowball. Doubted, doubted.

All. Order.

Precise. Mr. Blower.

Blower (*rises, flourishes his handkerchief, blows his nose, strikes an attitude*). M-r-r-r-r. Foreman, and genteelmen of the jury, it is with spontaneous emotion that I rise to address you. You, genteelmen, with me, have looked upon a touching scene to-day. We have seen an enlightened citizen of this great republic, which, like the light of yonder firmament, attracts the attention of the whole world. We have seen him dragged from the bosom of his family and placed at the bar, at the bar, gentlemen, there to answer to grave and serious charges. It is evident that in the mysterious depths of that little back shop something has been concocted. The government says "Powder;" the defendant says "Shot." Powder and shot! "Powder" or "shot," in this case. One possesses the power to blow the human frame into infinitesimal particles; the other cures all ills that flesh is heir to. Can we pause and deliberate? Look at that man, dragged from the bosom of his family; his wife and children —

Jolly. Beg your pardon, Blower. Popgun is single.

Blower. Hey? Dragged from the paternal mansion. Hear the cry of the agonized and aged mother of the prisoner, as she stands upon the doorstep and screams, "My child! Bring back my little Popgun!"

Jolly. Wrong again, Blower. He's neither father nor mother.

Blower. Hey! Poor orphan! without a friend in the world! Can we turn our backs upon him? No. Let us be merciful. Let us indorse his patent medicine, and carry from this room a verdict of Not guilty. Then shall the tears of the orphan be squelched in gratitude, and the blessings of future generations of Popguns follow us.

O'Rourke. Begorra, that's a teching appeal.

Precise. Now, Mr. O'Rourke, your turn.

O'Rourke (*rising*). I ax yer pardon, judge, Mr. Foreman, and gintlemen all. Wid the blood of forty ginerations of O'Rourkes a seethin' with patriotic emotion in me bosom, d'ye mind; with faylings of gratitude for the fray gifts of life, liberty, and the pursuit of happiness, guaranteed by this moighty republic, which, as I look back into the future, is iver prisint in all its glory, d'ye mind. Could I be so base as to dash myself foreninst those illigant laws that crush the wake and guard the strong? By the grane sod of ould Ireland, niver! If that thaif of the wurld, Popgun, has transgressed the law, let him swing. And what for would he be mixing saltpatre and — and — and brimstone, and — and charcoal, if not to blow up somebody. Medicine, is it? It's my opinion that we'd better bring in a verdict of Guilty, and hang him, wid a recommendation to mercy, provided forty doses of his Medical Dead Shot bring him to life afther he's been dead and buried siven days. Thim's my verdict, judge. (*Sits*.)

Jolly. That's a reviving verdict.

Precise. Mr. Punster.

Punster (*rising*). Mr. Foreman, and gentlemen of the jury, the party popularly known in this suit as Popgun is a small affair, but I do not wonder that he kicks against this attempt of the government to charge him with powder he never made. How would you like it yourselves, gentlemen? Imagine yourselves Popguns, and happy in the disposing of butter, cheese, and — and hairpins to a needy community. Upon a luckless occasion, you sell ten cents' worth of powder to a red-headed urchin on the eve of our glorious independence. The awful crime is repeated; and, by the power of government, you innocent Popguns are incarcerated on a grave charge. You hear nothing but powder; you are loaded with reproaches and powder; it is rammed down your throats, until, like Popgun, you burst with indignation. Have we not heard from the lips of competent witnesses the amazing power of his Dead Shot? An old man had suffered forty years with influenza; the Dead Shot stopped it forever. An old lady, bent double with the rheumatism, was made straight by its power. A young mother, whose tender infant had wailed night after night, was loud in its praises. Gentlemen, this suit comes from the malice and jealousy of an envious rival. Gentlemen, this is a conspiracy. Let us clear Popgun of the charges under which he labors, by applying the match of justice to his overloaded soul. Then will he go off triumphantly, scattering destruction among his enemies, and give a good report of our deliberations. (*Sits*.)

Snowball (*jumping up*). See here, white folks, what's de use? what's de use?

Precise. Mr. Snowball, you're out of order.

All. Go on, Snowball. Fire away.

Snowball. Mr. Foreman and gemblem. Of course it am. Why not? And, if not, wherefore? I ax you. If de blessed Constitution of dese ere United States ob America don't permit the humblest of her sex to choose de proper medicines for dar physical systems, wedder it be gunpowder or gunpowder tea, what's de use ob bein' citizens and citizenesses of dese here republic? I ax you. Who's Popgun? Am he, or am he not, a phusician? I ax you. I don't care what his moral perquisites be, wedder he vote de demicratic or de bobolition. Does he cure de squills which air am flesh to? I ax you. When dat ar old man, which my white brudder alluded to, had de influendways, did he stop his sneezin? I ax you. When dat ar old woman hobble to him wid de rheumatics, did he straighten her out? I ax you. When dat ar baby squaked in its slumbers of midnight, did Popgun's Dead Shot fix it? I ax you. If so, and you find it so, — and I ax you to find it so, — you are forced to acquit Popgun as a medical dedical sturgen and phusician — ob course you am; for don' de stolid phalanx of justice circumbend every man on Columbia's footstool, wedder black or white, male or female? and de aurora borealistic splendors of eternal vigilance abide in de scrutinized recesses of de enlightened jury-room? I ax you.

O'Rourke. Begorra! send for an interpreter.

Precise. Mr. Short.

Short (*comes down to table*). It's my opinion, gentlemen, there's been a great deal of time and gas wasted in our deliberations. I've got very few words to say on this subject. Popgun manufactured an article which the government said was gunpowder. Popgun denies it. That is the question for us to decide. We were shown in the court-room a sample of this disputed article. It looked like gunpowder; it smelt like gunpowder; it felt like gunpowder. I took away the box. Here it is. (*Produces box.*) Some of you think it is not gunpowder. I propose to give it a practical test. (*Places box on table, takes off cover, takes a match out of his pocket.*)

Timorous. What! You're not going to fire it off!

Short. Don't be alarmed. There's only a pound or two. It can't do much damage.

Strongfist. You'll blow us all up!

Jolly. The man's crazy.

O'Rourke. Begorra, there! Aisy wid yer pranks.

All. Stop him! Stop him!

Short. Here she goes. (*Draws match across table.*)

All. Help! Murder! Officer! Put him out, &c. (Timorous *crawls under table;* Snowball *jumps up into chair and* makes *frantic attempts to crawl up the wall;* Doubtful *runs into corner, pulls* Paunch *up to cover him;* Blower *gets down and covers himself with a chair;* Precise *stops his ears, and crouches in a corner;* Strongfist *and* Punster *seize* Short, one on each *side;* O'Rourke *seizes* Short *by coat-tail behind;* Jolly *and* Slow *try to get behind each other.*)

Precise. Would you murder us?

Strongfist. Blow us to pieces?

O'Rourke. Call in the judge.

Short. Let me go, I tell you. (*Kicks* O'Rourke, *strikes* Precise *and* Strongfist, *and sends them to the floor.*)

O'Rourke. I'm kilt intirely.

All. Help! Murder! Help!

Short (*holding the match*). Now, gentlemen of the jury, here is a convincing test. Shall I apply it, or are you ready with a verdict?

All. No. Yes. Verdict. Verdict.

Short. Gentlemen, what is your verdict, guilty or not guilty?

All. Guilty.

Short. All right. Mr. Foreman, make out your papers. (*Blows out match. All resume seats.*)

Timorous. Well, I never had such a scare in all my life.

O'Rourke. By me soul! I say a wake a comin' for the last of the O'Rourkes.

Snowball. By golly, I'm all ob a hot chill in my backbone.

Precise (*who has been writing*). Gentlemen, listen to your verdict. " We find the defendant, Peleg Popgun, guilty."

Jolly. " So say we, all of us."

All. Ay. Ay.

Short. Then there's no further use for this box of sawdust, I suppose.

All. Sawdust?

Short. Exactly. You thought 'twas gunpowder. No matter. I *saw* I could throw *dust* in your eyes with it. I can't say much for your argument. You're like all the rest of this universal Yankee nation — anxious to fasten your tongue tackle on to every question. There's a very plain case here, which might have been a very knotty one but for the sawdust, which has brought you to terms, and thus proved a better medicine than Popgun's celebrated Dead Shot.

CURTAIN.

THE SEVEN AGES.

A TABLEAU ENTERTAINMENT.

[*Arrangement for Home Representation.* — Across the middle of the longest room in the house stretch curtains to separate in the middle and draw apart. You thus have a room for audience and a stage for performers. The stage should be divided in like manner by curtains to separate in the middle, giving a stage in front for performers, behind for tableaux. The rear or tableau stage should be draped with dark cloth (purple is best); there should be entrances on both sides, that the characters in the tableaux may pass on and off without being seen. Should two rooms with folding-doors between be used, the curtains between the audience and the stage can be dispensed with and the doors used instead.

The performers are directed as though standing on the stage facing the audience. R means Right, L Left, C Centre.]

SPEAKING CHARACTERS.

PAUL PERPLEX, an Artist.
FACT, a "Stubborn Thing."
FANCY, the Artist's Pet.
REASON, the "Calm-Eyed."
The NURSE, the SCHOOLBOY, the LOVER, the SOLDIER, the FATHER, the JUSTICE, the PATRIARCH.

COSTUMES.

PAUL. Dressing-gown or velvet jacket, smoking-cap, white pants, slippers.

FACT. Long brown robe, fastened at the waist with a rope, iron-gray wig, full beard.

FANCY. Female, gay dress, bright ribbons, floating hair.

REASON. Female, plain white dress, floating hair.

The NURSE. Calico dress and cap.

The SCHOOLBOY. Roundabout jacket, short pants, white stockings, rolling collar and cap.

The LOVER. Light pants, black velvet coat, wide collar spread over coat-collar, long black hair, black mustache.

The SOLDIER. Military uniform: red coat, blue pants with gilt stripes, sash, and sheathed sword at side.

The FATHER. Blue coat with brass buttons, dark pants, white vest, white necktie, gray wig, gray side-whiskers.

The JUSTICE (corpulent). Brown coat, breeches and top-boots, figured waistcoat, cane.

The PATRIARCH. Dressing-gown, nankeen pants, slippers, white waistcoat, long white hair, wrinkled face.

PART I.

PROLOGUE.

[Acted on the stage nearest the audience, front of the second set of curtains which are closed.]

SCENE. — *The painter's studio. Easel, R., with canvas on it.* PAUL *seated in front of it, with pallet and brush in hand.*

Paul. Mysterious canvas, on thy ghastly face,
My trembling pencil fails to leave a trace.
Behind thee lie rich treasures of delight,
Waiting the mystic-touch to charm the sight,

THE SEVEN AGES.

TABLEAU 1.—THE INFANT.
COSTUMES.

1. Brown dress, white apron.
2. White dress, cherry ribbons.
3. Dark dress; baby, white dress.
4. White dress, blue ribbons.
5. Dark pants, white vest, figured dressing-gown.

Waiting the master-hand to break the seal
And loose the beauties which thou dost conceal.
In vain I seek thy stubborn guard to break,
In vain I pray thy tenants to forsake
Their prison cells, and with a generous glow,
On a poor artist their sweet smiles bestow.
Alas! All vain; aloof they flickering stand,
Mocking the weakness of my unskilled hand.
O for some mighty power to break the chain,
To tear the veil, and give my fancy rein!

Enter FANCY, R.

Fancy. Here at your call, my master.
Paul (rises).   Do I dream?
Fancy. Perhaps; no matter, it doth really seem
By your remarks that some one's wanted here.
So I've dropped in to offer you my aid.
My name is Fancy.
   Paul.   Dear delightful maid,
Welcome, thrice welcome! Thy bewitching face
With rays of glory fills this gloomy place.
   Fancy. That's very pretty, — rays of glory. Fine
Young man, you are a follower of mine;
I read it in those dreamy eyes, that wavy hair,
That sighing bosom, and that languid air.
How can I serve you? Speak, and you shall find
Fancy a mistress bountiful and kind.
   Paul. O gracious mistress, I would win a name,
I long for glory, and I sigh for fame.
Upon the canvas 'tis my fond desire
To fasten beauty, homage to inspire.

THE SEVEN AGES. 191

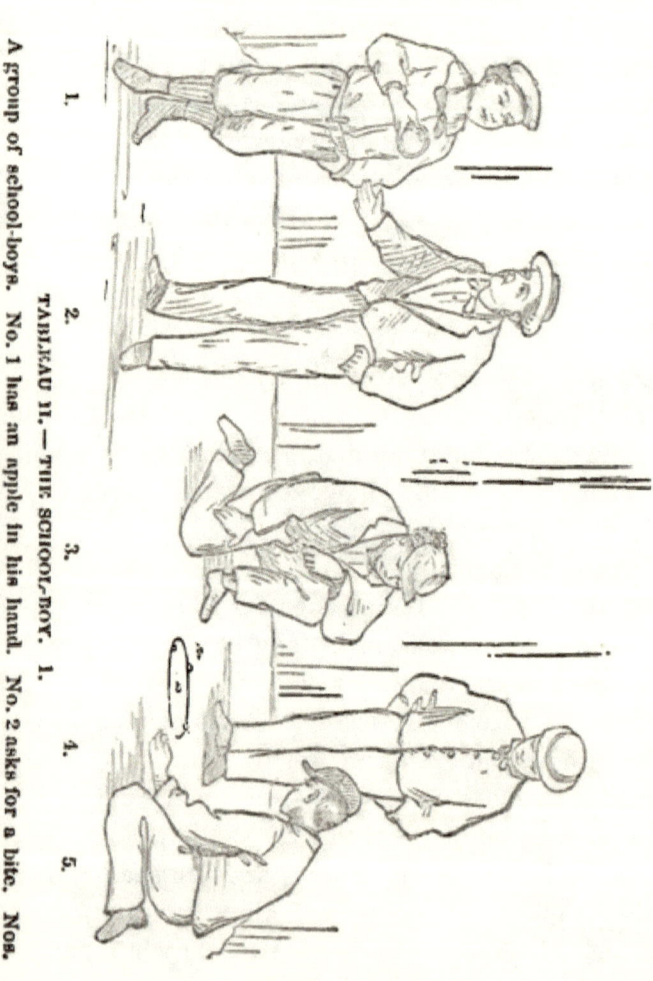

TABLEAU II.—THE SCHOOL-BOY.

A group of school-boys. No. 1 has an apple in his hand. No. 2 asks for a bite. Nos. 3, 4, and 5 are playing marbles. Costumes dark, with bright neckties.

Alas! my hand is weak; I strive in vain
The dancing, flickering shadows to enchain.
    Fancy. Then come with me; my realm is beauty's
        home;
There all unchecked the master spirits roam,
Gather bright laurels from the rainbow mints,
That color-freighted pour the choicest tints.
Come, revel in my fleecy, cloudland bower;
There may be found the talisman of power.
    Paul. Bright seraph, I am thine; or near or far,
I'll follow, follow thee forever —

        Enter FACT, L.

    Fact.   Bah!
Humbug! Ne'er listen to the wily maid.
Vanishing vapors make her stock in trade;
There's naught substantial in the realm she rules,
Shadows and moonshine are the toys of fools.
Turn back with me and deal in stubborn facts;
Stern hardy life's the loadstone that attracts
The master spirits of the brush and pen,
Who reap bright laurels by portraying men.
    Paul. And who are you? your garb is very queer,
Your features rugged, and your speech severe.
    Fact. Men call me Fact.
    Fancy.   He is a stubborn thing,
With neither taste nor beauty, quick to fling
His gloomy mantle over Fancy's play,
And with the cry of "Duty" bear away
Her choicest spirits. Fie upon thee, knave
Base and ignoble! thou art Labor's slave.

THE SEVEN AGES. 193

TABLEAU III. — THE SCHOOL-BOY.

The changes need very little explanation. No. 1 has given No. 2 the apple for a bite. Nos. 3 and 5 have quarrelled; and No. 4 is watching for a chance to snatch the marbles while the fighters are busy. No. 6 is a new character, — a bright little girl, dressed prettily, who, at the stroke of the bell, appears suddenly between curtains at back.

Fact. Nay, neighbor Fancy, thine's a saucy air,
A biting tongue for one so debonair:
Labor's my master, that I free avow;
The lordly monarch of the forge and plough,
The mighty builder and the broadcast sower,
Who rears and fashions with a matchless power.
Painter, to win a name, come, rove with me,
Mid Labor's subjects on the land and sea.

Fancy. Nay, nay, forbear; the path is rough to tread,
Fact's pictures are with ugliness o'erspread;
The sweating, delving busy life of care
Can show thee nothing fanciful or fair.

Fact. 'Twill show thee duty with its aims and ends,
Wherein much gloom with genial brightness blends.
If thou be wise, let Fancy cloudward go;
She's but a meteor, out of place, below.

Fancy. Well, you're polite.
Fact.   Thank you.
Paul.   No more;
On my account ne'er quarrel I implore.
I thank you both for the expressed desire
With power my lagging pencil to inspire.
You, Fancy, point me to a fairy wold;
You, Fact, a stronger, sterner realm unfold; —
Now which to choose, I'm very much in doubt.

   Enter REASON, C. (*between curtains*).

Reason. Well, my good friend, I've come to let you out.
Paul. Another stranger.

THE SEVEN AGES. 195

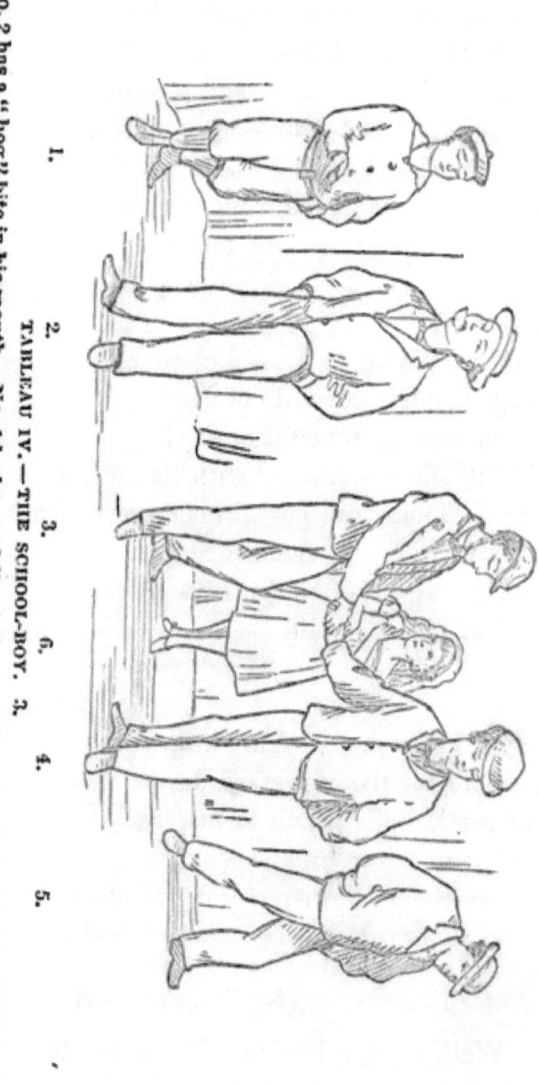

TABLEAU IV.—THE SCHOOL-BOY.

No. 2 has a "hog" bite in his mouth. No. 1 looks ruefully at the small portion left in his hand. No. 6 is joining the hands of the combatants. No. 5 is creeping off with the marbles. When properly rehearsed, these make effective tableaux. The music should be varied to suit the picture.

Fact. Ah, good neighbor Reason,
You're always near.
   Fancy. She's never out of season,
And always welcome; let her wise decree
Settle the difference betwixt you and me.
   Paul. Madam, your visit seems quite *apropos.*
Will it please you some good counsel to bestow
On a poor artist, and for him decide
Which, Fact or Fancy, he shall take as guide?
   Reason. Why not take both? I think, my painter
      friend,
You'll find that Fact and Fancy closely blend.
No scene of beauty and no work of skill
But needs them both perfection to instil.
The realm that Fancy pictures as divine
Stern Fact can match with one as good and fine;
In fields that Fact obscures with smoke and steam,
Fancy's embedded jewels brighter gleam.
Both are your friends; let them united serve,
And what they picture do you well observe.
Ne'er heed their quarrels, they but flirt and flout;
The very best of friends sometimes fall out.
So set to work and clothe the form of Fact
In Fancy's gayest raiment to attract,
Then will you tread the path that leads to fame,
And in its inmost temple carve your name.
Come, Fact, be stirring, let the painter gaze
On healthful life in all its devious ways.
Shakespeare, the foremost of poetic sages,
Has given to man a scale of seven ages;
Disclose them to our fame-desiring friend,

THE SEVEN AGES. 197

TABLEAU V. — YANKEE COURTSHIP. 1. Bright red dress, calico apron, hair arranged in old-fashioned style. 2. Short pants, heavy boots, plaid vest, large-checked necktie, blue coat with brass buttons, bell-crowned hat.

With brightest hues that Fancy's art can lend.
To gain his triumphs all your powers combine,
And let your hands his brow with laurel twine.
 Fact. She argues fairly.
 Fancy.   Justly, to my mind.
I give consent.
 Fact.   And I.
 Paul.   You're very kind.
I am your servant, lead me as you will;
I long at Genius' fount to drink my fill.
 Reason. Then forward. Industry all thirst assuages.
Take your first lesson from the seven ages.
(FACT *takes* PAUL'S *right hand and points* R. FANCY *takes his left,* REASON *steps behind* PAUL, *and points* R. *Curtain falls on picture.*)

PART II.

THE SEVEN AGES.

Curtain rises as before; the first stage is bare, the second curtains closed.

Enter the NURSE, *with babe in her arms.*

 Nurse. "You'd scarce expect one of his age
To speak in public on the stage,"
So I suppose it's really very *natteral*
That for his speech his *Nuss* should be collateral.
Well, he's an infant, bless his precious eyes
(Don't squirm so, deary, I'll keep off the flies),

THE SEVEN AGES. 199

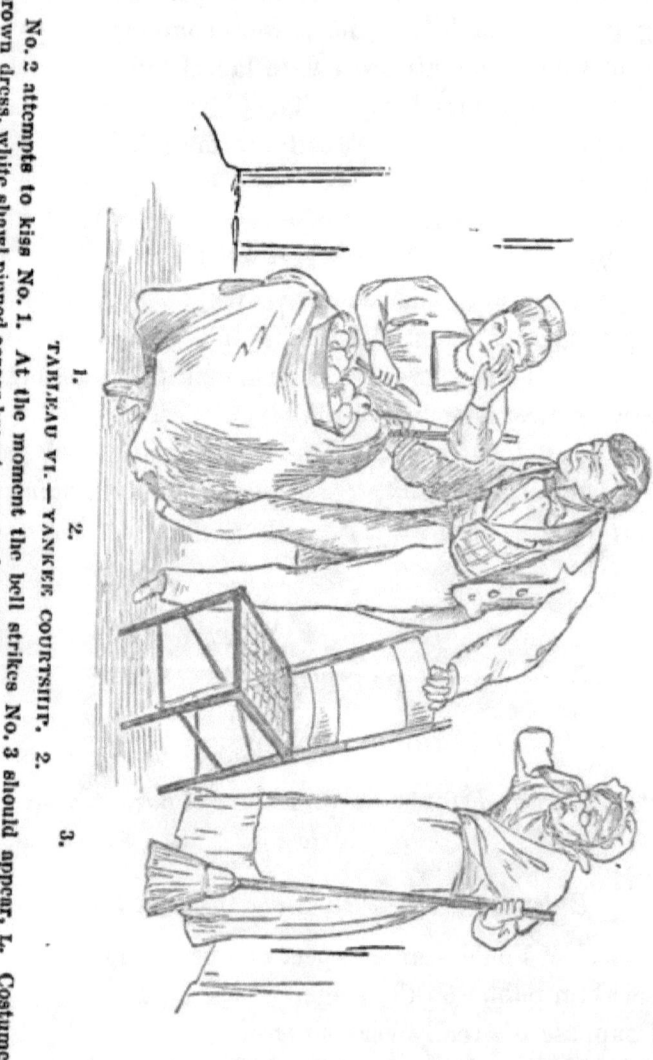

1.   2.   3.

TABLEAU VI.—YANKEE COURTSHIP. 2. At the moment the bell strikes No. 3 should appear, L. Costume faded brown dress, white shawl pinned across breast, cap, and spectacles. No. 2 attempts to kiss No. 1.

A little cherub — (*Child cries.*) Don't begin to squall,
You never can deceive the dears at all;
They know they are not angels, because why?
Angels will never drop down from the sky
To play at human babbies. Massy knows!
When their first little game is pains and woes,
O deary me, I think they are a trial!
Dosing with catnip-tea and *pennyrial*,
And walking nights, now isn't it severe
On us poor nurses who receive 'em here?
" The cry is still they come," for all of that, —
Bouncers and pigmies, skeleton and fat.
One half survive, the rest are taken off
By measles, chicken-pox, and whooping-cough.
Yet bless 'em, how we love 'em! (*Child cries.*) Don't
    you cry, —
He's stuck his big fist in his little eye.
Now say good night. (*Child cries.*) His speech is
    said,
Exit to " put him in his little bed."   [*Exit*, R.
(*Music* — "*Hush, my babe, lie still and slumber,*" *Piano. Curtains at back open, disclosing* Tableau I. *The curtains should be open time enough to count, moderately, fifteen, then closed slowly. Music continues till fall of curtain.*)

Enter the SCHOOL-BOY, L.

  School-boy. To school, or not to school, on time, or
    late,
We boys oft find a question for debate.
Study is irksome, good behavior's stiff,

THE SEVEN AGES.

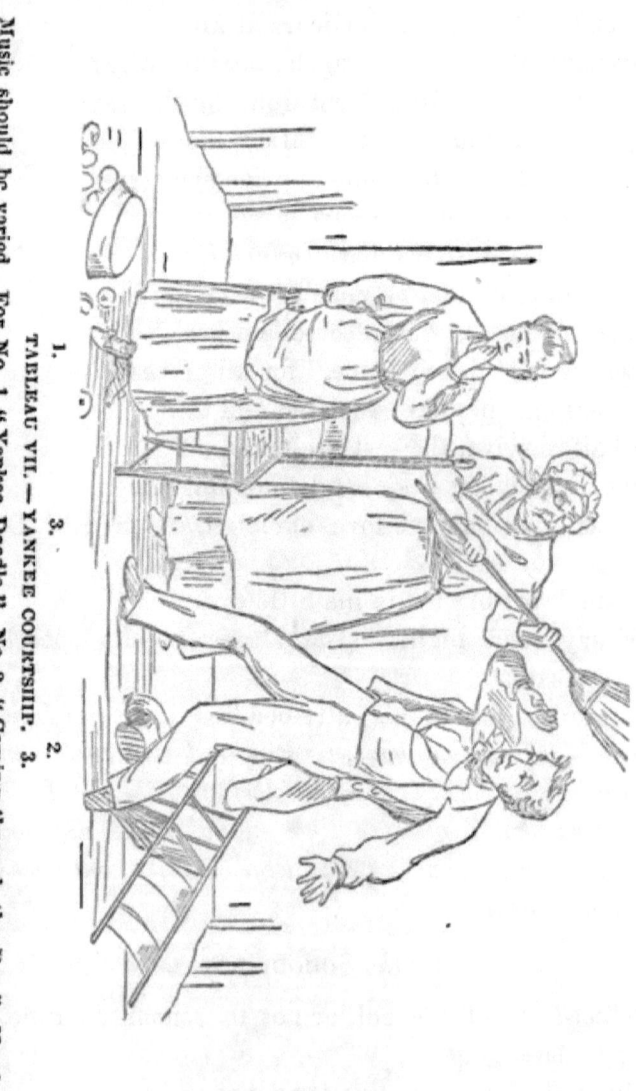

TABLEAU VII.—YANKEE COURTSHIP.

1.   3.   2.

Music should be varied. For No. 1, "Yankee Doodle." No. 2, "Coming through the Rye." No. 3, "O dear, what can the matter be?"

And old Dame Learning's often in a miff;
'Twixt marks and merits wavering and fickle,
She sternly rules us with a rod in pickle,
Impresses strong her lessons on our backs,
Welted with energy and sealed with whacks.
"Boys will be boys," we hear the old folks say.
If they speak true, why rob us of our play?
For where's the boy, except he be a fool,
Who, of his choice, would ever go to school?
His brains to crush 'neath heaps of Roman dust,
All that remains of that great empire "bust";
To choke and struggle with ill-fated Greece,
In vain attempt to conquer e'en a peace,
When sport and exercise their strong arms bare,
And woo him to the water and the air.
The light boat waits impatient on the tide,
Green fields their carpets spread on every side,
Broad oaks their shadows fling across his way,
The ball and bat are eager for the play,
The free air thrills him; naught can hold him back,
Except the haunting fear of "Hooking Jack,"
And something better, — born of ancient lore, —
"The path to fame lies through the school-house door."

[*Exit*, R.

(*Music. Curtains at back open, disclosing Tableau II. After Tableau II. has been shown the usual time, a bell should be struck, when, without the curtain being dropped, the characters instantly change positions to Tableau III. Change, at stroke of bell, to Tableau IV.*)

THE SEVEN AGES. 203

TABLEAU VIII.—THE SOLDIER.

This Tableau represents an officer (No. 4) attacked by Zouaves (Nos. 3 and 5). The officer's costume should be red coat, white pants, red sash, dark cape lined with blue thrown over shoulder. Nos. 1 and 7 are private soldiers, dressed in blue. The Zouaves (Nos. 2, 3, 5, and 6) are dressed in white clothes, only relieved by red sashes around the waist. No. 1 has No. 2 by the throat, and is pointing a pistol at him. Nos. 3 and 5 are in the act of charging bayonets. No. 6 has his gun aimed at No. 1. No. 7 has his musket clubbed in the act of striking No. 6.

At the fall of the curtain, enter, L., *the* LOVER. *He speaks and gesticulates in a burlesque, lackadaisical manner.*

Heigh-ho! heigh-ho! Ah me! good gracious!
Cupid doth feed with appetite voracious
Upon my bleeding heart. O Blousabelle,
Your sparkling eyes enslave me with a spell.
I am enraptured with your beauteous face;
Enthralled, bewitched, by your enchanting grace.
O darling Blousa! honey-drop of sweetness!
Pink of perfection! violet of neatness!
Would I could press thee to this manly breast!
Soft-pillowed there thy golden curls to rest, —
Thy tender form to guard forevermore,
Devouring words within thy ears to pour,
To make this dull earth bloom like paradise.
Heigh-ho! ah me! now wouldn't it be nice?
Over a picture of successful love
My longing eyes too oft delighted rove,
Let me rehearse for your amusement here
How Zekiel wooed and won his Hulda dear.
(*Recitation of Lowell's poem,* " *The Courtin'.*" *Exit* LOVER, R. *Lively music. Curtains at back open, disclosing Tableau V. After the usual time, strike the bell, and the characters change positions to Tableau VI. At sound of bell, change to Tableau VII. Curtain falls.*

Enter SOLDIER, L.

Soldier. When Peace, the olive-crowned, with ashen face,
Forsakes her throne, and to grim War gives place;

THE SEVEN AGES.

TABLEAU IX.— THE FATHER.

This group represents "Virginius and his Daughter," and should be made to imitate marble. The costumes should be white; unbleached cotton cloth is best. Wigs can be made by fitting "skull-caps" close to the head, and fastening upon them imitation of hair made of tambour cotton. The flesh should be thickly covered with white chalk. Have everything white. Place the characters well back.

When Treason stalks abroad, when Riot roars,
When Crime grows rampant, and Rebellion soars,
The Soldier, armed and mailed with martial power,
Stands forth the master-spirit of the hour.
The loud drum thrills him with its wild alarms,
The clash of steel his manly bosom warms,
The whirr of bullets and the cannon's roar
Make the hot blood in quicker currents pour,
Till, filled from crown to toe with bloody zeal,
No foeman can resist his crushing heel.
Up! on the ramparts, where with fierce assail
And deadly purpose, ploughs the iron hail;
Down! in the pit where ambush lieth low,
Fearless, defiant, leaps he on the foe.
So brave, so valiant, Glory doth delight
To wreathe his brow with laurels green and bright.
But when across the field of Labor's life
Peals the loud trump, dread harbinger of strife;
When through the workshop, busy marts of trade,
Through student's study, 'neath the classics' shade,
Through fashion's halls, where folly rules the hour,
Through homes that cherish love's domestic power,
Sounds the shrill notes that wake the hearts of all
To hurry forward at their country's call,
Sternly as Patriot he doth nobly stand
Against all foes to guard his native land.
A nation's gratitude, with smiles and tears,
Freshens his memory all the coming years;
And grand old Freedom, midst her brightest joys,
Points proudly to her gallant soldier boys.

[*Exit*, R.

THE SEVEN AGES. 207

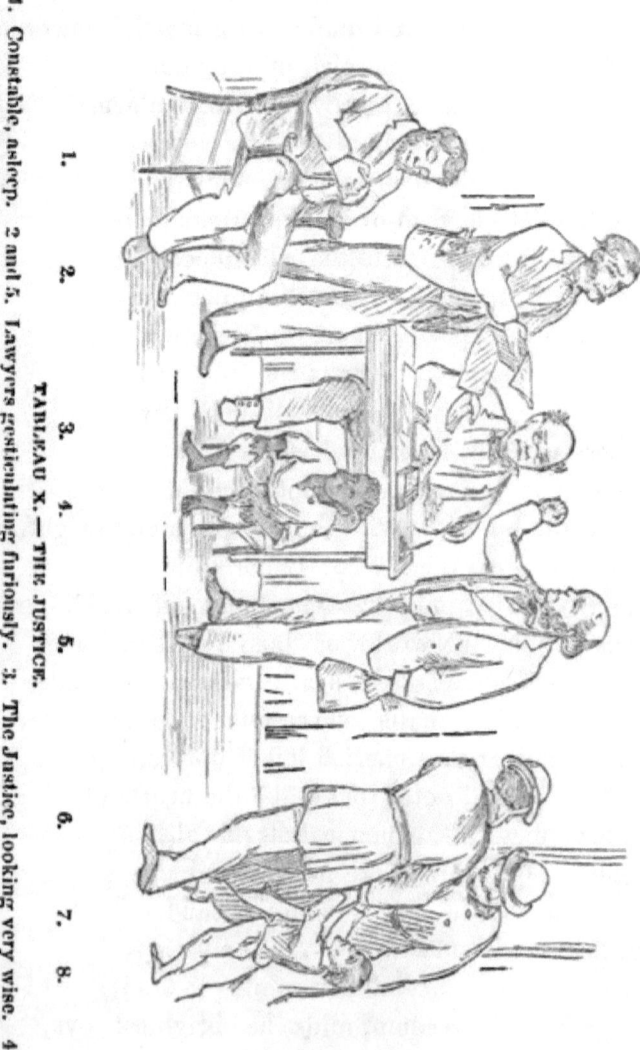

TABLEAU X.—THE JUSTICE.

1. Constable, asleep. 2 and 5. Lawyers gesticulating furiously. 3. The Justice, looking very wise. 4. The Culprit, a little darkey, looking at the lawyer with eyes rolled up. 6 and 8. Constables dragging a small boy. Costumes modern.

(Curtains at back are drawn, disclosing Tableau VIII. Do not follow strictly the positions in the drawing, but make the picture animated and striking. Music should be of a martial character. Curtain falls.)

Enter the FATHER, L.

Father. And what's a father? Some say an old fellow
With hair turned gray, and features turning yellow,
Full of his aches and pains, — a queer old chap
For whom his family don't care a rap,
Save that he pays the bills, keeps out of sight,
And locks the house up carefully at night.
Some say a tyrant, ruling with a sneer,
All frowns and wrinkles, with a voice severe
For youthful follies, and a stinging snap
When pealing laughter robs him of his nap.
And some say — bless them! — he's earth's paragon,
The kindest mortal that the sun shines on;
For all our woes, the ever-ready friend,
With kindly heart, to cheer and comfort lend.
Of all our joys, so ready e'er to share,
Warmed by his smile, they seem more bright and fair.
On all our secrets locks the trusty door,
And proves himself a confidant secure
For all our follies, eager to advise,
Lenient, forgiving, generous, and wise.
Half-way betwixt the cradle and the grave,
Washed by a sea of troubles, wave on wave,
The father takes his place, a beacon-light
To guide the wayward bark of youth aright.

THE SEVEN AGES.

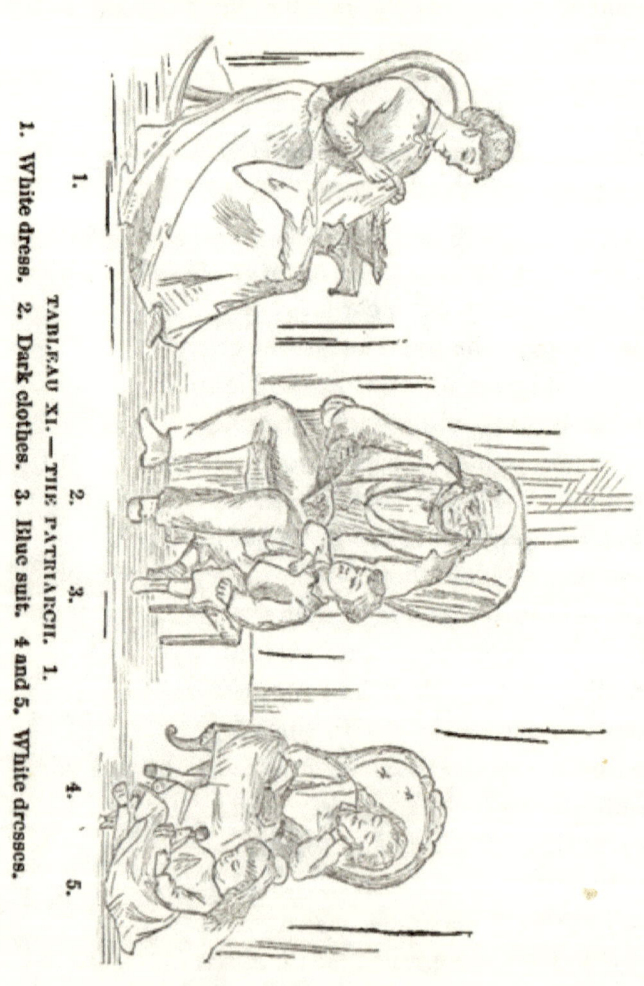

TABLEAU XI.—THE PATRIARCH. 1. White dress. 2. Dark clothes. 3. Blue suit. 4 and 5. White dresses.

The fierce and angry winds of strife may roar,
Misfortune's sullen clouds may hover o'er,
Yet through the darkest night of fear and woe,
The light of love, with calm and steady glow,
Flashes upon the tossed and sin-opprest,
A talismanic harbinger of rest.
Honor the father! History's bright page
Records his sacrifice in every age.
Turn backward to the ancient Roman days,
When stern Virginius did the world amaze.
When wicked Sextus — vile and crafty knave! —
The fair Virginia sought to make his slave,
The noble father, with his cruel knife,
Her honor saved at cost of her dear life;
Look on this picture, let its teachings prove
Fathers can slay as well as save for love.   [*Exit*, R.
(*Sad music. Curtains open, disclosing Tableau* **IX**.
  Curtain falls.)

              Enter the JUSTICE, L.

  Justice. Well, what's the matter? Burglary or theft?
Why am I rudely of my rest bereft?
Whose hencoop's plundered? Hey? whose ducks and
    geese
Have sloped with some despoiler of the peace?
What murderous youngster has been breaking bones,
Or smashing windows with obdurate stones?
Hey? No complaint? well, this is very queer;
I thought I heard a call for " Justice " here,
And I'm that high, official dignitary,
Learned, *pompostuous*, disciplined, and wary,

THE SEVEN AGES.

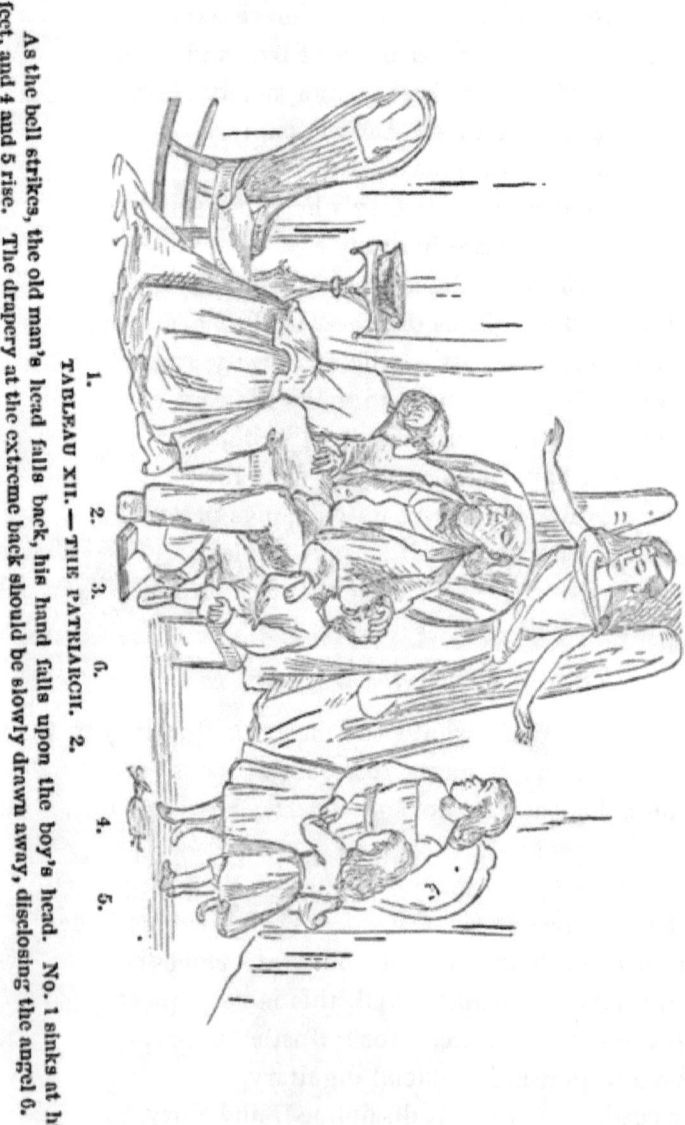

TABLEAU XII.—THE PATRIARCH.

As the bell strikes, the old man's head falls back, his hand falls upon the boy's head. No. 1 sinks at his feet, and 4 and 5 rise. The drapery at the extreme back should be slowly drawn away, disclosing the angel 6.

Whose frown doth terrify the sneaking scamp
With dreams of iron bars and dungeons damp.
Ahem! the *squeak* of law is in my tread;
From off my path wild urchins slink with dread;
The biggest blackguard of a saucy crew
Shuts fast his mouth whene'er I come in view;
The straight-laced deacon with his stiffened back,
The learned doctor, the successful quack,
The gifted parson, and the man of wealth,
Admiring glances cast at me by stealth,
Because I hold the scales that win or lose,
And make them bend whichever way I choose, —
That is — of course — by *interlectual* sway.
I'm always right, — the scales the right obey, —
And so I'm ready to enforce the laws,
And find a verdict in a righteous cause,
Provided that the culprit is not rich,
For in that case my fingers always itch
To place across the bridge of this wise nose
A pair of spectacles with golden bows. [*Exit*, R.
(*Music. Curtains open, disclosing Tableau X. Curtain falls.*)

Enter the PATRIARCH, L.

Patriarch. " Last scene of all, which ends this strange
       eventful history,
Is second childishness, and mere oblivion."
Nay, nay, good master Shakespeare, thou art wrong,
For richest joys around the aged throng.
Upon the record of ascending years,
Oft flecked with sunshine, blotted oft with tears,

Where can be found so kind and true a friend
As keen-eyed Memory, who doth freely lend
Unto the " seventh age " her matchless power,
To deck and glorify the sunset hour?
Upon the patriarch she doth free bestow
Her brightest jewels plucked from long ago :
Pleasures of youth, deep buried in the past,
Wakened to life, come merrily trooping past ;
Triumphs of manhood, with new laurels crowned,
And prouder bearing, thickly gather round.
The babe, the youth, the lover, soldier, sage,
Each in his time displays again his age ;
Each at the summons will repeat his part,
And all are welcome to the old man's heart.
What scene of happiness so pure and bright
As " home, sweet home," the temple of delight,
Wherein the patriarch as an honored guest
Beloved, respected, finds a welcome rest,
Until the Master's messenger of peace
Shall bid life's sentinel his watch to cease !
Then ends the journey, then earth's race is run,
Then the *eternal* age is entered on. [*Exit*, R.
(*Music*, "*Home, sweet Home.*" *Curtain opens, disclosing*
 Tableau XI. Bell strikes, and change to Tableau
 XII. Music sad and soft until the curtain falls.

CURTAIN.

THE BOSTON DIP.

A COMEDIETTA, IN ONE ACT.

CHARACTERS.

Mr. Moses Mulligrub, once Proprietor of a Fish-cart, now a rich Speculator.
Monsieur Adonis, a Dancing-Master.
Mr. Richard Dasher, a Fast Man.
Mr. Lavender Kids, an Exquisite.
Mrs. Moses Mulligrub.
Miss Ida Mulligrub.
Miss Eva Mulligrub.

COSTUMES.

Full Evening Dress.

Scene. — *Handsome drawing room in* Monsieur Adonis's *Academy. Entrances,* R., L., *and* C. *Lounges,* R. *and* L. *Screen,* L. *corner, back. Two chairs,* R. *and* L. *of door in flat.*

Music, as curtain rises, Straus's waltz, "Beautiful Blue Danube." MISS IDA *and* MISS EVA *discovered waltzing, introducing " The Boston Dip." They waltz a few moments, then stop. Music ceases.*

Ida. Now, isn't that delightful?

Eva. Delightful! It's positively bewitching. Bless that dear Monsieur Adonis. He deserves a crown of roses for introducing to his assembly the latest Terpsichorean novelty. O, we shall have a splendid time to-night!

Ida. Especially as those charming waltzers, Messrs. Richard Dasher and Lavender Kids, "the glass of fashion and the mould of form," are to honor us with their presence.

Eva. Yes, indeed. What would the dance be without them?

Ida. Not worth the trouble of dressing. But don't you think that Mr. Dasher is a little too attentive to Miss Eva Mulligrub, — eh, sister?

Eva. Not more attentive, certainly, than is Mr. Lavender Kids to her charming sister, Miss Ida Mulligrub. — Eh, sister?

Ida. But seriously, Eva, I begin to think that you are carrying this matter a little too far. Mr. Dasher might reasonably expect, from the partiality you unhesitatingly show for his society, and the smiles you bestow upon him, to be considered your lover.

Eva. You begin to think. Why, bless you, Ida, I've thought and thought and thought, for a long time, that

THE BOSTON DIP.

were I Mr. Lavender Kids, I should pop the question at once, so undeniably entranced are you by his attentions.

Ida. Eva!

Eva. Ida!

Ida. You're talking nonsense.

Eva. Well, you began it.

Ida. But you know you like Mr. Dasher.

Eva. To be sure I do. He's the best waltzer in the city. Graceful, agreeable, and decidedly good-looking.

Ida. And you would marry him?

Eva. Not unless he asked me, and then —

Ida. And then —

Eva. I should remember that he is considered a fortune-hunter, that he is too fond of horses, that possibly he might have an eye on father's bank-book, that I don't want such a husband, and should very sweetly, calmly, but decidedly say, No, thank you, Mr. Dasher.

Ida. Exactly what I should say to Mr. Kids, without the sweetness and calmness.

Eva. I hope we shall not have the chance, for then, of course, we should lose their society — and they are such superb waltzers.

Ida. But what in the world could have possessed mother to have us come so early. Hurry, girls, hurry! And here we are before the hall is lighted.

Eva. I'm sure I don't know. It's one of her whims. One would hardly think that, at her age, she would care for dancing.

Ida. But she does. I caught her to-day attempting a waltz before the glass in her room; and such work as she did make of it!

Eva. She's not very nimble with her weight of years and flesh, but she would come to-night, and without father, too.

Ida. Catch him in such a place! No doubt he's already snoring at home in his easy-chair, speculating on corner lots in his dreams.

Eva. Better that than the old life, dragging a hand-cart through the streets, and shouting, "Cod! haddock! halibut! eel — eel — eel — eels!"

Ida. Why, Eva, don't speak of that; and such a noise, too.

Eva. Who cares. Everybody knows what we once were, and I, for one, am not going to be ashamed of father's old occupation. He has made money in an honest way: so let us have no false pride, Ida. "Cod! haddock! halibut! eel — eel — cel — eels!"

Enter MRS. MULLIGRUB, C.

Mrs. M. Well, I never! Eva Mulligrub, I'm blushing with shame, petrified with mortification, and stunned with grief, to hear such words as those proceeding from your lips. I never heard such language before, never.

Eva. Why, mother! And I've heard father say those very words brought you to the window many a time when he passed; that they were the bait by which you were caught, and that you were the best catch he ever made.

Mrs. M. Fiddle-de-de! That's his twaddle. We're above such language now. But come, girls, fix me up! I'm all coming to pieces. Is that what's-its-name behind all right, and this thingumbob on my neck, and the what-you-may-call-it on top of my head? Dear me, I'm all in a pucker.

Ida. Everything about your dress is charming, mother.

Mrs. M. Well, I'm glad on't. Now girls, look here, I've made an assignment with Munseer What's-his-name to-night.

Eva. A what?

Ida. Assignment? You mean an appointment.

Mrs. M. Well, it's all the same. I'm going to learn to do that dipper thing, if I die for it.

Eva. I don't understand.

Ida. She means The Boston Dip.

Mrs. M. That's it — where you go tipping about, while the fiddlers play Struse's Beautiful Blue Dan-*u*-by.

Eva. You, mother, learn to waltz!

Mrs. M. And why not? There's Mrs. What's-her-name gets through it, and she's older and heavier than I. I'm going to learn it. What's the use of having money if you can't spin round like other folks. But don't say a word to your father. Bless me, how he would roar! But he's safe at home, snoozing in his chair by this time. I've arranged it all. I've engaged this drawing-room for my own party, and when you're all dancing in the hall, Munseer A— A— what's-his-name will slip in here, and practice the waltz with me, and nobody will know anything about it until I'm deficient.

Ida. Proficient, mother.

Mrs. M. Well, what's the difference? It's all arranged. I'm not going to make a fool of myself before folks when I can pay for private lessons.

DASHER *appears*, C.

Dasher (loud). Eureka!

Mrs. M. (starting). Good gracious! You what?

Dasher. "Fortune favors the brave." Like Cæsar, I came, I saw, and I'm overcome. May I come in?

Mrs. M. Certainly, Mr. Dasher. Your presence always adds a charm to our — what's-its-name — circular.

Ida. Circle, mother.

Mrs. M. Well, what's the odds?

Dasher. Thank you, Mrs. Mulligrub. You are arrayed like an empress; Miss Ida, your costume is only eclipsed by your charming face; Miss Eva —

Eva. "Last but not least in our dear love," must of course be divine; so spare my blushes and your breath. (*Sits on lounge,* R.)

Dasher. Thank you. And now congratulate me. I threw down my pen, after a hard fight with figures, to seek the lonely recesses of my bachelor's quarters, heartily sick of life, when it suddenly occurred to me that this evening Monsieur Adonis gives one of his charming assemblies. Perhaps, thought I, there I may find rest for my weary brain from the figures of the ledger, which are dancing in my head, in the figures of the dance. But did I dream of falling into such charming society? No; most emphatically and decidedly, no. Therefore, like Cæsar —

Mrs. M. And pray, Mr. Dasher, who is this Cæsar you're making such a fuss about?

Ida. Why, mother!

Mrs. M. La, child, there's nobody of that name I'm acquainted with.

Ida. You know, mother, Cæsar was the great Roman general, who —

Mrs. M. La, yes; Mr. Dasher was only speaking metagorically. Cæsar was the man who crossed the what's-its-name, and was stabbed by a brute.

Eva. Never mind Cæsar. Here's my card, Mr. Dasher. Of course your name will be the first I shall allow upon it.

Dasher (*sits on lounge beside* EVA). Am I to be so highly honored. (*Takes card.*)

Eva. For a waltz, and only one.

Mrs. M. La, child, don't be so unscrupulous. You'll dance till you drop if you get a chance.

Ida. Hush, mother.

Mrs. M. Now what's the matter with you? Mr. What's-his-name will dance with you, too. Don't be so anxious.

Ida. O, dear, was there ever such a torment. (*Sits on lounge,* L.)

Enter KIDS, C.

Kids (*with glass to his eye*). Now, weally! Have I stumbled into the bodwaw of a bevy of enchanting goddesses? — have I, weally?

Ida. O, Mr. Kids!

Eva. You have, weally, Mr. Kids.

Dasher. Lavender, my boy, how are you?

Kids. And will the divine goddesses permit me to entaw, to disturb their tableaw of beauty with my horwid figgaw?

Eva. Yes, trot your horwid figgaw in, Mr. Kids.

Mrs. M. Eva, I'm astonished at such language *as* those. Mr. Kids, we are delighted to see you.

Ida. Yes, indeed, Mr. Kids. I've kept my card for you.

Kids. Divine creachaw, you overpowaw me — you do, weally. (*Sits on lounge beside* IDA, *and takes her card.*) Just one waltz?

Eva. As many as you please, Mr. Kids.

Mrs. M. Now that's what I call generous. I wonder where Mr. — no, Munseer — Adonis can be. (*Retires up.*)

Eva. Mr. Dasher, how can you tell such falsehoods, when you know, that I know, that you know, we were to be here to-night.

Dasher. What a knowing young lady. It's one of the frailties of masculine nature, Miss Eva. I'm glad I was not George Washington, for I should certainly have spoiled that hatchet story by a lie. Now I am here, dear Miss Eva, overpowered with the burden of a weighty secret, I am going to disclose it. I — I —

Kids. I say, Dashaw, I've had my bwains surveyed to-day.

Dasher. Have you? I didn't know you had any.

Kids. Yaas, several. Destwuctiveness, combativeness, idolitwy —

Dasher. Ideality.

Kids. Yaas, it's vewry wemarkable how those phwenological fellaws lay out your bwains, and name them just like — aw — stweets.

Dasher (*aside*). They must have labeled some of yours " No Thoroughfare."

Eva. O, don't talk about brains, Mr. Kids. The discussion of such a subject might fly to your head.

Dasher. And so light is the material there, cause a conflagration.

Kids. Yaas, yaas, like a Mansard woof. And, Dashaw, I've got a diwectory of my bwains, and it's deucedly clevaw; for if an ideah gets into my bwains, I can trace it out in the diwectory, and tell just where it lies, you know, and know just where to find it. Deuced clevaw.

Dasher (aside). 'Twould die of starvation before you found it.

Mrs. M. (comes down). Ah, here's Munseer Adonis at last!

Enter MONSIEUR ADONIS, R.

Mons. A. Charmant, charmant, leedies and gentimen, I kees your hands. You do me proud. I feel ze glow of satisfaction in ze inermost inside of zis bosom, when you do me ze *grande honneur* to grace my salon wiz your presence. I feel ze glow all ovar.

Mrs. M. O, Munseer Adonis!

Eva. Politest of Frenchmen.

Ida. Paragon of dancing-masters.

Mons. A. Pardon me, *charmant* medmoiselles and adorable madam, if ze modest blush of shame paint my cheek wiz ze hues of ze roses. I am ze humble instrument of ze divine art which gives ze grace to ze figure, and ze airy lightness to ze beautiful toes of madam and ze *charmant* medmoiselles.

Eva. Now, Munseer Adonis, we are all impatience. When will the dance begin?

Mons. A. On ze instant. Ze company have assemble in ze grande salon. When madam and her friends make ze grande entrée, zen will ze music strike ze signal.

Ida. We are all ready.

Mrs. M. Munseer Adonis, one word with you.

Mons. A. Wiz ze uttermost pleasure. Am I not ze slave of ze matchless madam (*aside*) and her money. (*They retire up stage, and converse.*)

Dasher. Miss Eva, I must have an interview with you this evening. I have much to say. Meet me here in half an hour.

Eva. Certainly. I'll slip away at the first opportunity.

Dasher. Thank you. The first dance is mine, you remember.

Kids. Aw, Miss Ida, I must speak with you alone; I must, weally. There's something on my bwain — no — on my bweast, that must be welieved. Don't go. Stay behind with me.

Ida. And lose the first dance? — No, indeed.

Kids. Weally, I couldn't ask that. Couldn't you contwive to meet me here alone?

Ida. At the first opportunity. I'll do my best. (*Rises.*) Eva, one moment.

Eva (*rises and comes*, c.). Well, dear?

Ida. Don't you think, Mr. Kids wants me to meet him here alone.

Eva. Does he? The same thought must have wandered into his bwain that crept into Mr. Dasher's, for he expects me to meet him here alone.

Ida. Do you know what it all means?

Eva. Certainly — proposals.

Ida. And will you permit Mr. Dasher —

Eva. No, indeed. Marry that fickle thing? Never!

Ida. Exactly my mind. Mr. Kid's a fool.

Eva. But, like **Mr. Dasher,** a splendid waltzer. We cannot afford to lose them.

Ida. Indeed we cannot. Partners are so scarce.

Eva. They want father's money.

Ida. But they must not have his daughters.

Eva. No, indeed. You watch me, and I'll watch you, and there'll be no proposals. (*Retire to* R. *and* L. Monsieur Adonis *and* Mrs. Mulligrub *come down stage.*)

Mrs. M. And you got my note, Munseer Adonis?

Mons. A. Ah, madam, I have it next my heart. (*Produces an envelope, opens it, takes out note, puts envelope in his pocket. Reads.*) "Meet me in the private drawing-room when ze company are waltzing. Do not fail me. Hannah Mulligrub." Zat is all it say.

Mrs. M. But you know what it means. I am anxious to learn "The Boston Dip." Were I to come to your school I should be laughed at, but here, while the company are waltzing, no one would know it, and the inspiring music would aid me. I don't want to make a fool of myself, you understand.

Mons. A. Certainly. All zat I shall remember. I have written on ze back of ze note "Boston Dip." I put him in ze pocket wiz my handkerchief, so zat when I pull him out to wipe my face ze note will arrest my attention, and I shall fly to you, madam. (*Puts note and handkerchief in his pocket.*)

Mrs. M. O, you Frenchmen are so inveterate.

Dasher. Come, Monsieur Adonis, the dance, the dance! I'm all impatience (*aside to* Eva) for its end.

15

Kids. Weally, the delay is vexatious; it is, weally. (*Aside to* IDA.) Meet me here, you know.

Mons. A. Pardon me, I am all impatience. *Charmant*, madam, shall I have ze pleasure. (*Offers his arm to* MRS. MULLIGRUB.) Ze night is ver warm, ver warm. (*Music,* "*Beautiful Blue Danube.*" MONSIEUR ADONIS *takes out his handkerchief. The note falls on stage. He wipes his face, passes out door,* R., *followed by* DASHER *and* EVA, KIDS *and* IDA.)

Enter MULLIGRUB, C.

Mulligrub. So, so, here we are, Mrs. Mulligrub, unexpectedly, and no doubt unwelcome. You imagine the old codger snoozing away at home, but here he is, and wide awake too. It's about time the head of the house knew what is going on. And here's where the money goes. Well, who cares? There's lots of it, so let it fly. But I've a wonderful curiosity to know how my Hannah carries herself among all these fine snobs, so I'm bound to have a peep. (*Goes towards door,* R. *Sees note on carpet.*) Hallo! what's this? a billy-deux? (*Picking it up.*) Where's my specs? (*Reads.*) "Meet me"— ho, ho! here's a nice little plot — (*reads*) — "in the private drawing-room" — that's here — (*reads*) — "while the company are waltzing. Do not fail me. Hannah Mulligrub." My wife! Ye gods and little fishes! my wife. "Do not fail me." Is this the reward of my generosity? My wife! What does it mean? Who is the scoundrel that is tampering with the affections of Hannah, and the peace of Moses Mulligrub? (*Turns note over.*) "Boston Dip." Who's he? "Boston Dip." There's a name. I've heard of the "Manchester Pet," and the "Dublin Baby," but the "Boston Dip," — confound him, let me get hold of him, and I'll Christen him with a dip that will drown him. Here's nice goings on! A respectable wife, and a mother, too, making an appointment with an individual bearing such a name as that — "Boston Dip." He shall not fail you, Mrs. M., but he must meet me too. I'll not stir from this place until I know what this means. This comes of letting women roam abroad when they should be kept at home. O, Mrs. Mulligrub! if I don't cut down your pin money for this my name's not Moses Mulligrub. I'll not leave you a pin to stand on. (*Takes chair; slams it down,* C.) "Boston Dip." (*Sits, and jumps up.*) Gracious! he must be a sparrer, and that's his fighting name. No matter, let him come on. (*Sparring.*) The old man's a little out of practice, but he's game. (*Sits; folds his arms.*) If this little party does not end in a shindy, it won't be my fault.

DASHER *backs in,* R., *waving his handkerchief.*

Dasher. Does she mean to come? I cannot attract her attention. (*Backs up still, waving his handkerchief.*) Why don't she come? (*Backs against* MULLIGRUB'S *chair, sending it over, and* MULLIGRUB *on to the floor.*) I beg your pardon.

Mulligrub (*picking himself up*). Sir!

Dasher. I really beg your pardon. Did you break anything?

Mulligrub. No, sir; but I shall presently break the peace and your head.

Dasher. I beg you won't do anything of the kind. It was an accident; and besides, you are trespassing here.

Mulligrub. O, I am! And pray, sir, will you be kind enough to explain the meaning of that remark?

Dasher. Certainly. This is Mrs. Mulligrub's private drawing-room, where none but her friends are allowed to enter.

Mulligrub. Indeed! (*Aside.*) This must be "Dip." (*Aloud.*) Well, sir, I am one of her friends — a particular friend.

Dasher. I see: an old friend of the family. You're just the man I want to see. Yes, sir, the moment I set eyes on you I said to myself, "There's a man who can serve me."

Mulligrub. Indeed — (*aside*) with a broken head.

Dasher. Yes, sir. You know old Mulligrub?

Mulligrub (*aside*). Old Mulligrub! (*Aloud.*) Intimately.

Dasher. Good. I've never seen him, but people say he's immensely rich. What do you say? Will he cut up well?

Mulligrub (*aside*). "Cut up!" Confound his impudence.

Dasher. I've particular reasons for wishing to know. I may say, I am very much attached to a member of his family, you understand. I'm not mercenary; but you know times are hard, and to make a respectable show in society, have a nice house, a half dozen fast horses, and all that sort of thing, requires money. Now, what I want to know is this, will the old man shell out?

Mulligrub. Shell out? Look here, young man, for

coolness you certainly would take the premium at the largest display of frozen wares in Alaska. If I don't answer your polite questions, it is because your audacity has so astounded me, that, hang me, if I know whether there is an old Mulligrub to " cut up " or " shell out " at all. (*Aside.*) It must certainly be " Dip."

Dasher. O, you won't tell. Hush! there's somebody coming — somebody who I am particularly anxious to meet alone, you understand. Just step out of that door (*pointing*, C.), that's a good fellow.

Mulligrub. Sir, I shall do nothing of the kind.

Dasher. But you must — only for a moment, and then you shall return. (*Pushes him back.*)

Mulligrub. Sir, do you know who I am?

Dasher. Certainly; a friend of the family; and, as a friend of the family, when the time comes you shall know all. Now go, that's a good fellow. (*Pushes him back to door,* C.)

Mulligrub. But, sir, I shall not. (*Aside.*) Stop. I'll watch. (*Aloud.*) Very well, sir; as I seem to be in the way, I will retire.

Dasher. I knew you would — you're such a good fellow.

Mulligrub. Good fellow! (*Aside.*) Confound his impudence. [*Exit,* C.

Dasher. Ha, ha! Got rid of him. (*Comes down stage.* MULLIGRUB *enters,* C., *and steps behind screen.*) Now for a tender interview with Miss Eva, ending in a proposal, which I know she will accept. (*Enter* EVA, C.) I knew you would come.

Eva. Because I promised. O, Mr. Dasher, that waltz was delightful.

Dasher. Indeed! I am glad you enjoyed it. If it gave you pleasure I should be satisfied, though my heart is heavy, and the waltz had little inspiration for me.

Eva. Dear me, Mr. Dasher, you look as melancholy as an owl. What has gone wrong?

Dasher. Nothing — everything — Miss Eva. I am on the verge of a precipice, a frightful precipice. (MULLIGRUB's *head appears above screen.*)

Mulligrub (*aside*). There's "Dip" and — Eva, as I live!

Eva. I don't understand you, Mr. Dasher.

Dasher. Upon the verge of a frightful precipice I totter. Beneath me are the whitened bones of many a mortal. If I fall not a tear will be shed for me.

Mulligrub (*aside*). Nary a tear, young man.

Dasher. 'Tis the valley of disappointed hopes.

Mulligrub (*aside*). Dip's getting grave.

Dasher. Into this must I fall, unless the succoring hand be stretched forth to me.

Mulligrub (*aside*). The sucker!

Dasher. You, Miss Eva, you — admirable, divine, angelic — can stretch forth that hand to save Dasher from dashing himself into the valley.

Eva. Mr. Dasher, have you been drinking?

Dasher. Draughts of bliss from the fountain of love: basking in the sunshine of your presence. O, Miss Eva, will you save me?

Eva. Once again, Mr. Dasher, I tell you I do not understand you.

Mulligrub (*aside*). 'Twould puzzle a Dutchman.

Dasher. Have I then been mistaken? have those little

delicate attentions which I fondly imagined were gaining for me a corner on your heart — ah, I mean in your heart — been wasted on the desert air?

Mulligrub (*aside*). Dip's getting airy.

Dasher. On the brink of a precipice I stand —

Mulligrub (*aside*). On the rocks again, Dip.

Dasher. Can you see me rush headlong to ruin, angelic Eva.

Mulligrub (*aside*). Dip's getting high —

Dasher. You are the star of my destiny; you are the prize for which I strive, you are the divinity of my adoration. Here on my knees — (*Falls on his knees* L. *of* EVA.) I swear nothing shall part us.

Enter IDA, R., *hurriedly.*

Ida. O, quick, quick, Eva! I've got you such a partner! He's all impatience. Quick! the music is just about to commence. I wouldn't have you lose him for the world.

Eva. But Ida —

Ida. Don't stop to talk. Come quick! quick! (*Drags her off*, R.)

Mulligrub (*aside*). Ha, ha! Dip's left on the brink again.

Dasher (*jumping up*). Confound that girl! I've lost the chance. This comes of making a long story about a very short question. The precipice was a failure. I'll go and pump the friend of the family. (*Exit*, C. MULLIGRUB *comes from screen.*)

Mulligrub. That can't be Dip, after all. He's after Eva. But he can't have her. Thanks to his confidential assurance, I can send him over the precipice into the valley of disappointed hopes in short order.

Enter KIDS, C.

Kids. Now weally, I saw Miss Ida enter this woom, positively saw her, and now she's gone. Hallo! an intrudaw. Sir, I have not the honow of your acquaintance. This woom is the wesort, the westing-place of a bevy of divine goddesses. No masculine mortals are allowed to entaw here.

Mulligrub. Show! then you are not a masculine mortal, I take it.

Kids. Sir, you are impertinent. I am — I am a particular fwiend of the lady who is the lawful possessor of this wesort.

Mulligrub (*aside*). Can this be Dip? (*Aloud.*) Sir, I am a particular friend of the lady in question, being the brother of her husband's brother.

Kids. Weally, the bwover of her husband's bwover. 'Pon honow, that's a sort of cwoss-eyed welation.

Mulligrub. What do you mean by that? Do you doubt my right to be here?

Kids. Hey? wight? — no, no. (*Aside.*) He must be a witch welation. (*Aloud.*) Do you know Mr. Mulligwub?

Mulligrub. Intimately.

Kids. I say, would it be a good inwestment to wun away with a membaw of his family?

Mulligrub (*aside*). It must be Dip. Shall I mash him? No, no, the proof first. (*Aloud.*) Splendid! Can I help you?

Kids. Well, I don't know. He's a wough specimen, and he so vulgaw. Sold fish in a handcart, too. I detest fish, it's on such a low scale. Now isn't that good? It's owiginal, too. I don't like the odaw. Dreadful low people, but then, there's lots of money. Yaas, I think I will sacwafice myself.

Mulligrub (aside). I'll sacrifice you, you monkey. (*Aloud.*) But tell me, who is the favored member of the family?

Kids. Hush! somebody's coming. You must wetire.

Mulligrub. What, and lose the fun? No, I thank you.

Kids. You must, weally. The lady is coming. It would shock her delicate nerves were you to be pwesent at the interview. So go, that's a dear fellah. (*Pushes him back,* C.)

Mulligrub (aside). He calls me a good fellah. Shall I fell him on the spot? No, I'll wait; vengeance can afford to wait.

Kids. Do wetire, and, when it's all ovaw, I will call you. (*Pushes him back,* C.) Good fellah.

Mulligrub. You'll call me when it's all over. (*Aside.*) I'll be on hand while it's going on. [*Exit,* C.

Kids. There, the bwover of the husband's bwover is excluded from the apartment of the wife of the bwover's husband — no, that ain't it, it's the bwover's wife's husband — no, or — (MULLIGRUB *enters,* C., *and gets behind screen.*) Here she comes, lovely as a poppy, because she's got a rich poppy. That's good — owiginal, too.

Enter IDA, R.

Ida. Here I am, Mr. Kids, to fulfill my promise.

Kids. Yaas, Miss Ida, like the bounding fawn that — that — weally, I forget what the bounding fawn was doing — O, weally, bounding, of course. That's very good — isn't it? — owiginal, too. But where was the bounding fawn bound? that's the question.

Ida. I wish I could answer your question, but, not being versed in natural history, I am unable to say.

Kids. Weally. Well, never mind the fawn. Listen, O, listen! I'm a miserable wetch, I am.

Ida. Miserable? you?

Kids. Yaas, weally. I'm standing — I'm standing, — where am I standing? — O, on the bwink of a howid pwecipice.

Mulligrub (*sticking his head above screen*). Hallo! another brink, another precipice, and — Ida, as I live.

Ida. La, Mr. Kids, what a dangerous position.

Mulligrub (*aside*). Kids; then it's not Dip, that's certain.

Kids. O, dweadful, dweadful. But you can save me.

Ida. How, Mr. Kids?

Kids. That's the ideah, Miss Ida; for when a fellah is on the bwink of such a pwecipice, as the pwecipice I am on the bwink of, the best way to save him is to push him ovaw.

Ida. Well, that's certainly an original idea.

Kids. Yaas, it is an owiginal, idea — mine, too — I found it in my bwain, with the help of the diwectory. When a fellah's on the bwink of matwimony, of course his safety and his happiness is secured by his being pushed into it. You see my ideah.

Mulligrub (aside). Deuced clumsy one.

Ida. But how can I help you?

Kids. By pushing me ovaw. Miss Ida, you are bewitching, you are lovely, you are divine, and on my knees I ask you (*falls on his knees* L. *of* IDA) to give me a push.

Mulligrub (aside). Confounded jackass.

Ida. But, Mr. Kids, I don't understand. You're so — so — (*Aside.*) Where can Eva be? (*Aloud.*) You say you are on the brink of a precipice.

Kids. Howid, howid; and if you consent to be —

Enter EVA, R.

Eva. Quick, quick, Ida! mother's fainted.

Ida. You don't mean it?

Eva. Yes, yes, come quick! What are you waiting for?

Ida. But Mr. Kids is on the brink of a precipice.

Eva. Let him stay there. Come with me. (*Drags* EVA *off*, R.)

Mulligrub (aside). Won't somebody be kind enough to remove that precipice?

Kids (rising). Yaas, weally, that owiginal ideah will kill me, I know it will. I must go and bathe my head in Cologne, I must weally. Miss Ida didn't push well; in fact, I don't believe she's fond of pushing fellah's ovaw, I don't, weally. [*Exit*, C.

Mulligrub (comes from behind screen). I don't think that's Dip — I don't, weally. Egad! those girls of mine are determined not to be caught by chaff. I wonder if I can say as much for the old lady. I wish she would make her appearance. This must be the room. Ah, here she comes. Now for something interesting. (*Runs behind screen.*)

Enter MRS. MULLIGRUB, R.

Mrs. M. The fiddlers are tuning up for a waltz, and if Munseer Adonis is to keep his word now is the time. I wonder what Moses would say if he knew what I was about. But he can't know. He's safe at home, and there's certainly no harm in obtaining a graceful *inquisition* to my other accomplishments. (*Music, Beautiful Blue Danube, soft and low.*) There they go. O, isn't that splendid. (*Waltzes about stage in a very awkward manner.*)

Mulligrub (*with head above screen*). What's the matter with Hannah? She's bobbing about the room like a turkey with's its head off.

Enter MONSIEUR ADONIS, R.

Mons. A. Charmant, charmant! (*Music stops.*) Madam, you are ze ecstasy of motion. You have ze grace of ze antelope, and ze step of ze fairy.

Mrs. M. O, don't! You have come —

Mons. A. Wiz ze "Boston Dip," as I have promise.

Mulligrub (*aside*). "Boston Dip." That's him — the scoundrel!

Mrs. M. O, I'm so nervous.

Mulligrub (*aside*). You ought to be, you hypocrite.

Mons. M. Zar is not ze least occasion. We are here alone.

Mulligrub (*aside*). Not quite, Dip, not quite.

Mons. A. No one will dare to enter here. Zar is none to look at you but I, and am I not discretion itself, madam?

Mrs. M. O, you are the soul of honor.

Mulligrub (aside). Humbug!

Mons. M. Now, zar is no time to lose. Permit me. (*Takes her hand and leads her* C.)

Mulligrub (aside). Dip's taking her hand. I shall choke!

Mons. A. Put your left hand in mine — so.

Mulligrub (aside). She obeys him. Ah, faithless Hannah!

Mons. A. Zat is good. Do not tremble — zar is no danger.

Mulligrub (aside). Don't be so sure of that.

Mons. A. Now, my arm around your waist — so.

Mulligrub (aside). O, perfidious Hannah!

Mons. A. Now let your head drop upon ze collar of my coat. Ah, zat is good, zat is exquisite.

Mulligrub. She presses his collar, and my cholar is rising. I shall choke with rage.

Mons. M. All right. Now, one, two, three, and off we go.

Mulligrub (*pushing the screen over on to the floor. Discovered standing in a chair, with doubled fist*). Stop! (*Very loud.*)

Mrs. M. Ah! (*Screams, and falls into* MONSIEUR ADONIS'S *arms.*)

Mons. A. Sacre! Who calls so loud?

Mulligrub. An injured husband.

Mrs. M. (*jumping up*). O, it's Moses!

Mulligrub. Yes, it is Moses! Moses the deluded; Moses the deceived; Moses the betrayed; Moses on the brink of a precipice.

Mons. A. Moses! — Who be Moses?

Mrs. M. My husband.

Mons. A. Monsieur Mulligrub! O, ze light break upon my head.

Mulligrub (*jumping down*). Tremble, rascal! You're discovered. Woman, begone! O, Hannah! can I believe my eyes. You — you make an appointment with such a miserable, contemptible, sneaking cur as that? But I'll be revenged, rascal! (*Takes* Monsieur Adonis *by throat.*) Blaster of peaceful families (*shaking him*), I'll have your life!

Mons. A. Help! help! I am choke all over too much! Help! help!

Mrs. M. O, Moses, spare him!

Mulligrub. Never! I'll shake the life out of him. Rascal!

Mons. A. Help! somebody, quick!

Mulligrub. Scoundrel!

Mons. A. Help! help! He squeeze my windpipe all too much.

Enter, R., Ida *and* Eva.; C., Dasher *and* Kids.

Eva. Father here?

Ida. And fighting?

Dasher. What is the meaning of this?

Kids. Weally, a wow, a wiot, a wumpus!

Mulligrub. Meaning of it! Look at this miserable wretch! — this thing who answers to the name of "Boston Dip."

All. "Boston Dip."

Mons. A. Sar, you insult me. My name is Monsieur Achilles Adonis.

Eva. And "Boston Dip" is the name given to the latest movement of the waltz.

Mulligrub. What, not the name of an individual? Then, what is the meaning of that? (*Shows note.*)

Mons. A. Zat is my note, monsieur.

Mrs. M. Yes, written by me to Monsieur Adonis, asking him to give me a private lesson here.

Eva. And father thought it a love affair? O, father!

Ida. A man with the name of "Boston Dip!" O, father!

Dasher. Friend of the family, you've made a mistake.

Kids. Yaas, dipped into the wong man. Now isn't that good — owiginal, too.

Mulligrub (*looks at each in a foolish manner, then takes* MRS. MULLIGRUB *by the hand; leads her* C., *and kneels*). Hannah, I'm on the brink of a frightful precipice. I've made a fool of myself. Forgive me, and let's go home.

Mrs. M. I think you have, Moses.

Dasher. There's not the least doubt of it.

Kids. Yaas, Moses into the bull-wushes! That's good — weally owiginal, too.

Mulligrub (*rising*). Monsieur Adonis, I beg your pardon for my rudeness. I will make amends, ample reparation. Greenbacks shall shower upon your classic academy. To you, gentlemen, I need make no apologies. You see the old man has "cut up," and perhaps may be made to "shell out." I don't think my girls will be able to assist you on that precipice. With your permission, I will retire.

Eva. Don't go, father. Stay and enjoy yourself.

Ida. And see us waltz. We have splendid partners.

Mons. A. Proficient in all ze elegancies of ze art.

Mrs. M. Moses, I'm ashamed of you. You're really *proficient* in the usages of fashionable depravity; but I'll forgive you, and make you acquainted with my new flame, one which you so grievously mistook, my harmless pet, "The Boston Dip." (*Music,* Beautiful Blue Danube. MR. MULLIGRUB *bows, and retires up,* C. Waltz, MONSIEUR ADONIS *and* MRS. MULLIGRUB; DASHER *and* EVA; KIDS *and* IDA.)

CURTAIN.

THE DUCHESS OF DUBLIN.

A FARCE.

CHARACTERS.

DR. ADAM ACONITE, a Young Physician.
FRANK FRISKEY.
OLIVER OLDBUCK, rich and gouty.
SILAS SHARPSET, a Speculator.
DENNIS DOOLAN, a Widower.
PETER PLUMPFACE, with a bad cough.
ANNIE ACONITE, the Doctor's Sister.
LUCY LINDEN, a Milliner.
MISS ABIGAIL ALLLOVE, an Autograph Hunter.
MAGGIE MULLEN, "The Duchess of Dublin."

COSTUMES.

DR. ACONITE. Black suit, white necktie, light side whiskers, and light wig.
FRANK. Dark coat and vest, light pants, roundabout hat.
OLDBUCK. Gray wig, blue coat with brass buttons, double-breasted vest, white neckerchief, foot swathed in bandages, cane.

SHARPSET. Gray suit, red cop wig, full red beard, Kossuth hat.
DENNIS. Red wig, blue overall suit, rusty white hat.
PLUMPFACE. Made up fat, very red face, dark, old-fashioned suit. Eye-glasses attached to a string, which drop from his nose when he coughs.
ANNIE. Neat morning dress.
LUCY. Tasty street dress and hat.
ABIGAIL. Close-fitting black dress, hair "a la Grecian," black lace cape, broad straw hat, red nose.
MAGGIE. Neat dress of a kitchen girl, sleeves rolled up.

SCENE. — DR. ACONITE's *office. Table,* C., *with a display of vials, one or two books, writing materials, &c. Chair,* L. *of table. Two chairs back. Small table,* R., *with chair beside it.*

MAGGIE *discovered dusting. Her left hand is wrapped in a thick covering.*

Maggie. 'Pon my sowl, it's the docthor's a jewel, that he is! Didn't I burn me wid the hot fat, that made me howl wid the pain uv it? And didn't the blissid docthor tind me loike his own sisther — wid the cooling and haling salve for me fisht, and the wee sugar pills for the faver that was burnin' me up intirely? And didn't the blissid crayther, wid the bountiful heart in 'im, charge niver a cint for it, or sthop it out uv the wages uv a poor girl, as many a hathen would do, bad luck to 'em. To be sure he did; and, by that same token, it's Maggie Mullen would run the wide worrld over for the sakes uv him. Och, but it's little docthoring he has onyhow, and perhaps I did him a sarvice giving him the practice loike. Will, if the sick folks only knew how handy he is, there'd be little rist for the sole uv my fut answering the bill.

Enter FRISKEY, L.

Friskey. Hallo, Maggie! Where's the doctor?

Maggie. Sure it's at his brikfast he is. Can't you lit him have a little pace for his sowl? What wid bein' up all night, and runnin' to sick folks all day, it's little rist he finds onyhow.

Friskey. That's right, Maggie. Keep up a show of business if there is none. But I'm in the secret.

Maggie. Sacret, is it? Sure there's none.

Friskey. Ah, we know, Maggie, that our friend the doctor has yet to get his first patient.

Maggie. Indade you're wrong there, Masther Frank. Haven't I been under his charge, and don't I know the skilful arts uv him? Indade I do, and can give him the highest characther.

Friskey. O, I forgot that, Maggie. He's made a commencement. How's your hand, Maggie?

Maggie. As comfortable as it can be wid the finest midical attention.

Friskey. That's good. Well, I'll wait for him. (*Sits at table; takes up newspaper.*)

Maggie. That's right, sir. He'll be glad to say ye's. But mind, don't interfare wid his business. Don't tak his mind off the purshuit uv patients, for it's much they're wanted, ye's can belave. [*Exit*, R.

Friskey. I do *belave* it. Now here's a man who has

passed a splendid examination, received his diploma, and settled down in his native village to practise medicine, but so set are the good people that they will never patronize him until age and experience have fitted him to be their medical adviser. Stuff and nonsense! While he is growing he must starve, unless some way is found to move their stubborn will. Not a patient — no, I'm wrong — there's his free patient, Maggie, " The Duchess of Dublin," as Lucy and I facetiously call her. A free patient! If we could only contrive to get one of the high and mighty snobs of the village into his clutches, we'd physic him until the whole population flocked to his office. (*Knock*, L.) Come in. (*Enter* LUCY LINDEN, L.) Ah, Lucy, come in. How d'ye do? (*Shake hands.*)

Lucy. Where's Adam?

Friskey. The first of men is at his breakfast, replenishing his exhausted system before renewing the toil of practice.

Lucy. You're too bad, Frank. The dear fellow must not be laughed at. You know he has no practice.

Friskey. O, there you're wrong. The first patient has been found.

Lucy. You don't mean it? Who is it — Squire Prim, or Aunt Lucy Spear, Mr. Plumpface, or Mr. Oldbuck? Do tell me. I'm dying to know!

Friskey. A person of greater importance. One with a high-sounding title.

Lucy. Title — Judge Higgins? General Proof? You mysterious fellow, why don't you tell me.

Friskey. It's " The Duchess of Dublin."

Lucy. O, pshaw! Maggie Mullen. Frank Friskey,

you're a torment. I really thought 'twas some distinguished character.

Friskey. Well, the duchess had a fine *characther* from her last place. By Jove! an idea.

Lucy. Get rid of it, Frank; it's dangerous.

Friskey. Hush! This is really a magnificent idea. Our doctor must have patients, for several reasons: First, he is engaged to a beautiful young lady, whom he will not marry until his practice will allow him to support her as he desires —

Lucy. Just as if I cared. I'm sure I'd rather help him up hill, than to wait for the elegant mansion he hopes to rear on the summit.

Friskey. There *you* are interested. In the second place, his sister is engaged to a fascinating young gentleman, ahem! and him she will not marry until her brother can afford to let her leave his house, of which she is the toiling mistress.

Lucy. And there *you* are interested.

Friskey. Exactly. Therefore we are both interested in increasing the doctor's practice as soon as possible.

Lucy. The sooner the better

Friskey. Now listen to me. Suppose that a high-born lady, a titled lady of Europe, should visit this country; should pass through this village; should suddenly be taken sick. The aid of our good friend the doctor is required. He is called in. The news spreads like wildfire through the village. Patients flock to his office. His fortune is made, and we are happy in our loves.

Lucy. Ah, but where can we find such a patient?

Friskey. She's here beneath this humble roof — " The Duchess of Dublin," *incog.*

Lucy. Why, Frank, what a desperate idea!

Friskey. Desperate cases require desperate means. What say you, will you join me?

Lucy. In what way?

Friskey. We will leave this house at once, separate, you go to the right, I to the left. Drop in here and there quite accidentally, and, in confidence, disclose the interesting news that "The Duchess of Dublin," *incog.*, is in the skilful hands of Dr. Aconite. Magnify it a little, and await the result. I am confident that before night Adam will be as happy as a rush of complicated disorders can make an M. D.

Lucy. Capital! only if we are found out —

Friskey. We'll laugh it off as a capital joke. If, in the mean time, Adam gets a good patient, he'll make his way to a good practice.

Lucy. It's an absurd idea to exalt our Maggie to so high a position. Should anybody see her —

Friskey. Ah, but nobody must see her. The duchess is *incog.* You must communicate in the strictest confidence, and have it distinctly understood that not a word must be said to the doctor about his grand patient.

Lucy. I understand, and you may depend upon me; only if the worst comes I shall throw all the responsibility upon you.

Friskey. And I'll agree to take it all. Come, let's set out.

Lucy. Without seeing Adam?

Friskey. Yes, for I shan't trust you with him until you are fully committed to this arch plot. Come.

Lucy. What, would you rob me of a sight of my Adam?

Friskey. Eve-n so. Am I not robbed of the sight of my Annie?

Lucy. Not even one embrace?

Friskey. As a substitute embrace me. (*Throws his arms around her.*)

Lucy (*screams*). You horrid wretch! (*Runs off,* L., *followed by* FRISKEY.)

DR. ACONITE *appears,* R.

Dr. A. Am I awake? My friend, my bosom friend, with his arms about my affianced bride! Pills and powders! pestle and mortar! am I awake? Well, it's my usual luck. Day by day I've seen my stock of provisions sensibly decrease. I have this morning devoured the last fishball that could be manufactured from the slender stock of codfish and potatoes. It has vanished, and so has my love, with the friend of my bosom. There's nothing left for me now but to make a few slender meals of my sugar-coated pills, fricassee the canary, and then slowly but surely starve. (*Sinks into chair,* L.)

Enter ANNIE ACONITE, R.

Annie. Well, brother, what would you like for dinner?

Dr. A. Dinner? ha, ha! Dinner! Well, what say you to roast turkey with cranberry sauce?

Annie. Brother!

Dr. A. Or roast goose, with guava jelly?

Annie. Brother!

Dr. A. Or roast buffalo, with venison steak, devilled kidneys, and salmon, with oyster sauce on the half shell.

Annie. Adam, are you crazy?

Dr. A. Why not? Our dinner must be an imaginary one, so let's have it as costly and luxurious as possible. There's nothing in the larder. Let's be extravagant, and cook it all.

Annie. Why, how you rave! Is the money all gone?

Dr. A. Every cent.

Annie. But the butcher?

Dr. A. Would carve me with his meat-axe if I asked for credit.

Annie. Then I'll try him. He won't carve me. Now don't be despondent. We have always had a dinner, and, depend upon it, you shall to-day.

Dr. A.

> "O Woman, in our hours of ease,
> Uncertain, coy, and hard to please;
> But, when the dinner seems to lag,
> You'll have it, if you boil the puddin'-bag."

Annie, why don't you marry Frank Friskey?

Annie. Adam, why don't you marry the little milliner?

Dr. A. Because I have no patients.

Annie. And I have patience to wait until you get them before I marry Frank.

Dr. A. But I never shall have a patient. There's a dead set against me. They're determined I shall not cure or kill anybody until I kill myself with waiting.

Annie. Not so bad as that, Adam. Be patient, and wait.

Dr. A. O, humbug! My instruments are all getting

rusty, my pills old, my plasters cracking, and my drops drying up. Hang it, I'll go and doctor myself for amusement. (*Knock*, L.)

Annie. Hush! Perhaps there's a call.

Dr. A. The undertaker, perhaps, in search of a job. Come in.

Enter DENNIS, L.

Dennis. The top uv the mornin' to ye's. Is the docther man in — I donno?

Dr. A. Yes, I'm the doctor.

Dennis. Is that so? Yer rivirance, if ye plaze, Squire Croony wants ye's quick. The ould missus's howlin' in the pangs uv insinsibility, the young masther's took wid the jumpin' croup in his skull, and the babby's got the janders — an' it's pisoned they all are intirely.

Dr. A. What, Squire Croony?

Dennis. The same, yer rivirance, onto the hill beyant.

Dr. A. O, you've made a mistake. He wants Dr. Allopath.

Dennis. Niver at all, at all. It's Dr. Ac — Ac — Acraoniting I was to sind.

Dr. A. (*jumping up, and pulling off his dressing-gown*). My coat — quick! quick! (ANNIE *runs off*, R.) Maggie, Maggie, my hat and cane! Here's luck. (*Enter* ANNIE, *with coat. He jumps into it.*) You're sure he sent for me?

Dennis. To be sure I am.

Dr. A. Glory! glory! Rich Squire Croony! I'm a fortunate man. Where's my medicine case? (*Runs to table,* R., *and takes it.*) My good man, I'm terribly afraid you've made a mistake.

Dennis. Troth, I'm afraid they'll all git well afore you git there.

Dr. A. That would be fatal — ahem! — to me. I'm off. I'll return at the earliest possible moment. Should anybody call, let them wait. Tell them I am suddenly called to my rich patient, ahem! Squire Croony. (*Going off*, L.)

Enter MAGGIE, R., *with* DR. ACONITE'S *hat and cane.*

Maggie. Sure, docther, you're not going widout yer hat?

Dr. A (*returning*). That would be a mistake. (*Puts on hat.*) You're sure, my man —

Dennis. O, bother! Would ye lave them all to die suddenly wid a long illness?

Dr. A. I'm off. Glory! glory! Luck! (*Dances to door*, L., *then suddenly stops, straightens himself, and puts on a serious face*). Professional dignity, ahem! (*Struts off*, L.)

Annie. Maggie, remember, if anybody calls, "The doctor has been called to Squire Croony." [*Exit*, R.

Maggie. That I will — the dear docther! The luck's a-coomin'.

Dennis. Ah, ye's the fine gurl! Sure ye's remind me uv Donnybrook fair, in the ould counthry, wid ye's rosy cheeks, and pearly teeth, as white as — as — as — tombstones.

Maggie. Ah, will, will! It's the blarney-stone ye've kissed, sure, in the ould counthry.

Dennis. To be sure I have, colleen. Ah, bliss the ould sod! Sorry's the day I lift it, wid my own purty wife, Molly, who's been dead and gone the year, an' me wid the childers wid their bills open for food loike the little birds —

Maggie. 'Tis a widerer ye's are?

Dennis. A lone widerer, wid a tear in one eye and the other wide open tight for a purty girl to fill the sitivation made vacant by the absince of my Molly.

Maggie. Is it lonesome ye are?

Dennis. Lonesome is it? Begorra! ye may will say that. Sure there's not blankets enough to kape the chill out uv me heart, whin I wake in the night and miss the music uv Molly's snore — for she had a powerful organ, and could pipe "St. Pathrick's Day" through her nose widout missing a note. Could ye's riccommend me?

Maggie. Troth, I don't know what ye mane.

Dennis. To a nice, respectable gurl that wouldn't mind incumbrances in the shape of nine as purty childers as iver built stone huts or made dirt pies, the darlints.

Maggie. Troth, I think ye've give nine good raisins why no smart gurl would loike to take the head uv yer establishment. She'd be loike the ould woman that lived in a shoe.

Dennis. An' ye couldn't be prevailed upon yeself to share my fortunes?

Maggie. What's that, ye loonytic? Away wid ye's. I'll have none uv yer Molly's childers distractin' my shlumbers. So ye can take yer hat, misther, and yer lave to onct.

Dennis. O, now, pity the sorrows of a poor lone, afflicted widower.

Maggie. Git out er that, or I'll break yer skull. Away

wid ye's. (DENNIS *runs off*, L. *Runs into* OLDBUCK, *who enters.*)

Oldbuck. O, murder! my foot! you villain! you scoundrel!

Dennis. I ax yer pardon. Sind me the bill. [*Exit*, L.

Oldbuck. Confound you for a blundering fool! Girl, give me a chair. (MAGGIE *sets chair*, R. C. OLDBUCK, *groaning, hobbles to it, and sits.*) Now, then, where's the doctor?

Maggie. Sure he's at Squire Croony's.

Oldbuck. Squire Croony's — O, that foot! Why, he must have a pretty good practice.

Maggie. Ye may will say that. He hasn't ate a morsel for three days, nor slipt for a wake.

Oldbuck. Now that's a lie — O, my foot! Bring me a footstool — do you hear? Quick!

Maggie. What's that?

Oldbuck. A footstool, quick, or I'll break this cane —

Maggie (*snatching cane from him*). Ye'll be civil, so yer will, or out uv this house ye go.

Oldbuck. Give me that cane — O, my foot! You torment.

Maggie. Be aisy now, misther, and till yer business.

Oldbuck. I want the doctor.

Maggie. He's away wid dacint sick folks, that don't howl and break canes, and the loike, ye ould hathen!

Oldbuck. Do you know who I am?

Maggie. I niver set my two eyes on ye's before the day, and I niver want to again.

Oldbuck. You're a saucy jade — O, my foot!

Maggie (*poking his foot with the cane*). Does it burn.

Oldbuck. O! O! murder! Do you want to kill me?

Maggie. Kape a civil tongue in yer head, and I'll do ye's no harm.

Oldbuck. When will the doctor return?

Maggie. Soon as he's kilt or cured the sick folks at Squire Croony's.

Oldbuck. Has he any patients in the house?

Maggie. Yis, one. (*Aside.*) Sure, I'm his patient; that's no lie.

Oldbuck. Ah! Male or female?

Maggie. Well, from my sowl, ye's a mighty inquisitive ould chap. It's a famale.

Oldbuck (*aside*). Ah, it's true then. Sh! Come here, my good girl. (MAGGIE *approaches him, and hits his foot.*) O, my foot! You clumsy —

Maggie (*poking his foot with the cane*). Does it burn?

Oldbuck. O! O! O! Will you be quiet?

Maggie. If ye'll kape a civil tongue.

Oldbuck. I'm dumb. But tell me — this patient — who is she? I'll be secret.

Maggie. Sure, ye's mighty mysterious. It's myself.

Oldbuck. You? (*Aside.*) They said she was *incog.* This must be her. And now I look at her, there's a certain grace about her, a queenly air — O, it's the duchess. (*Aloud.*) Your grace —

Maggie. What's that?

Oldbuck. Pardon me, your grace, I failed to recognize, in this mean attire, the high-born lady, which your highness must be.

Maggie. The ould fellow's looney. (*Pokes his foot with the cane.*)

Oldbuck. O! O! my foot!

Maggie. Will ye's kape a civil tongue?

Oldbuck. Ten thousand pardons. I forgot your disguise.

Maggie. Disguise is it? Troth, it's my belafe that it's yerself is disguised intirely — in liquor.

Plumpface (*outside*, L., *coughing violently*). Where's (*cough*) the (*cough*) doctor? (*Enters,* L.)

Oldbuck. Old Plumpface, confound him!

Maggie. The doctor, is it? Troth, he's away on a call. He'll soon return. Take a cheer. (*Hands him chair,* L. *He sits.*)

Plumpface (*coughs*). O, this infernal cough! I'm in the last (*cough*) stages of a decline. (*Coughs.*)

Maggie. The docther'll cure ye's in a jiffy.

Oldbuck. Not that cough. Egad, he's kept it up for twenty years, and grows fat on it. Hallo, Plumpface! I thought Allopath was your medical adviser.

Plumpface. He's a swindle. (*Cough.*) He does me no good. (*Cough.*) I'm going to try the new one. (*Cough.*)

Oldbuck. Humbug! Keep your money. There's nothing the matter with you. You've tried twenty doctors. They bleed your pocket, and add power to that infernal cough.

Plumpface. Humbug yourself! (*cough*) hobbling round (*cough*) with that (*cough*) foot wrapped up. (*Cough.*) Stay at home and diet. (*Cough.*)

Maggie. Ye'll make a die of it some day, sure, wid that watchman's rattle in ye's throat.

Plumpface (*to* MAGGIE). Here (*cough*), I want to whisper to you. (*Cough.*)

Maggie (*comes close to him.*) D'ye call that a whisper?

Plumpface. Hush! (*Cough.*) Don't let Oldbuck hear. (*Cough.*) How is she? (*Cough.*)

Maggie. What she d'ye mane?

Plumpface. Hush! The doctor's (*cough*) patient here.

Maggie. Is it mysilf? Troth, I'm pickin' up lively.

Plumpface (*aside*). Her? Can she be the duchess? It must be, *incog.* Your grace. (*Cough.*)

Maggie (*aside*). Your what?

Plumpface. I'm delighted to (*cough*) meet your highness. (*Cough.*) When did you leave the old country? (*Cough.*)

Maggie. The ould counthry, is it?

Oldbuck. Here, this way. (*Aside to* MAGGIE.) Plumpface is an old fool. Don't mind him, your grace.

Maggie. Will, 'pon my sowl, if here isn't a couple of the quarest ould chaps I iver met. O, here's the docther. (*Gives* OLDBUCK *his cane.*)

Enter DR. ACONITE, L. Exit MAGGIE, R.

Dr. A. The ice is broken. I've cured four individuals in ten minutes. My fortune's made. (*Comes,* C.)

Plumpface (*jumping up*). O, doctor (*cough*), my cough!

Oldbuck (*jumping up*). Dear doctor, my foot — O!

Plumpface. Please attend to me first. (*Cough.*)

Oldbuck. No, I arrived first, and claim your attention first.

Plumpface. It's a lie. I sent an hour ago. (*Cough.*)

Oldbuck. He's a humbug. That cough's hereditary.

Plumpface. You villain! (*Shakes fist at* OLDBUCK.)

Oldbuck. You swindler! (*Shakes fist at* PLUMPFACE.)

Dr. A. (*stepping between them*). Gentlemen, be calm. 'Tis the proud boast of medical science that it can settle all difficulties, mental as well as physical. You need my aid; but such are the claims upon my time that I cannot, without doing injustice to my numerous patients, attend to you at present. Give me your address, and I will call upon you at the earliest possible moment.

Oldbuck. I am Squire Oldbuck.

Dr. A. (*aside*). The rich squire — good!

Plumpface. And I am Peter Plumpface. (*Cough.*)

Dr. A. (*aside*). The great manufacturer — good!

Oldbuck. I can pay handsomely.

Plumpface. I can pay liberally.

Dr. A. Gentlemen, you shall receive my early attention. You will pardon me, but I have a patient in the house who requires my immediate attention.

Oldbuck (*aside*). "The Duchess of Dublin."

Plumpface (*aside*). The Dublin duchess. (*Cough. Aloud.*) My dear doctor, I have heard of your skill. May I depend upon you?

Dr. A. At the earliest possible moment.

Oldbuck. You will give me early attention?

Dr. A. Immediate.

Oldbuck. Then I'll hobble home at once. Good day,

doctor. (*Aside.*) When old Plumpface is out of the way, I'll slip back again. [*Exit*, L.

Plumpface (*coughs*). I know your skill, doctor (*cough,*) and shall depend upon you. Good day. (*Cough. Aside.*) I'll come back and quicken his memory when Oldbuck is out of sight. [*Exit*, L.

Dr. A. (*rubbing his hands*). Ha, ha! that's a capital joke. Dr. Aconite, poor physician, turns two of the richest men out of his office to wait his pleasure! But that's the right way. 'Twill never do to be too anxious. Egad! they're rich acquisitions; for, though I have never met them, that cough and that gouty foot have been the rounds of the medical fraternity. Wonder how they happened to drop in upon me? No matter; I can cure them both in time. Ah, Time, you are the doctor's best friend, for you pay as you go. Luck's come at last, and that imaginary dinner shall be a real, substantial feast, to mark the day when Dr. Aconite took his first fee.

Enter SHARPSET, L.

Sharpset. **Heow d'ye dew.** You're Dr. Aconite, I reckon?

Dr. A. I am.

Sharpset. **Jes' so.** Wall, I'm Silas Sharpset, E. s. q., the founder and proprietor of the " Excelsior Perambulating Museum of Wonderful, Whimsical, Extraordinary, and Eccentric Living Curiosities."

Dr. A. Indeed!

Sharpset. Jes' so. You'll find in my wonderful collection studies of human nater in every variety. The remarkable and only original living fat girl, seven years of age, who has attained the enormous weight of seven hundred and seventy-seven pounds by a daily diet of molasses candy and gum drops.

Dr. A. Remarkable, indeed!

Sharpset. Jes' so. Also, the only real living skeleton, aged thirty-nine, weight seventeen pounds and three ounces, who lives on oatmeal gruel, eaten by the spoonful, once in forty-eight hours, who kin crawl through a stovepipe of six inches diameter, and dance the Cachuca in a quart measure.

Dr. A. Ah, that's too thin.

Sharpset. Jes' so. Then there's the man born without either arms or legs, who can lift a hogshead with his teeth, and write a remarkably legible hand with his back hair, which he wears in a cue for that purpose.

Dr. A. Cue-rious, indeed.

Sharpset. Jes' so. Then there's the bald-headed accountant, with his head so full of figures that he can run up the longest account in no time, and, by the force of his stupendous intellect, make the sum total appear in round figures, visible to the naked eye, on the top of his head.

Dr. A. A calculating baldhead.

Sharpset. Jes' so. But the assortment is too numerous to mention. I kin only say, that for variety, versatility, and invention, this collection is unsurpassed, and kin be seen in all its beauty for twenty-five cents a head.

Dr. A. Well, sir, what is your business with me? My time is precious.

Sharpset. Jes' so. Wall, then, to come to the p'int. You've got a nat'ral living curiosity, and I want it.

Dr. A. I've got a curiosity? So I have — a curiosity to know what you mean.

Sharpset. Jes' so. Mighty secret, but it's no use, doctor; it's all over town. You'll have to give in, so you might as well make the best terms you kin with me, for I've greater facilities for exhibiting the critter than any other live man. Jes' so — Silas Sharpset, E. s. q., can't be beat.

Dr. A. Exhibiting the critter, Mr. Sharpset? There's a wildness in your eye that betokens insanity. You are laboring under a wild hallucination. Go hence. Soak your feet, wrap a wet towel round your head, and return to your couch at once.

Sharpset. Jes' so. Keep it up, doctor. But it won't fool me. The critter's here. Turn her over to me, bag and baggage, and I'll pay you a thousand dollars down.

Dr. A. A thousand dollars — you'll pay me? Be calm, my friend, be calm. You betray unmistakable symptoms of a disordered mind. Will you oblige me with a little explanation?

Sharpset. Jes' so.

Dr. A. Who is the "critter" that you are in pursuit of?

Sharpset. The duchess, of course. Why, consarn it, it's all over town.

Dr. A. The duchess? Ah, yes, poor man, lunacy always takes high flights. Ah, who is the duchess?

Sharpset. Jes' so. Doctor, do you see anything of a verdant hue in this optic? (*Finger on left eye.*) It's no use. "The Duchess of Dublin" is in this house; is under your charge. Now do the handsome thing. I'll put her up as an extra attraction, charge double price, and divide profits. There's an offer.

Dr. A. By doubling your price on "The Duchess of Dublin"? Now, you must excuse the question, but who is "The Duchess of Dublin"? and what have I to do with "The Duchess of Dublin"?

Sharpset. Consarn it, mister, are you a fool?

Dr. A. Now gently, friend. Be calm, be calm. (*Aside.*) O, he's very crazy!

Sharpset. Humbug! Will you, or will you not, accept my offer? Half profits for the duchess. Sharp's the word! Quick, or you lose it!

Dr. A. My dear friend, it wouldn't hurt you to lose a little blood. My lancet's handy.

Sharpset. Jehoshaphat! do you take me to be an idiot?

Dr. A. You'd better go home. Your wife and children are expecting you. No doubt the little folks are chanting, with their childish voices, "Dear father, dear father, come home."

Sharpset. Jes' so. You can't pull wool over my eyes, doctor. Silas Sharpset is sharpset by name and sharpset by nater. You can't fool me. You've got a prize, and want to keep it for yourself; but if I don't set the populace howling round your door, and make you show up the duchess, then you can shave my head, and lock me up for life. No monopolies here in living curiosities while Sharpset's around — not if he knows it: jes' so. [*Exit*, L.

Dr. A. He's gone — home, I hope. He's very mad. Why don't his friends take care of him. It's dangerous to let a man run round with such horrid ideas as are rambling through his brain. The fat girl, the living skeleton, the bald-headed accountant, and "The Duchess of Dublin." 'Pon my word, the idea of my having under my charge a duchess! O, it's absurd. The man's crazy; he must be looked after; I'll follow him (*takes hat*), and see that he does no damage. (*Goes to door*, L.)

Enters, suddenly, Miss Abigail Alllove, *with a large book under her arm. Seizes* Dr. Aconite *by arm, and drags him down,* C.

Abigail (*mysteriously*). You are — are you? — or am I mistaken?

Dr. A. Eh? You may be right, you may be wrong, or you may be mistaken.

Abigail. You do not answer me; and I, poor lone orphan that I am, tremble in your presence.

Dr. A. Eh? Are you often alone? Miss, or madam, let's drop this nonsense. Have you any business with me? I am Dr. Aconite.

Abigail. You are the friend of the unfortunate; the guide of suffering humanity to havens of rest; the healer of broken hearts; the finger-post that points the way to the mansion of health. O, human angel, list to my woes.

Dr. A. Madam, or miss, I shall be happy to aid you with my professional skill.

Abigail. Professional skill? Away with it. I want it not. I want sympathy, friendship, love.

Dr. A. Ah, indeed. Then I'm sorry I cannot help you. They are not in my line.

Abigail. List to a tale of grief. At the age of four I lost my mother, at the age of ten my father, at the age of fifteen my sister, at twenty my only brother, at twenty-five my uncle, at thirty —

Dr. A. O, stop, stop, stop! Spare me. I didn't kill them. I haven't been in practice a year. You must see I had no time for such slaughter.

Abigail. I am alone in the world. No relatives, no friends, " no one to love," — only this. (*Shows book.*)

Dr. A. And pray what is that?

Abigail. A treasure millions could not buy. A pearl of matchless value — my life, my friend, my love — my autograph album.

Dr. A. O, indeed, is that all? And you want my autograph? With the greatest pleasure. (*Attempts to take book.*)

Abigail. Away! Do not profane it with your touch. None but the noble stain its spotless pages.

Dr. A. Ah, indeed! Pardon my presumption.

Abigail. No, only the divine wielders of the pen, the classic movers of the artistic brush, the noble toilers with the gracing chisel, the seraphic sons and daughters of song, kings, emperors, queens, the high-born and the great can dot their i's in Abigail Alllove's autograph album.

Dr. A. Decidedly select.

Abigail (*opening book*). Behold the autograph of the Emperor of China.

Dr. A. (reading). " Will you come and take tea in the arbor. Te he ! " Ah, did you te-ease him for that?

Abigail. The name of the Emperor of the French.

Dr. A. (reading). " Put out the light, and then put — Napoleon." Which he did. Very good.

Abigail. The Queen of Sheba.

Dr. A. (reading). " Anything on this board for ten cents. Saloma." Attentive to business, very.

Abigail. Dr. Livingstone.

Dr. A. (reading).

" On, Stanley, on,
Were the last words from Livingstone."

Original, very.

Abigail. Joshua Billings.

Dr. A. (reading). " Duz time fli in fli time? Josh Billings." That's a very bad spell.

Abigail. Alfred Tennyson.

Dr. A. (reading).

" When I can shoot my rifle clear
To pigeons in the skies,
I'll bid farewell to pork and beans,
And live on pigeon pies."

A. Tennyson."

Abigail. Exquisite poet !

Dr. A. I admire his taste.

Abigail. Now, dear doctor, I would add one other name to my valuable collection. You can aid me. Will you? O, say you will — will you? and take the burden from the heart of a lone orphan.

Dr. A. Madam, or miss, I should be very happy to assist you —

Abigail. O, rapturous answer! O, noble disciple of Æsculapius! The lips of the lone orphan will bless you; the tears of the lone orphan shall bless you; the smiles of the lone orphan —

Dr. A. Be calm, be calm. In what way can I assist you?

Abigail. You have beneath your roof a noble lady —

Dr. A. Eh?

Abigail. From a foreign clime. You hold her here in secret. Let me but get her name in my autograph album, and Abigail Alllove will die happy.

Dr. A. Noble lady? (*Aside.*) Another lunatic.

Abigail. Yes, the name of "The Duchess of Dublin."

Dr. A. The — dickens! Stark, staring mad. My dear young lady, you are laboring under a hallucination. Go home at once. Call your friends.

Abigail. Alas! I have no friends. Did I not tell you I am a lone —

Dr. A. Yes, yes; but call in the neighbors, the kind neighbors —

Abigail. But the duchess! I must see the duchess. The hopes, the fears, the life of a lone orphan —

Dr. A. Lone orphan, go home; let me alone. I have no duchess, know no duchess. You are deceived. No, no, dear, go home.

"Be it ever so humble, there's no place like home."

Abigail. O, you wretch! You mean, contemptible

quack. You have read my album, my precious volume, and now refuse my request.

Dr. A. But, my dear young lady —

Abigail. Don't come near me! You've broken the heart of a lone orphan. You're a base, ungrateful, ugly, miserable pill-box! and I hope you'll never live to own an autograph album — there! [*Exit,* L.

Dr. A. Good by, lone orphan. Now there's a case that requires immediate attention. Poor thing! I ought not to have let her go until her friends appeared. (*Enter* DENNIS, L. *Stands in door, beckoning to* DR. ACONITE.) Hallo! who's that?

Dennis (*mysteriously*). Sh! sh! (*Creeps down,* C., *beckoning to* DR. ACONITE.)

Dr. A. Well, what is it?

Dennis. It's all right, docther, it's all right.

Dr. A. Well, I'm glad to know that, at any rate.

Dennis. Yis, I'll not brathe a word. It's from the owld counthry I am.

Dr. A. That's very evident.

Dennis. An' it's mysilf that would give the worrld to sit my two eyes on her. Now, docther, it's a lone widdyer I am, an' would ye's go for to do me a kindness?

Dr. A. To be sure I would.

Dennis. Hiven bliss ye! Thin fich her out. Let me faist my eyes on her beautiful face, her illigant, dignified figure. Let me kiss the him of her magnificent dress, and hear her swate voice spake the brogue of the gim of the say.

Dr. A. What are you talking about? Who do you want to see?

Dennis. You know will what I mane — her grace, the noble, moighty, illigant "Duchess of Dublin."

Dr. A. What? "The Duchess of Dublin?" Out of my house at once, or I shall do you an injury.

Dennis. Faix, you don't mane it. Rob an Irishman of his right to pay his rispicts to a high-born lady uv his own counthry?

Dr. A. Do you see that door?

Dennis. Faix, I'm not blind.

Dr. A. Then get the other side of it at once. (*Takes cane.*) I've had enough of "The Duchess of Dublin."

Dennis. Is that so? Thin I'm the b'y to take her off ye's hands.

Dr. A. Will you leave this house?

Dennis. To be sure I will, afther I've seen her grace.

Dr. A. (*rushes at him with cane*). O, you will have it — will you?

Dennis (*backing to door*). Aisy, docther; I want none uv ye's medicine. But I'll say the duchess, so I will, wid ye's lave or widout it. [*Exit,* L.

Dr. A. Has the whole village gone crazy? or is this some infernal plot to drive me into hopeless lunacy?

PLUMPFACE *coughs outside, then enters,* L.

Plumpface. Doctor (*cough*), I thought you were coming to (*cough*) see me?

Dr. A. I'll be there in half an hour, Mr. Plumpface. Business of a very serious nature has detained me here.

Plumpface. Yes (*cough*), I know. She kept you.

Dr. A. She — Who do you mean?

Plumpface. O (*cough*), it's all right, doctor. I'm in

the secret. (*Cough.*) I've seen her; spite of her disguise, I knew her at once. (*Cough.*)

Dr. A. Knew her at once? Who, pray?

Plumpface. O, you sly dog! (*Cough.*) The duchess.

Dr. A. Heavens and earth! She here again?

Plumpface. She hasn't been away — has she? (*Cough.*)

Dr. A. Look here, Plumpface. Go home, quick! Go to your room, get into bed, and don't stir until I get there.

Plumpface. What's the matter now?

Dr. A. Your case has taken a serious turn. You are going to get rid of that cough. It's going to your head. You will be mad.

Plumpface. Mad? You don't say so! What a horrible idea! I'm afraid you're right. I haven't coughed for three minutes. O, doctor, is there no hope?

Dr. A. Don't stop to talk. Get home at once. (*Pushes him out of door*, L.) Run for your life. How he goes! The exercise will do his lungs good; but his head, poor fellow! He's got the duchess fever.

Enter OLDBUCK, L.

Oldbuck. I say, doctor, what's the matter with Plumpface? I met him, running. Is there a fire anywhere?

Dr. A. Yes, very near him — in his head. It has been turned.

Oldbuck. You don't say so. By what, pray?

Dr. A. By "The Duchess of Dublin."

Oldbuck. Egad! she's enough to turn anybody's head. But I say, doctor, how is she?

Dr. A. What?

Oldbuck. I'm mightily interested in her. How's she getting along? I've seen her, too.

Dr. A. O, this is too much. Oldbuck, look at that foot.

Oldbuck. What's the matter?

Dr. A. It's swelling fearfully. A dangerous symptom. It must be kept down. (*Steps on his foot.*)

Oldbuck. O, murder! Confound you, what are you doing?

Dr. A. Keeping down the swelling. (*Steps again.*)

Oldbuck. O! Do you want to murder me?

Dr. A. (*steps again.* OLDBUCK *avoids him, and runs round stage, crying out*). I tell you, there's no other way. (*Steps.*) Get home, quick! (*Steps.*) Quick! If the swelling continues (*steps*) 'twill reach a vital part. (*Steps.*) Go home! (OLDBUCK *runs out,* L., *crying out.*) He's gone. No more practice to-day. (*Locks door.*) O, that infernal duchess! She's nearly driven me mad, mad, mad! (*Sinks into chair.*)

Enter ANNIE, R.

Annie. O, brother, what does it all mean? The yard is filled with people.

Enter MAGGIE, R., *with broom.*

Maggie. And the fince is covered wid bys, roosting loike so many hins. I'll have them off, jist. (*Goes,* L.)

Dr. A. Stop! Don't open that door. My life's in danger if you open that door. (*Shouts outside,* "Hi! hi! The duchess! the duchess!") O, Lord! the whole village has got it — and got it bad. O, Annie, if you love me, send for Dr. Allopath, send for Judge Busted, or I am completely busted.

Annie. Brother, are you sick? What does this mean?

Enter FRANK *and* LUCY, R.

Frank. It means fame, fortune. O, it's glorious!

Dr. A. Glorious to have your front yard filled with a howling, yelling pack? Hear that. (*Shouts outside,* "Hi! hi! The duchess! the duchess!")

Frank. O, that's all right.

Dr. A. (*jumping up*). All right! And perhaps 'twas all right when I saw you a half hour ago with your arms around my affianced bride.

Annie. You did? O, Frank, how could you?

Frank. It's all right, I tell you. (*Shouts outside, as before.*) I can explain. But, in the mean time, we've work before us. Here, Lucy, just throw that cloud around your head so your eyes alone will be visible. (*She does so.*) That's good. Now, doctor, give Lucy your arm.

Dr. A. But I would like to know —

Frank. So you shall. In the mean time unhesitatingly obey me. Your professional reputation is at stake. Give Lucy your arm, go up stairs, open the window, step out upon the balcony, and gracefully bow to the assembled people. (*Shouts as before.*)

Dr. A. Yes, but this proceeding —

Lucy. Is strictly proper. Depend upon it, Adam, there is no other way.

Dr. A. If there is no other way, will you be kind enough to tell me what this way is?

Lucy. Right up stairs. Come.

Dr. A. But what is it about?

Lucy. About time we were up stairs — so come along. [*Exit*, Dr. ACONITE *and* LUCY, R.

Annie. Now, Mr. Frank Friskey, I should like to know —

Frank. Hush! (*Goes to door*, L. *Shouts as before.*) I hear them above. Now he opens the window. Good. (*Outside shouts*, "*Hurrah! hurrah! hurrah!*") Splendid!

Alice. Will you oblige me — (*Outside shouts*, "*Hurrah! hurrah! hurrah!*")

Frank. Good, good! Ah, now he's shutting the window.

Maggie. 'Pon my sowl, is it the prisident?

Frank. The crowd is breaking up. (*Knock at door*, L.)

Enter DR. ACONITE *and* LUCY, R.

Dr. A. Will anybody, male or female, be kind enough to look in my face, and tell me if I am Adam Aconite, or if I am not Acom Adamite.

Frank. I'll be back in a minute. (*Runs off*, R.)

Maggie. Sure it's the most mysterious mystery that iver took place. It bates the deluge, sure. (*Knock at door*, L.)

Lucy. Shall I open the door, doctor?

Dr. A. No — yes — don't mind me. I'm not myself. I'm out of my head. I'm mad, mad, mad! (*Sinks into chair.*)

Annie. O, brother! isn't this terrible? (*Knock*, L.)

Maggie. Bedad, there'll be a breakdown at that door, or I'm mistaken. (*Opens door.* OLDBUCK, SHARPSET,

PLUMPFACE, *and* DENNIS *tumble in on floor.*) Troth, is that a pelite way to inter the house? (*They pick themselves up.*)

Oldbuck. Introduce me, doctor.

Plumpface. No; me first, doctor.

Sharpset. I'll hold to my bargain.

Dennis. Presint me, docther.

Maggie (*swinging her broom round her head*). Shoo! Away wid ye's! Don't you say the docther's sick? (*They fall back.*)

Dr. A. (*rising*). Gentlemen, I am at your mercy. An hour ago I was the possessor of a noble intellect. Now, I am like the reed shaken by the blast. To whom shall I present you?

Oldbuck, Plumpface, Sharpset, Dennis. "The Duchess of Dublin."

Dr. A. "Monsieur Tonson come again." (*Sinks into chair.*)

Maggie. "The Duchess of Dublin." O, be aisy wid yer nonsinse. Sure there's nobody here that answers to that name at all at all.

Enter FRANK, R.

Frank. No, because her grace has just been driven away in her own carriage. I had the honor of bringing her here; I have had the honor to conduct her from this place, and to receive her thanks for the able manner in which she has been treated by Dr. Aconite.

Dr. A. (*comes down*, C.). Have you been taken, too, Frank? Alas! poor fellow!

Frank. O, it's all right! Listen to me. Annie!

Lucy! (*Beckons to them. They come down,* c. OLDBUCK, PLUMPFACE, SHARPSET, *and* DENNIS *come down.*) Your pardon, gentlemen, a little family secret.

Maggie (*swings her broom around her head*). Shoo! Ye are trespassing, d'ye mind! (*They retire.*)

Frank. Doctor, for all the trouble you have endured to-day, I, and I alone, am to blame. We are all interested in your success, and, to insure that success, Lucy and I put our heads together.

Dr. A. And your arms about each other — yes.

Frank. And concocted a scheme which has succeeded admirably. (OLDBUCK, PLUMPFACE, SHARPSET, *and* DENNIS *look at each other, then stealthily approach,* c.)

Maggie (*flourishing broom*). Shoo! Away wid ye's! Have ye's no manners, ye hathens?

Frank. You have your hands full of patients now, from the fact that it has leaked out that you had under your charge a high-born lady. You know that one good customer will attract others. Your success is assured, and our happiness, I trust, not in the distance, as it appeared to be an hour ago.

Dr. A. And you have deceived the trusty public, and given me position by a lie.

Frank. No, for "The Duchess of Dublin" is still under your roof. Have you forgotten the title I gave to Maggie? and she certainly was your patient.

Dr. A. I never thought of that, Frank. I owe you much. But if ever you attempt another such trick —

Frank. But I shan't. This one will give me a wife (*takes* ANNIE's *hand*), and there will be no more mischief in me.

Dr. A. Lucy, what have you to say for yourself?

Lucy. O, I'm delighted. It brings our wedding day so much nearer.

Dr. A. Well, I suppose I must be satisfied then. Gentlemen (*all come down* R. *and* L.), I have rather neglected my business to-day, but, having such a mysterious patient, I think you will pardon me. I intend, in the future, to give my attention strictly to village practice.

Oldbuck. It's all right, doctor. I'm proud to have as my physician a gentleman who has been the medical attendant of so distinguished a personage.

Plumpface. Yes, indeed, you've sent my cough off in a hurry, just by your advice; and if you can keep it from my head —

Dr. A. No fear, Mr. Plumpface. I'll cure your head in short order.

Sharpset. Say, doctor, can't you give me the address of the lady? I'll make her a splendid offer to take a position in my Living Curiosity Gallery.

Dr. A. No, that would be betraying profound secrecy.

Dennis. Sacrecy, is it? Be jabers, it's no sacret that she's gone. Ye've a sthrong lift in the profession, and I've a mind to engage ye's to docther the nine childer, if ye'll make the fays conform to the size uv thim.

Enter ABIGAIL, L.

Abigail. And has she gone? and am I bereft of her autograph? O, cruel doctor! to so basely deceive a lone orphan —

Dr. A. Now don't! Say no more about it, my dear miss — madam. It was a mistake. If you will pardon me, I will endeavor to obtain for you the autograph of the king of the Cannibal Islands, in red ink, made from the blood of a missionary.

Abigail. Will you? O, then I forgive you, with all my heart.

Dr. A. (*to audience*). Ladies and gentlemen, you have witnessed the success of Dr. Aconite during the last half hour in obtaining patients. It may possibly occur to you that they have been obtained by false pretences. But am I to blame? Maggie, come here. (Maggie *comes down* L. *of* Dr. Aconite.) I am seeking patients, and want a good recommendation. What can you say for me?

Maggie. Sure, ye's the illigant docther, so ye are, an' it's a plisure to be sick wid the chance of being cured or kilt by the loikes uv ye's.

Dr. A. You hear what she says. Can I hope for your support? Will you become my regular patients? If you will, it shall be my endeavor to serve you well; and you know I can bring a high recommendation from no less a personage than her grace, "The Duchess of Dublin."

Situations.

R.			L.
	Lucy.	Dr. Aconite.	
	Annie.	Maggie.	
Frank.		Abigail.	
Oldbuck.		Sharpset.	
Dennis.			Plumpface.

CURTAIN.

Plays for Amateur Theatricals.

By George M. Baker.
Author of "Amateur Dramas," "The Mimic Stage," "The Social Stage," &c.

DRAMAS.   *In Three Acts.*

My Brother's Keeper. 5 male, 3 female characters. 15c.

In Two Acts.

Among the Breakers. 6 male, 4 female characters. 15c.
Sylvia's Soldier. 3 male, 2 female characters. 15c.
Once on a Time. 4 male, 2 female characters. 15c.
Down by the Sea. 6 male, 3 female characters. 15c.
Bread on the Waters. 5 male, 3 female characters. 15c.
*The Last Loaf. 5 male, 3 female characters. 15c.

In One Act.

Stand by the Flag. 5 male characters. 15c.
*The Tempter. 3 male, 1 female character. 15c.

COMEDIES AND FARCES.

The Boston Dip. 4 male, 3 female characters. 15c.
The Duchess of Dublin. 6 male, 4 female characters. 15c.
*We're all Teetotallers. 4 male, 2 female characters. 15c.
*A Drop too Much. 4 male, 2 female characters. 15c.
Thirty Minutes for Refreshments. 4 male, 3 female characters. 15c.
*A Little More Cider. 5 male, 3 female characters. 15c.

Male Characters Only.

Gentlemen of the Jury. 12 characters. 15c.
A Tender Attachment. 7 characters. 15c.
The Thief of Time. 6 characters. 15c.
The Hypochondriac. 5 characters. 15c.
A Public Benefactor. 6 characters. 15c.

---

* Temperance pieces.

COMEDIES AND FARCES (continued).

THE RUNAWAYS. 4 characters. 15c.
COALS OF FIRE. 6 characters. 15c.
WANTED, A MALE COOK. 4 characters. 15c.
A SEA OF TROUBLES. 8 characters. 15c.
FREEDOM OF THE PRESS. 8 characters. 15c.
A CLOSE SHAVE. 6 characters. 15c.
THE GREAT ELIXIR. 9 characters. 15c.
*THE MAN WITH THE DEMIJOHN. 4 characters. 15c.
HUMORS OF THE STRIKE. 8 characters. 15c.
NEW BROOMS SWEEP CLEAN. 6 characters. 15c.
MY UNCLE THE CAPTAIN. 6 characters. 15c.

Female Characters Only.

THE RED CHIGNON. 6 characters. 15c.
USING THE WEED. 7 characters. 15c.
A LOVE OF A BONNET. 5 characters. 15c.
A PRECIOUS PICKLE. 6 characters. 15c.
THE GREATEST PLAGUE IN LIFE. 8 characters. 15c.
NO CURE NO PAY. 7 characters. 15c.
THE GRECIAN BEND. 7 characters. 15c.

ALLEGORIES. *Arranged for Music and Tableaux.*

THE REVOLT OF THE BEES. 9 female characters. 15c.
LIGHTHEART'S PILGRIMAGE. 8 female characters. 15c.
THE WAR OF THE ROSES. 8 female characters. 15c.
THE SCULPTOR'S TRIUMPH. 1 male. 4 female characters. 15c.

MUSICAL and Dramatic Entertainments.

THE SEVEN AGES. A Tableau Entertainment. Numerous male and female characters. 15c.
TOO LATE FOR THE TRAIN. 2 male characters. 15c.
SNOW-BOUND; OR, ALONZO THE BRAVE AND THE FAIR IMOGENE. 3 male, 1 female character. 25c.
BONBONS; OR, THE PAINT-KING. 3 male, 1 female character. 25c.
THE PEDLER OF VERY NICE. 7 male characters. 15c.
AN ORIGINAL IDEA. 1 male, 1 female character. 15c.
CAPULETTA; OR, ROMEO AND JULIET RESTORED. 3 male, 1 female character. 15c.

---

* Temperance piece.

www.ingramcontent.com/pod-product-compliance
Lightning Source LLC
Chambersburg PA
CBHW032118230426
43672CB00009B/1786